· 3 ·

Of Methods, Monarchs, and Meanings
A Sociorhetorical Approach to Exegesis

תורה נביאים כתובים

STUDIES IN OLD TESTAMENT INTERPRETATION

Series editors
Jeffrey S. Rogers, Furman University
Cecil P. Staton, Jr., Mercer University

תורה נביאים כתובים

תורה נביאים כתובים

STUDIES IN OLD TESTAMENT INTERPRETATION

·3·

*Of Methods, Monarchs,
and Meanings
A Sociorhetorical Approach
to Exegesis*

❏

Gina Hens-Piazza

❏

MERCER UNIVERSITY PRESS
·1996·

ISBN 0-86554-514-6 BS
                                    1182.5
                                    $.H46$
                                    1996 MUP/H399

Of Methods, Monarchs, and Meanings
A Sociorhetorical Approach to Exegesis
Copyright ©1996
Mercer University Press, Macon, Georgia 31210-3960 USA
Printed in the United States of America
First edition, October 1996

The paper used in this publication meets the minimum requirements
of the American National Standard for Information Sciences—
Permanence of Paper for Printed Library Materials,
ANSI Z39.48-1984.

Library of Congress Cataloging-in-Publication Data

Hens-Piazza, Gina, 1948–
Of methods, monarchs, and meanings :
a sociorhetorical approach to exegesis / Gina Hens-Piazza. — 1st ed.
xx-xxx pp. 6x9" (15x23 cm.) —
(Studies in Old Testament Interpretation ; 3).
Includes bibliographical references.
ISBN 0-86554-514-6 (alk. paper).
1. Bible. O.T.—Sociorhetorical criticism.
2. Bible. O.T. 1 Samuel XIV, 36-46—Ctiticism, interpretation, etc.
3. Bible. O.T. 2 Samuel XIV, 1-22—Criticism, interpretation, etc.
4. Bible. O.T. 1 Kings III, 16-28—Criticism, interpretation, etc.
5. Deuteronomistic history (biblical criticism).
I. Title. II. Series.
BS1182.5.H46   1996
220.6'01—dc20   96-24096   **CIP**

Contents

Preface

The following study proposes a sociorhetorical method for the interpretation of biblical texts. A preliminary study on the Elijah narratives (1 Kings 17–18) was the catalyst for this project. A rhetorical analysis of these stories in conjunction with a social science investigation of conflict among prophets surfaced unexpected correspondences. I lacked a theoretical framework and methodological avenue by which to assess these correlations. Two women and their work provided the impetus and laid the foundation for what I wanted to pursue.

First, Professor Phyllis Bird outlined an initial model for relating social data and narrative artistry in her 1989 study in *Semeia*, "The Harlot as Heroine: Narrative Art and Social Presupposition in Three Old Testament Texts." While my own project travels a somewhat different course than her study, Bird's contention that adequate interpretation requires the engagement of both literary criticism and social analysis supplied the necessary momentum to explore uncharted terrain. I returned to Bird's work many times for instruction and encouragement during the course of my research.

Second, Professor Phyllis Trible, who introduced me to rhetorical criticism, raised important questions and offered invaluable suggestions in the early phases of the writing. These helped to shape the form and focus of the study. Her own work on rhetorical criticism served as a benchmark for this endeavor.

Many fruitful conversations and constructive comments contributed to the completion of the study. The faculty of Union Theological Seminary in New York offered steady guidance during the project's preliminary stage as a dissertation. Professor George Landes contributed numerous suggestions on the study's organization, made helpful comments on the Hebrew translations, and suggested many improvements throughout the process. Like many of his students, I am conscious of owing him a debt that cannot be repaid. For his perseverance through many drafts, I am deeply grateful. Professors Julie Duncan and Vincent Wimbush also read and commented on the project. I am thankful for their efforts and contributions.

Professor Karen Barkey, of the Department of Sociology at Columbia University, was an indispensable reader and critic. Professor Barkey, who taught me theory and method in sociology, offered many important suggestions. For her willingness to assist with the manuscript and for her enthusiasm for interdisciplinary studies, I am most grateful.

My appointment to the faculty of the Jesuit School of Theology at the Graduate Theological Union in Berkeley spurred the expansion of the project to its present form. The enthusiastic interest and constructive remarks of my colleagues John Endres, S.J., and Sandra Schneiders, I.H.M., have been invaluable. John Donahue, S.J. contributed important suggestions on methodology. I am especially grateful to him for his ongoing interest in the progress of the work, for his comments and suggestions on the final draft, and for his friendship.

The entire faculty of the Jesuit School of Theology graciously devoted a colloquium to a critical appraisal of the study. Many fine suggestions from that discussion have been incorporated into the chapters. Finally, Dean David Stagaman, S.J., generously offered release time and editorial funding for the completion and publication of the work. This immense generosity of my colleagues in time, interest, and support has made possible the completion of the manuscript.

Others have also contributed to this endeavor. Nancy Haught and Bula Maddison provided skillful editing and technical assistance at different phases of the project. If I were to reference their contributions, every page would bear their names. The steady interest and encouragement of my friend Kathlyn Conway has been a treasured asset.

My family has been the mainstay during these past years of work. Each of them, in his or her own way, has made a contribution. Gabriel, the youngest, always encouraged me in my work by his spirited zest for life. Hannah, in the wisdom of her thirteen years, offered understanding and friendship along the way. Fred, by his interest, editing, enduring companionship, and love provided immeasurable assistance. My gratitude to him eclipses words. To him I dedicate this work.

G.H.P.

Abbreviations

AB	Anchor Bible
AJSL	*American Journal of Semitic Languages and Literature*
AnBib	Analecta biblica
ASTI	*Annual of the Swedish Theological Institute*
BAR	*Biblical Archaeology Review*
BASOR	*Bulletin of the American Schools of Oriental Research*
Bib	*Biblica*
BTB	*Biblical Theology Bulletin*
BZ	*Biblische Zeitschrift*
CBQ	*Catholic Biblical Quarterly*
Ebib	*Études bibliques*
ErIsr	*Eretz Israel*
ExpTim	*Expository Times*
HBT	*Horizons in Biblical Theology*
HTR	*Harvard Theological Review*
HUCA	*Hebrew Union College Annual*
ICC	International Critical Commentary
IDB	*Interpreter's Dictionary of the Bible*
IDBSup	*IDB Supplementary Volume*
Int	*Interpretation*
JBL	*Journal of Biblical Literature*
JJS	*Journal of Jewish Studies*
JNES	*Journal of Near Eastern Studies*
JQR	*Jewish Quarterly Review*
JSOT	*Journal for the Study of the Old Testament*
JSOTSup	JSOT supplement series
JSS	*Journal of Semitic Studies*
KAT	Kommentar zum Alten Testament
KD	*Kerygma and Dogma*
KHC	Kurzer Hand-Commentar zum Alten Testament

LCL	Loeb Classical Library
LXX	*Septuagint*, Rahlfs edition
MT	Masoretic text
NJBC	*New Jerome Biblical Commentary*
NIV	New International Version
NRSV	New Revised Standard Version
NovT	*Novum Testamentum*
RB	*Revue Biblique*
RSV	Revised Standard Version
SBL	Society of Biblical Literature
SBLDS	SBL Dissertation Series
SBLSP	SBL Seminar Papers
ST	*Studia Theologica: Scandinavian Journal of Theology*
TLZ	*Theologische Literaturzeitung*
UF	*Ugarit-Forschungen*
VT	*Vetus Testamentum*
VTSup	*VT* supplements
WBC	Word Biblical Commentary

Introduction

During the past century, the work of biblical scholars has been defined and, increasingly, specialized according to a wide array of different methodological approaches.[1] Historical critics survey the Scriptures for clues from which history can be reconstructed. Social science critics study the cultural matrix extrinsic to the texts. Source critics investigate the oral and written traditions behind the documents. Form critics classify individual literary units and search for their probable "setting in life."[2] Tradition critics study the origins, composition, and transmission of the biblical writings. New literary critics, structuralists, and even deconstructionists analyze the literary character of the narratives.

Such specialization has reaped important gains. Biblical studies has been emancipated from parochialism. Biblical scholars regularly collaborate with colleagues in other areas of the humanities. Study of the biblical text is a respected and funded enterprise within the public sector.

At the same time, methodological specialization has yielded conflicts and disparities within the biblical field. Synchronic approaches struggle to undermine diachronic methods.[3] A focus on context contrasts with a focus on text.[4] Literary analysis frequently involves setting aside the

---

[1]Paul Achtemeier and Gene Tucker identify this influx of new methods as the most characteristic feature of biblical studies at present. See Achtemeier and Tucker, "Biblical Studies: The State of the Discipline," *Bulletin for the Council on the Study of Religion* 3 (1980): 73ff.

[2]The expression "setting in life" is used here for Hermann Gunkel's phrase *Sitz-im-Leben*. As the pioneer of form criticism, Gunkel used this phrase to refer to the situation that produced and maintained a particular genre. See Gunkel, "Fundamental Problems of Hebrew Literary History," in *What Remains of the Old Testament*, trans. A. K. Dallas (New York: Macmillan, 1928) 60-64.

[3]E.g., in Walter Wink, *The Bible in Human Transformation* (Philadelphia: Fortress Press, 1973) 7-8, the author declares historical criticism bankrupt.

[4]E.g., R. Culley conducts a narrative analysis and D. Jobling conducts a structural analysis on the texts in Genesis 2–3. See Culley, "Action Sequences

research and conclusions of historical critics.[5] Different approaches to interpretation engender polarization on the determinancy or indeterminancy of meaning.[6] While such disagreements can be productive, they can also encourage fragmentation. Methodological specialization threatens to erect methodological ghettos.

In recent years, scholars have begun to address this situation. In 1977, at a colloquium at Carleton University, Ontario, John Dominic Crossan offered an assessment and prognosis.[7]

> My argument is that biblical study will no longer be conducted under the exclusive or even dominant hegemony of any one discipline such as historical philology or even of one discipline with two divisions,

---

in Genesis 2–3," SBLSP, vol. 1, ed. P. Achtemeier (Missoula MT: Scholars Press, 1978) 51-59; and D. Jobling, "A Structural Analysis of Genesis 2:4b–3:24," ibid., 61-69. By contrast, P. Bird and C. Meyers study the various contexts of the Genesis stories and how these contexts inform interpretation. See P. Bird, "Male and Female He Created Them: Gen. 1:27b in the Context of the Priestly Account of Creation," *HTR* 77 (1981): 129-59, and C. Meyers, "Gender Roles and Genesis 3:16 Revisited," *The Word of the Lord Shall Go Forth*, ed. C. Meyers and M. O'Connor (Philadelphia: American Schools of Oriental Research, 1983) 337-54.

[5]For a discussion of the incompatibility of literary and historical paradigms, see Hans Frei, *The Eclipse of the Biblical Narrative* (New Haven: Yale University Press, 1974) 150-54.

[6]B. Childs argues for the determinancy of the canonical meaning. See Childs, *Introduction to the Old Testament as Scripture* (Philadelphia: Fortress Press, 1979) 74-75. J. Barr criticizes Child's discussion. See Barr, *Holy Scripture* (Philadelphia: Westminster, 1983) 145 and 154. Influenced by Derrida, D. Jobling and M. Bal argue for the indeterminancy of texts' meaning. See Jobling, *The Sense of the Biblical Narrative—Structural Analyses in the Hebrew Bible II*, JSOTSup 39 (Sheffield: JSOT Press, 1986) 12-13, and Bal, *Lethal Love—Feminist Literary Readings of Biblical Love Stories* (Bloomingdale IN: Indiana University Press, 1987) 13-14.

[7]See John Dominic Crossan, "Ruth Amid the Corn: Perspectives and Methods in Contemporary Biblical Criticism," *The Biblical Mosaic—Changing Perspectives*, ed. R. Polzin and E. Rothman (Philadelphia: Fortress Press, 1982) 199-210.

philology and archeology, but will be studied through a multitude of disciplines interacting mutually as a *field criticism*.[8]

Other scholars have encouraged collaboration between specialized approaches to the biblical texts. Robert Culley invited those who focus on context to relate their approaches, aims, and interests to the text.[9] Rolf Knierim called for the correlation of the sociological study of Israel's history with the study of genres of the Old Testament literature.[10] Norman Gottwald proposes a "socioliterary-theological" approach to the Bible in the conclusion of his introductory textbook.[11]

Four recent studies on Old Testament texts have enlisted two or more methods in the interpretation of texts. In *Moses and the Deuteronomist*, Robert Polzin uses structural (synchronic) analysis to address source-critical (diachronic) issues.[12] In *The Sense of the Biblical Narrative II*, David Jobling combines social science criticism and literary structuralism to study Numbers 32 and Joshua 22.[13] In *Discovering Eve—Ancient Israelite Women in Context*, Carol Meyers conducts a literary analysis of Genesis 2–3 in conjunction with a social reconstruction of early Israel.[14]

---

[8]Ibid., 201.

[9]Robert Culley, "Exploring New Directions," *The Hebrew Bible and Its Modern Interpreters*, ed. D. Knight and G. Tucker (Philadelphia: Fortress Press, 1985) 190.

[10]Rolf Knierim, "Criticism of Literary Features," in ibid., 144.

[11]Norman Gottwald, *The Hebrew Bible—A Socioliterary Introduction* (Philadelphia: Fortress Press, 1985) 596-609. For a review of this proposal, see David Jobling, "Sociological Literary Approaches to the Bible: How Shall the Twain Meet?" *JSOT* 38 (1987): 85-93.

[12]Robert Polzin, *Moses and the Deuteronomist—A Literary Study of the Deuteronomic History* (New York: Seabury Press, 1980). See also the continuation of this work in Robert Polzin, *Samuel and the Deuteronomist: A Literary Study of the Deuteronomic History* (San Francisco: Harper & Row, 1989).

[13]David Jobling, "The Jordan a Boundary: A Reading of Numbers 32 and Joshua 22," SBLSP 19 (Chico CA: Scholars Press, 1980) 183-207, has since been revised and published in David Jobling, *The Sense of the Biblical Narrative—Structural Analyses of the Hebrew Bible II* (Sheffield: JSOT Press, 1986).

[14]Carol Meyers, *Discovering Eve—Ancient Israelite Women in Context* (New York/Oxford: Oxford University Press, 1988) 72-121. Further, Meyers's social reconstruction draws upon comparative studies from anthropology, as well as

In *David's Social Drama*, James Flanagan employs the metaphor of a hologram to juxtapose sociological, archaeological, and literary readings of the David saga.[15]

These projects represent a growing effort in biblical studies to integrate methods and so suggest new prospects for research and study. What methods can be interrelated feasibly? What are the points of intersection? How does one conduct a reading of a text using two or more methods concurrently?

Exploration of these questions on method occasions this study. It reviews two methods, rhetorical criticism and social science criticism, and defines an avenue for the collaboration of their findings. How can rhetorical criticism and social science criticism work together in interpretation? Do the congruences between the findings of these methods reveal an interplay between the social and rhetorical features of texts? Can the sociorhetorical interplay contribute to interpretation? These questions will be explored in two parts.

Part one offers a theoretical overview in three chapters. Chapter 1 explores rhetorical criticism. A discussion of the development of rhetorical criticism accompanies an elaboration of the method. Chapter 2 surveys social science criticism. An overview of the current social-science methods is followed by a discussion of one avenue for the appropriation of these findings. Chapter 3 defines the points of collaboration between these two disciplines. The concluding discussion details a sociorhetorical approach to exegesis.

Part two illustrates sociorhetorical interpretation. Chapters 4, 5, and 6 offer a sociorhetorical exegesis of three biblical texts: 1 Samuel 14:36-46, 2 Samuel 14:1-22, and 1 Kings 3:16-28. Though all these passages are situated within the so-called Deuteronomistic History, the choice of them was not governed by this common literary context. Initial probings into the story of the Judgement of Solomon (1 Kings 3:16-28) influenced the selection of texts. In this narrative, the matter of monarchical authority in a judicial context governed the social-science investigation. This focus served as criterion for the selection of two other stories—Saul's

---

archaeological findings.

[15]James Flanagan, *David's Social Drama—A Hologram of Israel's Early Iron Age* (Sheffield: The Almond Press, 1988).

judgment of Jonathan (I Samuel 14:36-46), and David's judgment on behalf of the Tekoite Woman (2 Samuel 14:1-22). In each account, a monarch exercises judicial authority. Practical considerations motivated restricting the scope of the social science inquiry. The containment of this aspect of the study assured that the focus on methods and their collaboration assumed priority in this discussion.

Finally, chapter 7 sets forth the conclusion. Drawing upon the outcome of the sociorhetorical studies in chapters 4, 5, and 6, this discussion maps out the discoveries. The results are catalogued according to three principles. Then follows a discussion of the factors which encumber and/or limit the proposed sociorhetorical approach. The work closes with a brief reflection on sociorhetorical criticism as "method."

Part One

Method and Theory

Rhetorical criticism and social-science criticism form two routes across the terrain of biblical studies. The course of these roadways continues to be explored. The following discussion joins these expeditions. Chapter 1 charts the early development of rhetorical criticism and maps its course. Chapter 2 reviews the various directions that social-science criticism has traveled and proposes an alternate route. Chapter 3 discloses a point of intersection for the findings of rhetorical and social-science criticism. A sociorhetorical method surveys and develops this crossroad.

Rhetorical Criticism

The recent emphasis on rhetorical criticism in biblical studies stems from the work of James Muilenburg.[1] Though an advocate of form criticism, Muilenburg became increasingly dissatisfied with the reduction of texts to representative categories. One must also take account of "the features which lie beyond the spectrum of genre."[2] He called for a consideration of the unique and individual characteristics with which traditions are composed. Narrative structure, stylistic features, and variations in traditional modes of speech stamp conventional forms with individuality. Literary sequences, parallelisms, and repetitions contribute to a text's originality.

> What I am interested in, above all, is understanding the nature of Hebrew literary composition, in exhibiting the structural patterns that are employed for the fashioning of a literary unit, whether in poetry or prose, and in discerning the many and various devices by which the predications are formulated and ordered into a unified whole. Such an enterprise I should describe as rhetoric and the methodology as rhetorical criticism.[3]

Muilenburg's own work on the biblical texts reflected these interests.[4]

---

[1]For a bibliography of Muilenburg's works, see R. Lansing Hicks, "A Bibliography of James Muilenburg's Writings," in *Israel's Prophetic Heritage*, ed. B. Anderson and W. Harrelson (New York: Harper & Row, 1962) 233-42; I. Jay Ball, Jr., "Additions to a Bibliography of James Muilenburg's Writings," in *Rhetorical Criticism: Essays in Honor of James Muilenburg*, ed., J. J. Jackson and M. Kessler (Pittsburgh: Pickwick Press, 1974) 285-87; and T. F. Best, "Additions to the Bibliography of James Muilenburg's Writings," in *Hearing and Speaking the Word*, ed. T. F. Best (Chico CA: Scholars Press, 1984) 448.

[2]J. Muilenburg, "Form Criticism and Beyond," *JBL* 88 (1969): 7.

[3]Ibid., 8.

[4]For an assessment of Muilenburg's work, see B. W. Anderson's introductory

His commentary on Second Isaiah disclosed the literary richness of
Hebrew composition.[5] In subsequent years, his work on such texts as the
Song of the Sea (Exod. 15:1-18) and Jeremiah illustrated an approach for
the study of this artistry.[6] His programmatic address, "Form Criticism and
Beyond," detailed this rhetorical method and its results.

For Muilenburg, two concerns direct a rhetorical appraisal. First, the
analysis must define the scope of a passage.[7] Elements of form[8] and
content govern this evaluation. Forms such as ring composition or ballast
lines delimit a literary unit. The introduction and resolution of a motif
enlists content in this determination. Second, rhetorical analysis studies
the structure and component parts of a passage.[9] Content provides the
subject matter with which to fashion a story. Forms such as repetition,
stanzas, and parallelisms structure this subject matter. The results of this
analysis are not merely for "the evaluation of literary manner but also for
hermeneutics."[10] Muilenburg's own work illustrated how the study of
these literary features informed interpretation.[11]

---

essay, "The New Frontier of Rhetorical Criticism: A Tribute to James Muilenburg," in *Rhetorical Criticism*, ix-xviii.

[5]James Muilenburg, "Second Isaiah," *Interpreter's Bible* 5, ed. G. A. Buttrick
et al. (Nashville: Abingdon, 1956, 1978) 381-419.

[6]E.g., see James Muilenburg, "A Liturgy on the Triumphs of Yahweh," *Studia Biblica et Semitica*, ed. W. C. van Unnik and A. S. van der Woude (Wageningen, Netherlands: H. Veenman en Zonen, 1966) 233-51; and "The Terminology
of Adversity in Jeremiah," *Translating and Understanding the Old Testament*, ed.
H. T. Frank and W. L. Reed (Nashville: Abingdon Press, 1970) 42-63.

[7]Muilenburg, "Form Criticism and Beyond," 9.

[8]Because the English word "form" can refer to two technical terms (*Gattung*
and *Form*) of German form criticism, clarification is warranted. In this study, the
word "form" refers not to *Gattung*, but to the broad category of formal
characteristics (*Form*) in literature. These include stylistics, structuring devices,
narrative patterns, and those characteristics that shape the literary unit.

[9]Muilenburg, 10.

[10]James Muilenburg, "A Study in Hebrew Rhetoric," VTSup 1 (Leiden: E. J.
Brill, 1953) 109.

[11]E.g., see J. Muilenburg, "The Intercession of the Covenant Mediator
(Exodus 33:1a, 12-17)," in *Words and Meanings*, ed. Peter R. Ackroyd and
Barnabas Lindars (Cambridge: Cambridge University Press, 1968) 159-81.

Muilenburg readily acknowledged that others before him had studied the literary artistry of the Bible.[12] Concern with the style and structure of the biblical writings dates to the beginning of the Christian era.[13] Hence, Muilenburg's programmatic appeal was not an innovation. Amid the shortcomings of form criticism, Muilenburg's proposed program of rhetorical criticism constituted a revival.

Historical Beginnings of Classical Rhetoric

The renaissance of rhetorical criticism in contemporary biblical studies traces its legacy to an ancient and richly variegated tradition. Two developments characterized the study of rhetoric in the classical period.[14] First, rhetoric developed as the "art of oration." As early as the fifth century B.C.E., Croax of Syracuse taught rhetoric as a judicial strategy for defending oneself in court.[15] Around the same period, the Sophists earmarked rhetoric as the academic discipline of oration. As entrepreneurs in education, the Sophists taught rhetoric as a strategy for winning academic debates, as well as a personal skill for survival in a competitive world.[16] Gorgias, who founded a sophist school at Athens in 427 B.C.E.,

---

[12]Muilenburg noted that "from the time of Jerome and before," biblical scholars were concerned with matters of composition and style. See "Form Criticism and Beyond," 8.

[13]E.g., Origen attends to metaphors and other figures of speech in his instructions on allegorical interpretation. See Origen, "De Principiis," in *The Ante-Nicene Fathers*, ed. A. Roberts and J. Donaldson (New York: Charles Scribner's, 1907) iv.i.9.

[14]For a history of classical rhetoric, see E. J. Corbett, "A Survey of Classical Rhetoric," in *Classical Rhetoric for the Modern Student* (New York: Oxford University Press, 1971) 594-630; V. Farenga, "Periphrasis on the Origin of Rhetoric," *Modern Language Notes* 94 (1979): 1033-55; and George A. Kennedy, *Classical Rhetoric and Its Christian and Secular Tradition from Ancient to Modern Times* (Chapel Hill: University of North Carolina Press, 1980).

[15]While a copy of Croax's teachings no longer exists, they are considered to be the source for the instructions on judicial oration in Aristotle, *Rhetoric to Alexander*, LCL, trans. H. Rackman (Cambridge MA: Harvard University Press, 1983) iii.40–iv.10.

[16]M. Untersteiner, *The Sophists* (Oxford: Basil Blackwell, 1953) 194-205.

outlined and defined various figures of speech as the means to this end.[17] Isocrates, his student, integrated the study of such techniques with the matter of actual delivery.[18]

In the fourth century B.C.E., Plato opposed these teachers of rhetoric.[19] He objected that the Sophists had sacrificed the substance of speech for appearances.[20] In *The Republic*, Plato even excluded the Sophists from his ideal commonwealth because their rhetorical curriculum corrupted youth.[21]

As a teacher in Athens (335–323 B.C.E.), Plato's student Aristotle, counteracted the low estimate of rhetoric as practiced by the Sophists.[22] In his three-volume treatise *The Art of Rhetoric*, Aristotle characterized rhetoric as "the means of persuasion."[23] Over and against the Sophists' concern with manner and delivery of words, Aristotle focused upon the prior task of composition. Logical argumentation, (judicial, deliberative, epideictic), modes of proof (logos, pathos, ethos), and virtuosity of the

---

[17]For figures of speech attributed to Gorgias, see *Diodorus of Sicily*, LCL, trans. C. H. Oldfather (Cambridge MA: Harvard University Press, 1950, 1962) xii.53.4. For a study of Gorgias's teachings on rhetoric, see R. L. Enos, "The Epistemology of Gorgias' Rhetoric: A Reexamination," *Southern Speech Communication Journal* 42 (1979): 35-51.

[18]E.g., in *Antidosis*, Isocrates defends himself in court and identifies the rhetorical techniques as he speaks. See Isocrates, *Antidosis*, vol. 2, LCL, trans. G. Norlin (Cambridge MA: Harvard University Press, 1982) i-cccxxii.

[19]Plato, *The Republic*, vol. 2, LCL, trans. P. Shorey (Cambridge MA: Harvard University Press, 1980) vi.491-92.

[20]For two dialogues in which Plato concentrated his attacks against the Sophists, see Plato, *Gorgias*, LCL, trans. W. R. M. Lamb (Cambridge MA: Harvard Univeristy Press, 1925) i.447-527; and *Phraedrus*, LCL, trans. H. N. Fowler (Cambridge MA: Harvard University Press, 1932) i.227-79.

[21]Plato, *The Republic*, vi.492.

[22]Aristotle, *The Art of Rhetoric*, LCL, trans. J. H. Freese (Cambridge MA: Harvard University Press, 1926). For an exposition of Aristotelean rhetoric, see K. Erickson, ed., *Aristotle: The Classical Heritage of Rhetoric* (Metuchen NJ: Scarecrow Publishers, 1974) and *Aristotle's Rhetoric: Five Centuries of Philological Research* (Metuchen NJ: Scarecrow Publishers, 1975); G. Kennedy, *The Art of Persuasion in Greece* (Princeton: Princeton University Press, 1963) esp. 52-124; and Kennedy, *Classical Rhetoric*, 60-82.

[23]Aristotle, *The Art of Rhetoric*, i.i.25-26.

effort were among his considerations.[24] Aristotle's theory and practice of rhetoric became the mainstay for further exposition of the discipline.

In subsequent years, collections of handbooks on rhetoric elaborated aspects of oration.[25] *On Style*, authored by Demetrius Phalarus at the end of the fourth century B.C.E., dealt exclusively with elocution and choice of words.[26] *Rhetorica ad Herennium* by Cicero (106–45 B.C.E.) offered a comprehensive treatise on delivery and memory.[27] One of the most extensive monographs on rhetoric, *Institutio Oratoria* by Quintilian (45–90 C.E.), detailed the rhetorical features of invention, arrangement, style, memory, and delivery.[28] Such works served the needs of private individuals, as well as public political figures and guided the manner of discourse.

Concurrent with these later elaborations of rhetoric, several factors occasioned a second development in the discipline. From about the fourth century B.C.E., an increase in the use of writing promoted widespread literacy.[29] Speeches, stories, and recitations were frequently solidified into

---

[24]Aristotle, *The Art of Rhetoric*, i.iii.i-ix.39.

[25]Kennedy, *Classical Rhetoric*, 18-24 and 86-107.

[26]Demetrius Phalarus, *On Style*, LCL, trans. W. Rhys Roberts (Cambridge MA: Harvard University Press, 1927, 1982) i-v.

[27]Cicero, *Rhetorica ad Herennium*, LCL, trans. H. Caplan (Cambridge MA: Harvard University Press, 1931) i-iv. Although Cicero's authorship is uncertain, he produced a significant number of works on rhetoric to justify crediting him with the work. See *De Inventione, De Optimo Oratorum*, and *Topica*, LCL, trans. H. M. Hubbell (Cambridge MA: Harvard University Press, 1949); and *De Oratore* and *De Partitione Oratoria*, LCL, trans. E. W. Sutton and H. Rackham (Cambridge MA: Harvard University Press, 1942). Also see comments in Kennedy, *Classical Rhetoric*, 90-99, and Corbett, 600-601.

[28]Quintilian, *Institutio Oratoria*, LCL, trans., E. Butler (Cambridge MA: Harvard University Press, 1922, 1979) esp. iii-ix. For a commentary, see G. Kennedy, *Quintilian*, Twayne World Authors Series (New York: Twayne Publishers, 1969).

[29]Aristotle notes the value of reading and writing. He observes that it serves moneymaking, household management, learning, and civic affairs. See Aristotle, *Politics*, LCL (Cambridge MA: Harvard University Press, 1978) viii.ii.15-17. For a study of the spread of literacy in this period, see William Harris, *Ancient Literacy* (Cambridge MA: Harvard University Press, 1989).

texts.[30] The replacement of the scroll with the leafed book (or codex) made manuscripts more accessible. The periodic suppression of free speech by political tyrants diminished the opportunities for oral discourse.[31] Gradually, the understanding of rhetoric as the "art of oration" expanded to include the "art of composition."

By the beginning of the second century B.C.E., monographs on rhetoric began reflecting the concerns of writing as well as of speech. At that time, Hermogenes's work *On Ideas of Style* defined twelve different qualities of style and illustrated each with examples from the classical literature.[32] At the end of the first century B.C.E., Dionysius Halicarnassus' study, *On Literary Composition*, explored various styles, structures, and elements of prose.[33] During the first century C.E., a Greek rhetorician's work, *On the Sublime*, detailed figures of speech, word order, and other aids to composition.[34] By the beginning of the Christian era, studies on rhetoric addressed matters of style, word order, effect, and figures of speech of oration and/or composition.[35] Rhetoric was firmly established as a discipline with two components parts—"the art of oration" and "the art of composition."

---

[30]Kennedy labels this "slippage of rhetoric into literary composition" as "letteraturizzazione." See Kennedy, *Classical Rhetoric*, 109.

[31]In a first century speech to the inhabitants at Rhodes, Dio Chrysostom characterized rulers as "harsh and savage," precisely because they "afford no entrance to words." See Dio Chrysostom, *The Twenty Third Discourse to the People of Rhodes*, LCL (Cambridge MA: Harvard University Press, 1979) xxxii.26.

[32]Hermogenes, "On Ideas of Style," in *Ancient Literary Criticism: The Principal Texts in New Translations*, ed. D. A. Russell and M. Winterbottom (Oxford: Clarendon Press, 1972) 561-79.

[33]Dionysius, *On Literary Composition*, LCL, trans. Stephen Usher (Cambridge MA: Harvard University Press, 1910) i-xxvi.

[34]W. H. Fyfe, trans., *Longinus on the Sublime* (Cambridge MA: Cambridge University Press, 1927, 1982) i-xliv.12. Although the actual author of this first-century work remains unknown, it is traditionally attributed to the third-century Greek philosopher Cassius Longinus.

[35]Mindful of the gradual nature of these developments, this periodization is somewhat arbitrary. As early as the 4th century, Aristotle had already noted this twofold development of rhetoric. See Aristotle, *The Art of Rhetoric*, iii.xii.1-2.

Rhetoric in Contemporary Biblical Studies

Rhetorical studies in contemporary biblical research manifests a congruence with this early history. Two models of rhetorical criticism which reflect the two developments in classical rhetoric guide the work of biblical scholars today. Classical studies on rhetoric as oration have influenced the formation of one approach. Classical studies on rhetoric as compositional artistry provide the backdrop for a second model.[36]

The work of classicist George Kennedy undergirds the first type of biblical rhetorical studies.[37] He employs the precepts of Aristotle and other ancient rhetoricians to evaluate the persuasive strategies of texts. Drawing upon Hellenistic definitions and classical categories of oratory, he proposes a five-stage program of rhetorical criticism. It includes an investigation and definition of the rhetorical unit, the rhetorical situation, the rhetorical argumentation, the rhetorical devices, and the rhetorical unit as a synchronic whole.[38]

Despite the delimited character of Kennedy's method, various kinds of studies, each with a distinct focus, have been conducted under his influence. For example, H. D. Betz's study of 2 Corinthians 8-9 analyzes the rhetorical unit and argumentative techniques of these chapters within the history of Corinthian correspondence.[39] J. Staley's project on the fourth

---

[36]For an overview of these two schools, see C. Black, "Rhetorical Criticism and Biblical Interpretation," *ExpTim* 100 (April 1987): 252-58. See also P. Trible, *Rhetorical Criticism—Context, Method, and the Book of Jonah* (Minneapolis: Fortress Press, 1994) 25-54, for a somewhat different organization of rhetorical projects in biblical studies as "art of persuasion" and "art of composition."

[37]See esp. G. Kennedy, *New Testament Interpretation through Rhetorical Criticism* (Chapel Hill and London: University of North Carolina Press, 1984).

[38]Kennedy, *New Testament Interpretation*, 33-38. Prior to Kennedy's proposal, two New Testament scholars were already working with models of rhetorical criticism which drew upon Aristotelean categories. See H. D. Betz, "The Literary Composition and Function of Paul's Letter to the Galatians," *NTS* 21 (1975): 353-79; and W. Wuellner, "Paul's Rhetoric of Argumentation in Romans," *CBQ* 38 (1976): 350-51.

[39]Hans-Dieter Betz, *2 Corinthians 8 and 9: A Commentary on Two Administrative Letters of the Apostle Paul*, Hermeneia (Philadelphia: Fortress Press, 1985) 35-36.

gospel investigates the implied reader in relation to the rhetorical design and progression of the text.[40] W. Kurz's analysis of Luke-Acts studies the development of rhetorical argumentation (invention) that Jesus is the Christ.[41] R. Jewett's study of Romans researches the rhetorical situation, namely, the Roman house-church to which this Pauline correspondence was directed.[42]

All of these projects claim affiliation with Kennedy's rhetorical program, and implicitly with Aristotelean theory. However, each study pursues only one or two of the five considerations of Kennedy's approach. Betz and Kurz trace the development of argumentation. Jewett reconstructs the rhetorical situation. Staley studies rhetorical design. These different foci indicate the wide range of considerations encompassed by Kennedy's rhetorical proposal.[43] The study of New Testament texts tend to dominate in this model.[44]

The classical studies on rhetoric with its attention to the "art of composition" form the backdrop for a second type of rhetorical criticism in biblical studies. James Muilenburg's definition and practice of the discipline shape this model.[45] Muilenburg was concerned with the scope, structure, and stylistic features of Hebrew composition. Yet, rhetorical analysis was for him "not merely an aesthetic exercise."[46] Literary forms are inextricably related to content. Muilenburg observed that,

---

[40]Jeffrey Staley, *The Print's First Kiss: A Rhetorical Investigation of the Implied Reader in the Fourth Gospel*, SBLDS 82 (Atlanta: Scholars Press, 1988).

[41]William Kurz, S.J., "Hellenistic Rhetoric in the Christological Proof of Luke-Acts," *CBQ* 42 (1980): 171-95.

[42]Robert Jewett, "Romans as an Ambassadorial Letter," *Int* 36 (1982): 5-20.

[43]For further discussion of Kennedy's program and its appropriation in New Testament studies, see B. Mack, *Rhetoric and the New Testament* (Philadelphia: Fortress Press, 1990).

[44]A notable exception is the monograph by Old Testament scholar Y. Gitay, *Prophecy and Persuasion: A Study of Isaiah 40–48*, Forum Theologiae Linguistics 14 (Rome: Linguistica Biblica, 1981). See also Rodney Duke, *The Persuasive Appeal of the Chronicler: A Rhetorical Analysis*, Bible and Literature Series 25 (Sheffield: Almond Press, 1990).

[45]See 9ff. for a discussion of his method.

[46]Muilenburg, "A Liturgy on the Triumphs of Yahweh," 250.

> It is the creative synthesis of the *particular formulation* of the pericope
> with its *content* that makes it the distinct composition that it is.[47]

Examination of these artistic or "particular formulations" in tandem with "content" guided Muilenburg's work.

Many different kinds of studies have been conducted under the influence of Muilenburg. His summons to consider the "particular formulation" beyond the genre defines the focus in some projects. These rhetorical studies attend primarily to matters of form in the scope, structure, and design of a text. For example, J. Lundbom's rhetorical study of Jeremiah assesses the prominence of inclusios and chiasms as the structuring devices of both the prophet's speeches and the book itself.[48] In a rhetorical analysis of Genesis 7, Martin Kessler attends to repetitions of key words and verbal roots, as well as the occurrence of formulaic word-pairs and inversions to delineate the literary scope and structure of the flood story.[49] David Clines offers a rhetorical analysis of Job 3–31 which examines the tone, topos, and verbal modality of Job's three interlocuters' speeches.[50]

Other rhetorical studies more expressly pursue Muilenburg's interest in the inseparability of form and content. In two collections of essays, Phyllis Trible's analysis of selected biblical texts exemplifies this agenda.[51] In her rhetorical assessment of the creation story (Genesis 2:4ff.), Trible characterizes the form of the first episode (2:7-8) as cyclic.[52] Four lines which describe God's action surround one line which describes the earth creature. Next, Trible observes how form collaborates

---

[47]Muilenburg, "Form Criticism and Beyond," 5; italics added.

[48]Jack Lundbom, *Jeremiah: A Study in Ancient Hebrew Rhetoric* (Atlanta: Scholars Press, 1975).

[49]Martin Kessler, "Rhetorical Criticism of Genesis 7," *Rhetorical Criticism: Essays in Honor of James Muilenburg*, 1-17.

[50]David Clines, "The Arguments of Job's Three Friends," in *Art and Meaning: Rhetoric in Biblical Literature*, ed. D. Clines, D. Gunn, and A. Hauser (Sheffield: JSOT Press, 1982) 199-214.

[51]Phyllis Trible, *God and the Rhetoric of Sexuality* (Philadelphia: Fortress Press, 1978); *Texts of Terror* (Philadelphia: Fortress Press, 1984); and *Rhetorical Criticism—Context, Method, and the Book of Jonah.*

[52]Trible, *God and the Rhetoric of Sexuality*, 79.

with content. "Four actions by Yahweh God determine and encircle the earth creature."[53]

Similarly, Toni Craven's rhetorical study of the book of Judith discloses the "creative synthesis" of form and content in narrative.[54] Craven's analysis of form illuminates the overall theological content of the book of Judith. The symmetries of form which demarcate the two major divisions of the book coincide with and delineate two separate theological considerations therein, namely, the identity of the true God, and the acknowledgment of Yahweh's superiority.[55]

Under the influence of Muilenburg, D. Patrick and A. Scult propose another course for rhetorical criticism.[56] Concerns of form and content become a means to the study of the persuasion of an audience. A rhetorical analysis of Genesis 1-3 illustrates this proposal. The form and content of these stories are scrutinized for the ways in which they establish and maintain a persuasive effect on an audience.[57] Like the first model of rhetorical criticism, differences also exist among rhetorical projects that study the art of composition.

In its current status in biblical studies, rhetorical criticism accommodates a host of different foci and approaches to texts.[58] However, this variety is not confined to or characteristic of rhetorical projects among biblical scholars alone. Today, literary critics also subscribe to different models and principles in the work of rhetorical analysis. These current interests and proposals were instigated by the work of one scholar more than thirty years ago. In 1965, Edwin Black assailed the long-standing traditional (Aristotelian) model of rhetorical criticism and raised questions about the viability of the discipline.[59] The critique sparked a renewed

---

[53]Ibid., 79.

[54]Toni Craven, *Artistry and Faith in the Book of Judith*, SBLDS 70 (Chico CA: Scholars Press, 1983).

[55]Ibid., esp. 47-64.

[56]Dale Patrick and Alan Scult, *Rhetoric and Biblical Interpretation* (Sheffield: Almond Press, 1990).

[57]Ibid., 79-80.

[58]For an overview of works in rhetorical criticism in biblical studies see D. F. Watson and A. J. Hauser, *Rhetorical Criticism of the Bible*, Interpretation Series (Leiden: Brill Press, 1994).

[59]E. B. Black, *Rhetorical Criticism: A Study in Method* (New York: Mac-

interest and study of rhetoric. Since that time, scholars have proposed numerous alternative understandings of rhetorical criticism.[60] In a recent project on methods, Scott, Brock, and Chesbro outline five separate conceptualizations of rhetorical criticism.[61] First, *the traditional* approach, which is speaker/text oriented, analyzes discourse according to Aristotelian principles of rhetoric. Second, an *experiential* approach concentrates on the orientation of the critic in the analysis. Third, the *dramaturgical* approach evaluates the symbols the critic uses to describe, interpret, and evaluate human communication. Fourth, the *sociological* approach locates, defines, and assesses the rhetoric within a societal context. Finally, the *postmodern* approach evaluates ideological interconnections within human communication. These different approaches indicate the complex nature of the discipline. Hence, what one does when conducting a rhetorical analysis requires specification. Brock, Scott, and Chesbro identify five areas along which to detail a rhetorical method.[62] These considerations include *focus, critical vocabulary, perspective* of the study, kinds of *judgments* being made, and the *end* to which the study is directed. An elaboration of rhetorical criticism as conducted in this study will be guided by these five concerns.[63]

---

millan, 1965). See also Marie Hochmuth Nichols' comments on the disagreement among literary critics over the definition of rhetoric. Marie Hochmuth Nichols, "Rhetoric and Style," *Patterns of Literary Style*, ed. J. Strelka (University Park: Pennslyvania State University Press, 1971) 130-43.

[60]Examples of new proposals include Thomas Frentz and Thomas Farrell, "Language-Action: A Paradigm for Communication," *Quarterly Journal of Speech* 62 (1976): 333-49; Janet Hocker Rushing and Thomas Frentz, "The Rhetoric of 'Rocky': A Social Value Model of Criticism," *Western Journal of Speech Communication* 42 (1978): 63-72; and Michael Leff and G. P. Mohrmann, "Lincoln at Cooper Union: A Rhetorical Analysis of the Text," *Western Journal of Speech Communication* 40 (1974): 346-50.

[61]B. Brock, R. Scott, and J. Chesebro, eds., *Methods of Rhetorical Criticism—A Twentieth-Century Perspective* (Detroit: Wayne State University Press, 1989).

[62]Ibid., 504-506.

[63]Craven, *Artistry and Faith*, also employs these guides in the exposition of her rhetorical program.

Rhetorical Criticism—Defining an Approach

Focus designates the point of reference that draws together the vari
ous parts of a study.[64] In this study, a focus on text subscribes to the
traditional model of rhetorical criticism. Like Muilenburg, this focus spotlights the art of composition in Hebrew narrative.[65] Scope and structure
govern this complex artistry. Scope defines the limits of a passage,
"where and how it begins and where and how it ends."[66] Structure discloses an inherent design and occasions the study of the component
parts.[67] Stylistic features such as parallelism, metaphor, assonance, and
repetition constitute these contributing elements.[68]

The Bible is a product of many stages and years of composition.
Because of this complex developmental history, elements of scope and
structure in Hebrew narrative may extend behind the received text. A
textual recension might provide the missing element in a parallelism, ring
composition, or chiasmus. In this study, rhetorical analysis does not
confine itself to the final form of the text. Textual recensions may also
be considered in the study of compositional artistry.

Critical vocabulary communicates the findings of a project.[69] This
rhetorical study enlists the nomenclature of literary criticism. Muilenburg,
who began his career as a teacher of English composition, employed
literary terms in his studies.[70] Repetitions, ring compositions, ballast or
climactic lines delimit the scope of a text. Chiasmus, strategic collocation
of particles, anaphora, and the placement of key words indicate compositional structure. Since Muilenburg's work, rhetorical critics in biblical
studies have continued to draw upon the terminology of the literary

---

[64]Scott, Brock, and Chesbro, *Methods of Rhetorical Criticism*, 504.
[65]Muilenburg, "Form Criticism and Beyond," 8.
[66]Ibid., 9.
[67]Ibid., 10-11.
[68]E.g., Muilenburg, "Second Isaiah," 386-93, considers the various stylistic
features of meter, assonance, imagery, etc., under the heading "Structure."
[69]Scott, Brock, and Chesbro, *Methods of Rhetorical Criticism*, 505.
[70]Bernard Anderson, "The New Frontier of Rhetorical Criticism. A Tribute
to James Muilenburg," in *Rhetorical Criticism—Essays in Honor of James
Muilenburg*, x.

field.[71] Literary studies from the past, as well as contemporary poetics, provide this specialized vocabulary. This shared terminology highlights the shared interests of literary and rhetorical studies. A consideration of perspective indicates their difference.

Perspective defines the vantage point from which one views the subject matter of a study.[72] A broad perspective constitutes the vantage point in literary criticism. Its view encompasses all the elements which qualify human discourse as literature. Genre, source, structures, stylistics, reader response, poetics are among its myriad considerations.

The perspective of rhetorical criticism here narrows. The inseparability of form and content limits its view. The study of scope, structure, and inherent design resides within these confines. This coherence of form and content not only governs the perspective of rhetorical analysis; it regulates the kinds of judgments which are made here.

Three kinds of *judgments* narrate the results in this study—*descriptive, interpretive, and evaluative.*[73] Descriptive judgments communicate the initial findings of this rhetorical study. The particular formulation of the scope, structure, and component parts of Hebrew composition along with its content require description. The meaning produced by the creative synthesis of these elements enjoins an interpretive judgment.

Fidelity to the form and content of the text moderates interpretive judgments. Finally, evaluative judgments assess the meaning set forth in the interpretation. In this study, the evaluative judgment assesses the import of theological meaning in the text. Such an evaluation corroborates the end toward which the study is directed.

Rhetorical analysis of biblical texts in this study serves a theological *end.* Undertaken as a strictly aesthetic enterprise, rhetorical criticism attends to artistry in composition. As such, rhetorical criticism need not consider the theological referent of this artistry. In this study, rhetorical

---

[71]See, e.g., Phyllis Trible, "Wisdom Builds a Poem: The Architecture of Proverbs 1:20-33," *JBL* 94 (1975): 509-18; J. Lundbom, *Jeremiah: A Study in Ancient Hebrew Rhetoric*; and George Rideout, "Prose Compositional Techniques in the Succession Narrative (2 Sam. 7, 9–20; 1 Kings 1–2)" (Ph.D. diss., Graduate Theological Union, 1971).

[72]Scott, Brock and Chesbro, *Methods of Rhetorical Criticism*, 505.

[73]Ibid., 16 and 505.

criticism is employed specifically as an exegetical tool in the study of biblical texts. It "reads meaning out of texts."[74] The confessional status of these texts invites and justifies the pursuit of their theological meaning. Their religious power in the lives of the faithful depends upon the ongoing exposition of the theological meaning.[75] Pursuit of theological meaning as the goal acknowledges the reason for which these texts were written and preserved.[76] Further, it attends to "their role and function . . . in the synagogues and churches today."[77] Rhetorical criticism in this study serves as a means to that end. Hence, rhetorical criticism, when explicitly employed in the work of exegesis, attends to the potential theological meaning housed in biblical texts.

---

[74]This definition of exegesis is faithful to the basic etymological meaning of the Greek verb *exegeomai*, "to lead out."

[75]See John Donahue, S.J., "The Changing Shape of New Testament Theology," *Theological Studies* 50 (1989): 334-35.

[76]On such grounds, George Landes argues that the intrinsic character of biblical exegesis is necessarily theological. See George Landes, "Biblical Exegesis in Crisis: What Is the Exegetical Task in a Theological Context," *USQR* 27 (1971): 273-98.

[77]Ibid., 275.

Social Science Criticism

Social science criticism, like rhetorical criticism, has recently received widespread interest and research in biblical studies.[1] Yet this approach is not new. At the end of the last century, Julius Wellhausen (1844–1918) and William Robertson Smith (1846–1894) each began evaluating belief systems, cultic practices, and religious institutions as social data.[2] Both scholars made attempts to describe aspects of the social world of ancient Israel.[3] In 1921, Max Weber, sociologist of religion, published his monumental work *Ancient Judaism*.[4] Weber's epic undertaking commenced the scholarly investigation of Israel's social world, including its primary texts, the Hebrew Bible. Over the years, three areas have constituted the

---

[1]For an overview of social science criticism in biblical studies, see H. F. Hahn, *The Old Testament in Modern Research*, 3rd and expanded ed. (London: S.C.M.; Philadelphia: Fortress, 1970); R. Wilson, *Social Science Approaches to the Old Testament* (Philadelphia: Fortress Press, 1984) 1-27; R. Culley, "Exploring New Directions," in *The Hebrew Bible and Its Modern Interpreters*, ed. D. Knight and G. Tucker (Chico CA: Scholars Press, 1985) 180-88; Carolyn Osiek, R.S.C.J., "The New Handmaid: The Bible and the Social Sciences," *Theological Studies* 50 (1989): 260-78; and R. E. Clements, ed., *The World of Ancient Israel* (Cambridge and New York: Cambridge University Press, 1989).

[2]J. Wellhausen, *Prolegomena to the History of Israel* (Edinburgh: A. & C. Black, 1885); and William Robertson Smith, *The Religion of the Semites: The Fundamental Institutions* (repr.: New York: Schocken, 1972; orig. pub. posthumously, 1927).

[3]Because of the focus of this study, it is particularly interesting to note that James Muilenburg wrote the prolegomenon (1-27) for William Robertson Smith's work. In it, Muilenburg noted the need for sociology to assume an "ampler place" in Old Testament study.

[4]Max Weber, *Ancient Judaism* (repr.: New York: Free Press, 1952); orig. pub. posthumously as vol. 3 of *Gesammelte Aufsatze zur Religion-Soziologie* (Tübingen: Mohr, 1921).

foci of scholarly investigations: *the social history of Israel, the structures and systems of Israelite society, and the social contexts of the biblical writings.*

First, projects on *the social history of Israel* investigate its life, culture, and institutions within a specified time period.[5] Their results describe the social changes, movements, and developments within this time frame. In his social history of Israel, Johannes Pedersen surveyed the evolution of Israel's religious notions from its tribal history to the postexilic era.[6] Roland de Vaux traced the development of four Israelite institutions (family, civic, military, and religious) throughout the biblical period.[7] Building on the hypothesis of George Mendenhall,[8] Norman Gottwald offered a social history of Israel's establishment in Canaan between 1250 and 1050 B.C.E.[9]

Second, studies on *the social systems and structures* of Israel investigate the origin, development, and/or function of these societal components within biblical Israel. Prophecy, tribalism, monarchy, the city, and cult are among frequent candidates for this kind of investigation. Based upon parallels with the Greek sacral leagues, Martin Noth detailed the

---

[5]The range of issues involved in the relationship between history and sociology is surveyed in Claude Levi-Strauss, "History and Anthropology," *Structural Anthropology*, trans., C. Jacobson and B. G. Schoepf (New York: Basic Books, 1963) 1-27; E. E. Evans-Pritchard, "Anthropology and History," *Essays in Social Anthropology*, ed. E. E. Evans-Pritchard (New York: Free Press, 1963) 46-65; and Robert Bellah, "Durkheim and History," in *Emile Durkheim*, ed. Robert Nisbet (Englewood Cliffs NJ: Prentice-Hall, 1965).

[6]Pedersen, *Israel, Its Life and Culture*, 2nd ed., 4 vols., trans. Mrs. Aslaug Møller (London: Oxford University Press, [2]1963–1964 [1]1926–1940; orig. Danish, 1920–1934). In an early review of Pedersen's volumes, G. Holscher was first to note the fundamental weakness of this study. Pedersen's analysis did not take into consideration the historical evolution of basic religious conceptions. See G. Holscher, *Theologische Studien and Kritiken* 58 (1937–1938): 238.

[7]Roland de Vaux, *Ancient Israel: Its Life and Institutions* (London: Darton, Longman & Todd, 1961; 2-vol. pbk. repr.: New York: McGraw-Hill, 1965).

[8]G. Mendenhall, "The Hebrew Conquest of Palestine," *Biblical Archaeologist* 25 (1962): 66-87.

[9]Gottwald, *The Tribes of Yahweh: A Sociology of the Religion of Liberated Israel 1250–1050 B.C.E.* (Maryknoll NY: Orbis, 1979).

tribal confederacy in Israel as an amphictyony.[10] Recently, Frank Frick presented a socioanthropological evaluation of the origin and development of "the city" in ancient Israel.[11] Using anthropological models, James Flanagan and Frank Frick have offered an analysis of the development and configuration of monarchy.[12] The origin, social function, authority, and ecstatic character of the prophets have also been topics for these kinds of explorations.[13]

Third, studies of *the social context of the Old Testament writings* examine the generative forces within a life setting for the emergence of a text. The work of form critics Herman Gunkel[14] and Sigmund Mowinckel[15] encouraged the investigation of this *Sitz im Leben*.[16] While many difficulties hamper the work, James Frazer's groundbreaking folklore studies have provided reliable textual evidence for the identification of the general sociocultural setting of oral traditions.[17] Recently, Robert Culley[18] and David Gunn[19] have explored the context and manner in

---

[10]Noth, *The History of Israel*, 2nd ed. (New York: Harper, [2]1960; [1]1958).

[11]Frick, *The City in Ancient Israel* (Missoula MT: Scholars Press, 1977).

[12]Flanagan, "Models for the Origin of Iron Age Monarchy: A Modern Case Study," SBLSP (Chico CA: Scholars Press, 1982) 135-56; and F. Frick, *The Formation of the State in Ancient Israel: A Survey of Models and Theories* (Sheffield: Almond Press, 1985).

[13]Peter Berger, "Charisma and Religious Innovation: The Social Location of Israelite Prophecy," *American Sociological Review* 28 (1963): 940-50; Robert R. Wilson, *Prophecy and Society in Ancient Israel* (Philadelphia: Fortress Press, 1980); B. O. Long, "Social Dimensions of Prophetic Conflict," *Anthropological Perspectives on Old Testament Prophecy*, ed. Robert Culley, *Semeia* 21 (1982): 31-53; and Thomas Overholt, "The Ghost Dance of 1890 and the Nature of the Prophetic Process," *Ethnohistory* 21 (1974): 37-63.

[14]Gunkel, "Fundamental Problems of Hebrew Literary History," *What Remains of the Old Testament*, trans. A. K. Dallas (New York: Macmillan, 1928) 57-68; and *The Legends of Genesis* (New York: Schocken, 1964).

[15]Mowinckel, *The Psalms in Israel's Worship*, trans. D. R. Ap-Thomas (New York: Abingdon Press, 1962).

[16]The term *Sitz im Leben* was Gunkel's phrase for "setting." See Gunkel, "Fundamental Problems of Hebrew Literary History," 61.

[17]James Frazer, *Folklore in the Old Testament* (London: Macmillan, 1918).

[18]Robert Culley, *Oral Formulaic Language in the Biblical Psalms* (Toronto:

which oral tradition developed. Robert Wilson has identified lineage systems as the broad context in which the segmentary genealogies in the Old Testament stories were created and preserved.[20] Influenced by the work of Mowinckel, N. Ridderbos[21] and A. Johnson[22] have earmarked and detailed "cult" as the defensible *Sitz im Leben* for some of the psalms.

As a result of the investigations within these three areas, social-science study of the Hebrew Bible has become an elaborate field. Research from sociology, psychology, economics, political science, and anthropology has contributed to the discipline. As a result, a variety of theories and methods is available for the study of Israel's social world. Amid these possible avenues of investigation, three approaches dominate social science research on the Hebrew Bible.[23]

The oldest method can be described as *constructive* in nature. Information derived from texts, archaeological remains, and/or ancient Near Eastern findings is used to establish Israel's social world. For example,

---

University of Toronto Press, 1967); "Oral Tradition and Historicity," in *Studies on the Ancient Palestinian World*, ed. J. W. Wevers and D. B. Redford (Toronto: University of Toronto, 1972); and "Oral Tradition and the Old Testament: Some Recent Discussion," *Semeia* 5 (1976): 1-33.

[19]D. Gunn, "Narrative Patterns and Oral Tradition in Judges and Samuel," *VT* 24 (1974): 286-317.

[20]Robert R. Wilson, *Genealogy and History in the Biblical World* (New Haven: Yale University, 1979).

[21]N. Ridderbos, "Psalmen und Kult," *Zur neueren Psalmenforschung*, ed. P. Neumann (Darmstadt: Wissenschaftliche Buchgesellschaft, 1976) 234-79.

[22]A. Johnson, *The Cultic Prophet and Israel's Psalmody* (Cardiff: University of Wales, 1979).

[23]For critical appraisals of methods in social science criticism, see Wilson, *Sociological Approaches*, 3-9, 28-29, and 81-83; N. Gottwald, "Sociological Method in the Study of Ancient Israel," in *Encounter with the Text: Form and History in the Hebrew Bible*, ed. M. J. Buss (Philadelphia: Fortress Press, 1979) 69-81; J. W. Rogerson, *Anthropology and the Old Testament* (Atlanta: John Knox Press, 1978); and Gerd Theissen, "Sociological Interpretation of Religious Traditions: Its Methodological Problems as Exemplified in Early Christianity," in *The Social Setting of Pauline Christianity: Essays on Corinth*, ed. J. H. Schutz (Philadelphia: Fortress Press, 1982) 175-200.

Roland de Vaux quarried the social data embedded in biblical texts.[24] He then used this information to explain practices, social constructs, or institutions in Israelite society.

In recent studies, *analytic* and *comparative* approaches are more frequently employed. The *analytic* approach enlists well-established categories from macrosocial theory, social psychology, and anthropology. Events, norms, or symbols in the text are explained according to these presiding theories and paradigms. For example, Norman Gottwald applies Marxist macrotheory to premonarchic Israelite society.[25] In another study, Robert Carroll makes use of cognitive dissonance theory from social psychology to interpret prophets.[26]

Comparative methods draw upon parallel situations and constructs. They may be contemporary with the biblical world or derived from comparable situations in other times and cultures. Burke Long enlists parallels from shamen studies in his project on prophetic conflict.[27] Thomas Overholt employs comparative data from millenarian sects in his investigation of apocalyptists.[28] The analogous subject matter informs the description and elaboration of these topics.

Each of these approaches *(constructive, analytic, and comparative)* has harvested abundant social data on the Hebrew Bible. A growing pool of information exists on the social history, structures/systems, and contexts of ancient Israel. The critic can readily draw upon this reservoir of information. However, the benefits of social science analysis need not be limited to clarifying and defining the extrinsic social world of ancient Israel. A clarification of the intrinsic world of narrative may also benefit from social science studies.

Though not necessarily a reflection of the social context of Israel, the biblical tale is a part of, a piece of, that social world itself. Social traditions, customs, institutions, roles, values, that are inscribed in the world of story derive their import from the extrinsic social context. The

---

[24]See de Vaux, *Ancient Israel: Its Life and Institutions*.

[25]Gottwald, *The Tribes of Yahweh*, esp. 389-463.

[26]Robert Carroll, *When Prophecy Failed: Cognitive Dissonance in the Prophetic Traditions of the Old Testament* (New York: Seabury Press, 1979).

[27]Long, "Social Dimensions of Prophetic Conflict."

[28]Overholt, "The Ghost Dance of 1890."

mention of a king's oath, the dialogue between a father and his son, or the description of a harlot's behavior in a story gain meaning with reference to their existence in the real world. Understanding their meaning in this social context illuminates their potential meaning in story. Thus, the findings of social science criticism can inform and clarify the narrative realm of story.[29]

Clifford Geertz's approach, "thick description," serves as an *analogy* for this kind of an investigation.[30] Borrowing from Max Weber, Geertz defines culture as "webs of significance."[31] Religious, literary, aesthetic, and economic conventions form these webs. Geertz calls the analysis of these webs "thick description." "Thick description" strives to discover, sort out, and detail the significant features, layers, and networks of human discourse, interactions, institutions, contexts, behaviors, conventions, and so forth. "Thick description" burrows deep into the labyrinth of a social world. It exposes the incongruities and raises questions. Moreover, these descriptions capture the uniqueness, significant import, and potential meaning of social reality itself.

By analogy, the social world in narrative lends itself to a kind of "thick description." The interchange between characters, the description of social roles and practices, the narration of an event are laden with social significance. Just as Geertz's "thick description" of a Javanese funeral discloses the cultural character of an urban context, so too a "thick description" of social referents in a tale can reveal the dynamics of a social exchange, the significance of a behavior, or the import of a custom narrated in the tale.[32] While anthropological field studies cannot be conducted on ancient manuscripts per se, the texts can function as an "anthropological field." The social referents in the biblical story make up this "anthropological field." Such features as characters' identities, the

---

[29]Similarly, Norman Petersen conducts a sociological study on the narrative world in Paul's letter to Philemon. See Norman Petersen, *Rediscovering Paul-Philemon and the Sociology of Paul's Narrative World* (Philadelphia: Fortress, 1985).

[30]See Clifford Geertz, "Thick Description: Toward an Interpretive Theory of Culture," in *The Interpretation of Cultures* (New York: Basic Books, 1973) 3-30.

[31]Geertz, "Thick Description," 5.

[32]Clifford Geertz, "Ritual and Social Change: A Javanese Example," *The Interpretation of Cultures* (New York: Basic Books, 1973) 142-69.

way they speak, the forms they use, the rituals in which they partake, qualify as these social referents.[33] Further, social traditions, conventions, institutions, roles, values, customs, expressions, and so forth, are inscribed in the content of a story. Together, these elements make up the larger complex social world implicit in the tale.

"Thick description" of the social realm of story attends to these referents. It teases out and details the potential layers and networks of the social world embedded in the tale. To do this, it draws upon the relevant data from constructive, analytic, and comparative studies of Israel. Analogous references and social clues in the larger narrative context contribute to this kind of a "close reading." In the resulting description, the social landscape within the tale appears. The social features of the narrative stand out. The social complexities within a story emerge.

Since the text is the "anthropological field," the description does not claim any mimetic kinship with the society in which the text developed.[34] While the text is the product of a society, it is not necessarily a reflection of that society.[35] Hence, this kind of "thick description" elaborates only the social world in the tale. It is not a social reconstruction of the allegedly real or historical Israel.

Accordingly, the critic assumes a role analogous to Geertz's definition of the anthropologist. "The anthropologist does not study villages. The anthropologist studies *in* the village."[36] Such a posture abandons claims of objective observation. Instead, the anthropologist is more "like

---

[33]Even literary critics note the social import of characters' speech, characterizations, etc. E.g., S. Bar-Efrat notes how "the speaker's or the interlocutor's social standing is often reflected in speech." See Bar-Efrat, *Narrative Art in the Bible* (Sheffield: Almond Press, 1984) 66-67.

[34]See also David Jobling, "Sociological and Literary Approaches to the Bible: How Shall the Twain Meet?" *JSOT* 38 (1987): 88, who observes that "literature and 'reality' are related, but not by 'reflection.' "

[35]Contra N. Gottwald, *The Hebrew Bible. A Socioliterary Introduction* (Philadelphia: Fortress Press, 1985) 32, who describes "the Hebrew Bible as a product and reflection of the social world."

[36]Geertz, "Thick Description," 22.

a literary critic."[37] Interpretation rather than observation characterizes their activity.[38]

The description of the social realm of a story is an interpretive activity. It exposes the significance and import of the social components therein. It also raises new questions with which to approach and appraise the biblical literature. Such descriptions of the social world of biblical narrative not only invite new interpretative insights; they also occasion a crossroad with the rhetorical dimensions of biblical narrative. The next chapter explores this intersection.

---

[37]Ibid., 9.
[38]Ibid., 9.

Sociorhetorical Interpretation

Currently, no major studies on the collaborative use of rhetorical and sociological methods on texts of the Hebrew Bible exist. By contrast, projects that employ a sociorhetorical analysis have been conducted within New Testament studies.[1] Influenced by George Kennedy, these studies employ the classical method of rhetorical criticism. They evaluate the persuasive capacity of New Testament rhetoric in conjunction with well-defined social situations.[2]

Norman Petersen examines the social roles of the characters in Paul's letter to Philemon.[3] An investigation of rhetorical forms in tandem with a sociological assessment enables Petersen to describe the relationships among the personae of the letter. In another study, Vernon Robbins offers a sociorhetorical analysis of Mark's gospel.[4] In Robbins' presentation, the rhetorical forms of the gospel verify Jesus' social role as teacher. In such projects, rhetoric functions in an adjunct capacity. The rhetorical assessment contributes to the sociological investigation. The reconstruction of the extrinsic social world in early Christianity is the goal in these studies.

---

[1]See S. Stowers, "Social Status, Public Speaking and Private Teaching: The Circumstances of Paul's Preaching Activity," *NovT* 26 (1984): 59-82; W. Wuellner, "Paul as Pastor: The Function of Rhetorical Questions in First Corinthians," *L'Apotre Paul: personalite, style et conception du ministere*, ed. A. Vanhoye (Leuven: Leuven University Press, 1986); and B. Mack, *A Myth of Innocence: Mark and Christian Origins* (Philadelphia: Fortress Press, 1988).

[2]B. Mack, *Rhetoric and the New Testament*, 24, anticipates abundant sociorhetorical studies along these lines in the coming years.

[3]Petersen, *Rediscovering Paul.*

[4]Vernon Robbins, *Jesus the Teacher: Sociorhetorical Interpretation of Mark* (Philadelphia: Fortress Press, 1984).

By contrast, the sociorhetorical approach described here targets the intrinsic "story world" of biblical narrative.[5] The realm of characters, setting, and plot makes up this "story world." The tale establishes its own spaciotemporal framework. Narrated discourse and direct speech of characters animate this reality.

This "story world" provides ample terrain for both social-science and rhetorical explorations. The social referents of the tale create an "anthropological field." Drawing upon the findings of social science studies, a "thick description" of these features defines and clarifies these social referents.[6] Moreover, literary conventions craft the content of this "story world." This artistry of form and content accommodates a rhetorical study.[7]

The integrity of the "story world" weaves together these social and rhetorical elements.[8] Social features such as identities, institutions, mores, behaviors, and laws are inscribed in the form and content of rhetoric. For example, the components of a religious practice might structure the content of a narrative. The description of a people's geographical boundaries might demarcate or coincide with the rhetorical boundaries of their story. The character of a relationship between a ruler and his subjects might be etched in the content and patterns of direct discourse.

---

[5]The concept of a "story world" is influenced by A. Eco's discussion and proposal of a "narrative world." See Alberto Eco, *The Role of the Reader: Explorations of the Semiotics of Texts* (Bloomington: Indiana University Press, 1979) esp. 220-26. M. H. Abrams provides historical background for the idea of a "story world." See Abrams, *The Mirror and the Lamp* (New York: W. W. Norton, 1958) 272-85. Wellek and Warren also recognize the notion of a "narrative world"/"story world." See Rene Wellek and Austin Warren, *Theory of Literature* (New York: Harcourt, Brace, and World, 1956) 212-25.

[6]See above, 27-30.

[7]See above, 20-22.

[8]See Giles Gunn, "The Semiotics of Culture and the Interpretation of Literature: Clifford Geertz and the Moral Imagination," *Studies in the Literary Imagination* 12 (1977): 109-28; B. Vickers, *Rhetoric Revalued* (Binghamton NY: Center for Medieval and Renaissance Studies, 1982) 14-15; and Joseph Gusfield, ed., *Kenneth Burke: On Symbols and Society* (Chicago and London: University of Chicago Press, 1989) 44.

Concurrently, rhetorical elements such as repetitions, narrative descriptions, parallels, and poetic formulations are ladened with social import and information. Repetitions might magnify the gravity of a behavior. Assonance may dramatize the tenor of an interaction. Patterns of direct discourse might challenge or undercut social decorum.

This apparent engagement between the social and rhetorical features of a story portends their collaboration in the interpretation of a text. What are these points of contact? What is the nature of their interconnection? How can these social-science and rhetorical insights be integrated in the reading of a text? The following sociorhetorical method addresses these questions and maps a route.

Biblical texts are products of borrowings, exchanges, imprints, and interactions with a social context. The metaphors, roles, identities, rituals, idiomatic expressions, and clothing move from one culturally demarcated zone to another. This does not assume the text mirrors its social setting. Rather, it implies that a text gains meaning with reference to a particular set of circumstances or surroundings. Hence, a sociorhetorical exegesis begins with an exposition of the social context referenced in the story. For example, a story about Saul issuing a judicial decision as king invites a description and, perhaps, qualification of kingship under Saul.

Next, three stages of analysis guide the exegetical journey through the text. The elaboration of the social components in a story constitutes stage one. This exposition or "thick description" of these social elements occurs as the referents are encountered in the text. Referents in the story may include a mention of a cultic ritual, the introduction of a king, the war practice of a judge, the hygienic observance of a woman, and so forth. Relevant constructive, comparative, and analytic studies within the social sciences on these matters are consulted. The findings of these studies clarify and detail the social element in a tale. Similar references in the surrounding narrative might aid this elaboration. For example, the reference to a widow in a story invites elaboration. Relevant studies on widows in ancient Israel make explicit the social and economic status of widows which the tale presumes. The presence and descriptions of widows in other biblical stories might also aid this elaboration. The resulting social description establishes an understanding of the identity of a widow in the social realm of the tale.

Upon completion of this initial exposition of the social world, the rhetorical assessment begins. In stage two, the rhetorical boundaries and structure of the story are delineated. Where the tale begins and ends frames the story unit. An elaboration of the rhetorical structure within these limits follows. The components of this structure (repetition, reversals, formulas, parallels, direct discourse, and so forth) guide the rhetorical assessment. In conjunction with the analysis of these forms, rhetorical criticism attends to the content of these forms. As more social referents are encountered, the rhetorical analysis pauses. Stage one, the social exposition, begins again.

As this two-stage analysis repeats itself, the social and rhetorical observations layer themselves like concentric interpenetrating circles. An assessment of these interconnections governs stage three of the method. This third stage occurs intermittently as the interconnections are encountered in the interpretative process. This stage explores how the social features and rhetorical elements interact. Does the rhetorical design coincide with the configuration of social elements in the tale? Is the social drama of the story reinforced by the rhetorical art? Does rhetoric shape, change, or animate a social dynamic in the narrative? Does rhetoric illustrate a social structure or custom? Are the social roles of characters in the story confirmed or undercut by the workings of rhetoric?

A brief example from the Elijah traditions (1 Kings 17–19, 21 and 2 Kings 1–2) will illustrate the three stages of sociorhetorical analysis. In the story of the episode on Mt. Carmel (1 Kings 18:20–40), Elijah the prophet overpowered the prophets of Baal. At the conclusion of this contest on Mt. Carmel (1 Kings 18:40), Elijah ordered the slaughter of these opponents. First Kings 19:1 opens with a summary of these events.

וַיַּגֵּד אַחְאָב לְאִיזֶבֶל

And Ahab told Jezebel

אֵת כָּל־אֲשֶׁר עָשָׂה אֵלִיָּהוּ

all that Elijah had done,

וְאֵת כָּל־אֲשֶׁר הָרַג

all whom he killed,

אֶת־כָּל־הַנְּבִיאִים בֶּחָרֶב׃
(1 Kings 19:1)

all the prophets with a sword.

In the first stage of the sociorhetorical analysis, an elaboration of the social world of the story occurs. To do this, one first identifies the social elements encountered in the text. Ahab's report to Jezebel in 1 Kings

19:1 offers a suumary of Elijah's victory over the Baal prophets. This encounter between the prophets of Baal and the prophet of Yahweh on Mt. Carmel qualifies as the social referent which invites elaboration.

Next, relevant studies conducted under the aegis of social-science criticism are consulted in order to draw out the unnarrated significance and details of this event. In his study on the social location of prophets, Robert Wilson identifies Elijah as a peripheral intermediary.[9] In contrast to central prophets, peripheral prophets had little status or credibility within the general public. In another study on prophetic conflict, Burke Long elaborates the social significance and consequences of confrontations between these intermediaries.[10] The prophet's sphere of influence increased according to the extent of his or her victory over rival intermediaries.[11]

Finally, this investigation yields a description of the social realm of the story. The episode which Ahab reports appears to be more than one prophet's challenge to the apostasy of Baalism and its influence. The contest between deities on Mt. Carmel enjoined a competition between prophets. The outcome of such contests had consequences for the social standing and status of both contenders.

In the second stage of a sociorhetorical assessment, the rhetorical analysis unfolds. How the form or literary artistry crafts the content is examined. In the rhetorical analysis one observes that the content of Ahab's speech reports the outcome and extent of Elijah's comprehensive victory. The form of this oration (the repetition of "all") demarcates three stages of his report. Moreover, the iteration dramatizes and reinforces the comprehensive scope of the prophet's feat.

Finally, the third phase examines how the rhetorical analysis and the social description might work together in the production of meaning. In this instance, the sociorhetorical interplay is revealing. The rhetorical

---

[9]R. Wilson, *Prophecy and Society in Ancient Israel* (Philadelphia: Fortress, 1980) 194-201.

[10]B. Long, "Social Dimensions of Prophetic Conflict," *Semeia* 21 (1982): 29-53.

[11]See also P. Fry, *Spirits of Protests* (Cambridge and New York: Cambridge University Press, 1976) 46, for further discussion of the social dynamics of prophetic conflict.

artistry (the repetition of "all") dramatizes and portends the social implications of Ahab's report. The "allness" of Elijah's victory forecasts a shift in Elijah's social standing, and an expected increase in his sphere of influence. The anticipation of such a shift yields irony in the upcoming episode. Elijah's comprehensive victory over the Baal prophets earns only isolation in the wilderness of Horeb.

In sociorhetorical analysis the nature of the inquiry varies for each text. The course of the analysis is governed by the progression of the story. The particular social and rhetorical elements in a story regulate the kinds of questions raised. The location of these elements in the story determines when the sociorhetorical interpretation occurs. Attention to rhetorical art coupled with a "thick description" of the social realm of the tale reveals these points of interplay and convergence.

In part two, a study of three texts illustrates the sociorhetorical method: 1 Samuel 14:36-46, 2 Samuel 14:1-22, and 1 Kings 3:16-28. How sociorhetorical analysis informs interpretation awaits discovery in the exegesis of these texts.

Part Two

The Sociorhetorical Exegesis of Texts

A Sociorhetorical Exegesis
of 1 Samuel 14:36-46,
2 Samuel 14:1-22,
and 1 Kings 3:16-28

The Improvidence of Royal Authority

A Sociorhetorical Exegesis of 1 Samuel 14:36-46

The biblical account of the Israelite monarchy depicts a hierarchically organized social structure. This vertical channel of power evolved from earlier stages in the social order. In the segmentary society[1] that preceded monarchy, various types of kinship groups carried out all economic, judicial, and military functions. With no overarching centralized authority, power relationships were horizontal.[2] According to the biblical narrative, individuals within tribes, clans, and families shared in the governance of society. Heads of families exercised judicial authority (Gen. 38, 24). Law codes attest to the judicial activity of tribal elders (Deut. 19:1-21; 21:1-9, 18-21; 22:13-21). Even military leaders conducted judicial hearings on the battle front (Josh. 7).

---

[1]E. E. Evans-Pritchard and M. Fortes, *African Political Systems* (London: University of Oxford Press, 1940) 13-14, first defined "segmentary society" as a tribe which was subdivided into a number of components.

[2]Discussions of early Israel's social structure may be found in G. E. Mendenhall, "Social Organization in Early Israel," *Magnalia Dei: The Mighty Acts of God*, ed. F. M. Cross et al. (Garden City NY: Doubleday, 1976) 132-51; C. H. J. DeGeus, *The Tribes of Israel* (Assen: Van Gorcum, 1976) 133-49; N. Gottwald, *The Tribes of Yahweh* (Maryknoll NY: Orbis Press, 1979) 239-92; and Niels Peter Lemche, *Early Israel: Anthropological and Historical Studies on the Israelite Society Before the Monarchy* (Leiden: E. J. Brill, 1985) 245-90.

The shift from these self-governing groups to the established bureau-cracy of kingship did not take place abruptly.[3] Chiefdoms arose as the interim order that facilitated the transition.[4] Situated between segmentary society and monarchic statehood, chiefdoms exhibited characteristics of both.[5] The Deuteronomistic portrait of Saul's administration illustrates this dual character.[6] As in segmentary society, leadership in Saul's ad-ministration was not specialized. No central ruling class carried out Saul's expanding responsibilities. In contrast to the delegation of responsi-bilities by kings, Saul himself carried out an array of political, judicial, and military tasks. He personally raised the support of a militia (1 Sam. 11:5-11). He led his own armies into battle (1 Sam. 13:2-3; 14:20-21). Judicial responsibilities also fell under Saul's direct auspices. He officiated as judge in the trial of the priests of Nob (1 Sam. 22:6-32). He

---

[3]On the rise of monarchy in Israel, see A. Alt, "The Formation of the Israelite State in Palestine," *Essays on the Old Testament History and Religion* (Garden City NY: Doubleday, 1968) 171-273; G. Mendenhall, "Monarchy," *Int* 29 (1975): 155-70; B. Halpern, *The Constitution of the Monarchy in Israel* (Chico CA: Scholars Press, 1981); A. D. H. Mayes, *The Story of Israel between Settlement and Exile* (London: SCM Press, 1983); and F. Frick, *The Formation of the State in Ancient Israel: A Survey of Models and Theories* (Sheffield: Almond Press, 1985).

[4]On the character of a chiefdom, see esp. C. Renfrew, "Beyond a Subsistence Economy: The Evolution of Social Organization in Prehistoric Europe," in *Reconstructing Complex Societies*, ed. C. B. Moore (Cambridge: American Schools of Oriental Research, 1974) 65-88; T. K. Earle, *Economic and Social Organization of a Complex Chiefdom: The Halelea District, Kahua'i, Hawaii* (Ann Arbor: Museum of Anthropology, University of Michigan, 1978); and James Flanagan, "Chiefs in Israel," *JSOT* 20 (1981): 47-73.

[5]E. Service, *Origins of the State and Civilization* (New York: Norton, 1975) 303-305; H. Claessen and P. Skalnik, "Limits: Beginning and End of the Early State," *The Early State*, ed. H. Calessen and P. Skalnik (The Hague: Mouton, 1978) 629; and Flanagan, "Chiefs in Israel," 50.

[6]Gottwald, *The Tribes of Yahweh*, 297-98; and F. Frick, "Religion and Socio-political Structure in Early Israel: An Ethno-Archaeological Approach," SBLSP 1979, ed. P. J. Achtemeier (Missoula MT: Scholars Press) 241 and 248, regard O.T. judges as chieftain figures. Flanagan, "Chiefs in Israel," 55-56, defines the transition to chieftains occurring in the period of Saul and David.

even conducted a hearing and issued a death sentence in the case of his own son Jonathan (1 Sam. 14:36-46).

Concurrently, accounts of Saul's rule record characteristics of a kingship. The biblical portrait of Saul resembled other ancient Near Eastern monarchs in their theocratic affiliations.[7] In Mesopotamia, kings were intermediaries between the gods and the people.[8] To this end, Saul frequently enlisted the services and counsel of prophetic and priestly liaisons of the divine (1 Sam. 14.18). The notion of divine choice characterized the reign of several Mesopotamian rulers.[9] Similarly, Samuel designated Saul as "the anointed by the Lord" at Saul's investiture (1 Sam. 10:1ff.). In Egypt, the Pharaoh presided at worship. Similarly, Saul officiated in the enactment of cult (1 Sam. 14:33-34; 13:8-9). Hence, Saul's tenure as leader combined elements of segmentary society, as well as features of kingship.

Prior to and during this time of transition, a covenant treaty with God constituted the core of Israel's identity.[10] This treaty established a bond between Yahweh and the community.[11] Such an agreement required the

---

[7]Theocratic claims legitimized kingship in the ancient Near East. See H. Frankfort, *Kingship and the Gods* (Chicago: University of Chicago Press, 1948). With reference to Israelite kings, see E. I. J. Rosenthal, "Some Aspects of the Hebrew Monarchy," *JJS* 9 (1958): 8-10; and T. N. D. Mettinger, *King and Messiah: The Civil and Sacral Legitimation of Israelite Kings* (Lund: C. W. K. Gleerup, 1976).

[8]Frankfort, *Kingship and the Gods*, 215-30.

[9]In Sumer, Lipit-Ishtar testified to his commissioning by the gods. See J. Pritchard, ed., *Ancient Near Eastern Texts* (Princeton: Princeton University Press, 1955) 159.

[10]For a discussion of the textual and historical evidence arguing in favor of covenant antedating kingship, see G. Mendenhall, *Law and Covenant and the Ancient Near East* (Pittsburgh: Presbyterian Board of Colportage of Western Pennsylvania, 1955); D. Hillers, *Covenant: The History of a Biblical Idea* (Baltimore: Johns Hopkins University Press, 1969); K. Baltzer, *The Covenant Formulary in Old Testament, Jewish, and Early Christian Writings* (Philadelphia: Fortress Press, 1971); and D. McCarthy, *Treaty and Covenant: A Study in Form in the Ancient Oriental Documents and in the Old Testament*, AnBib 21 (Rome: Pontifical Biblical Institute, 1963).

[11]G. Mendenhall, *The Tenth Generation: The Origins of the Biblical*

people's fidelity and obedience to God.[12] Sociologically, covenant culti-
vated a solidarity among the clans. Their common affliation with this
God reinforced their common identity as a people. How this covenantal
bond influenced the shape and scope of kingship is complex.[13] The
priority of this agreement necessarily influenced the character of the new
office. For example, the biblical narrative portrays Saul's kingship as
ordained by God. "The Spirit of God was upon him" (1 Sam. 10:9; 11:6).
At the same time, this appointment was conditional.[14] Saul's kingship was
premised upon his obedience to God (1 Sam. 12:14). As king, Saul must
remain faithful to God's covenant with the people. As king, he must
honor the sovereignty of Yahweh's kingship.[15]

The institution of kingship in Israel and its adaptation among a covenant people entailed change. Authority once concentrated within kinship

---

Tradition (Baltimore and London: John Hopkins University Press; 1973) 21;
N. Gottwald, *The Tribes of Yahweh*, 233; and R. Wilson, "Israel's Judicial
System in the Preexilic Period," *JQR* 74 (1983): 229.

[12]For an overview of the scholarly research since Wellhausen on covenant as
a religious and sociological entity, see E. W. Nicholson, *God and His People:
Covenant and Theology in the Old Testament* (Oxford: Clarendon Press, 1986).

[13]See W. Evans, "An Historical Reconstruction of the Emergence of Israelite
Kingship and the Reign of Saul," *Scripture in Context: Essays on the Comparative Method*, ed. W. Hallo, J. Moyer, and L. Perdue (Winona Lake IN: Eisenbrauns, 1983) 61-77; F. M. Cross, *Canaanite Myth and Hebrew Epic* (Cambridge: Harvard University Press, 1973) 219-73; and T. Ishida, *The Royal Dynasties in Ancient Israel* (Berlin and New York: Walter de Gruyter, 1977) 42-54.

[14]Cross, *Canaanite Myth and Hebrew Epic*, 220-21.

[15]Opinions are divided on the origin of the idea of Yahweh's kingship.
Because of the special relation of Yahweh's kingship to Jerusalem, scholars once
believed that God's kingship came into being after the kingdom of David was
established. See J. Gray, "Hebrew Conception of the Kingship of God: Its Origin
and Development," *VT* 6 (1956): 268-85; and L. Rost, "Konigsherrschaft Jahwes
in vorkoniglicher Zeit?" *TLZ* 85 (1960): 721-24. Other studies have produced
convincing arguments that the notion of Yahweh's kingship dates back to the
premonarchical traditions of Holy War. See G. von Rad, *Holy War in Ancient
Israel*, trans. M. Dawn (Grand Rapids: Eerdmans, 1991; 1958) 32; Ishida, *The
Royal Dynasties in Ancient Israel*, 38-39; Halpern, *The Constitution of the Monarchy in Israel*, 23-27, and J. Tigay, *You Shall Have No Other Gods: Israelite
Religion in Light of Hebrew Inscriptions* (Atlanta: Scholars Press, 1986) 77-78.

groups now shifted to one individual. With the centralization of power, the king managed an array of responsibilities. His rule required the cultivation of the people's trust and allegiance. The covenant between God and Israel necessitated the adaptation of the king's rule to the realm of God's sovereignty. At the same time, the people needed to endorse this human kingship. The community had to integrate their allegiance to the newly anointed monarch with an ongoing fidelity to the reign of God as king.[16]

The Deuteronomistic History recounts these events and embodies some of the social features of these transitions. The books of Joshua, Judges, Samuel, and Kings make up this literary corpus. Together, they trace Israel's story from the settlement in Canaan to the Exile.[17]

---

[16]These changes and the social tensions associated with the transition from tribal leadership to a monarchy are outlined in M. A. Cohen, "The Role of the Shilonite Priesthood in the United Monarchy of Ancient Israel," *HUCA* 36 (1964).

[17]In 1943, Martin Noth proposed that Deuteronomy–2 Kings was a theological history (the Deuteronomistic History = Dtr Hs). He argued for a single exilic author on grounds of stylistic and thematic unity. Noth's work countered the older view of these writings as a preexilic composition of the monarchy revised in light of the Judean exile (double-redaction hypothesis). See M. Noth, *The Deuteronomistic History*, trans. J. Douall et al. JSOTSup 15 (Sheffield: University of Sheffield, 1981). Since Noth's work, scholarly research on the Dtr Hs can be divided into two groups. First, some scholars accept Noth's proposal but refine its literary and theological insights. See O. Ploger, "Reden und Gebete im deuteronomistischen chronistischen Geschichtswerk," *Festschrift fur Gunther Dehn*, ed. W. Schneemelcher (Neukirchen: Erziehung, 1957) 34-49; G. von Rad, "The Deuteronomic Theology of History in I and II Kings," *The Problem of the Hexateuch and Other Essays*, trans. E. W. Trueman Dickman (New York: McGraw-Hill, 1966) 205-21; and H. W. Wolff, "The Kerygma of the Deuteronomic Historical Work," *Vitality of the Old Testament Traditions*, ed. W. Brueggemann and H. W. Wolff (Atlanta: John Knox Press, 1975) 83-100. A second group of scholars accept Noth's notion of a Dtr Hs but also sees evidence of a double redaction. See F. M. Cross, Jr., "The Structure of the Deuteronomistic History," *Perspectives in Jewish Learning* III (Chicago: Spectus College, 1967) 9-24, and "Themes of the Books of Kings and the Structure of the Deuteronomistic History," *Canaanite Myth and Hebrew Epic* (Cambridge MA: Harvard University Press, 1973) 274-89; D. N. Freedman, "Deuteronomic History," *IDBSup* (Nashville:

The books of Samuel specifically recount the shift from an amor-
phous social order to monarchic rule. Five units of story report this transition. First, the Shiloh traditions (1 Sam. 1–4) detail the decline of this
priesthood and the prominence of Samuel. Samuel will anoint the first
king. The second unit, the Ark Narrative (1 Sam. 4:1–7:1), which stands
as a cohesive independent story, recounts God's involvement in this
setting.[18] The third segment narrates the establishment of monarchy and
the emergence of Saul as the first king (1 Sam. 7:2–12:25). The fourth
section details his rejection as king (1 Sam. 13–15). Fifth, the extended
account of David's rise and reign concludes these works (1 Sam.
16–2 Sam. 24).

Israel's transition from a marginalized company of tribes to a centralized state entailed elaborate social change. The tensions, conflicts, alignments, and developments associated with this reconfiguration of power
impact and inform the form and content of the Samuel narratives. How
the form and content of these stories disclose, embody, corroborate, or

---

Abingdon Press, 1976); R. E. Friedman, *The Exile and Biblical Narrative: The
Formation of the Deuteronomistic and Priestly Works* (Chico CA: Scholars Press,
1981); R. D. Nelson, *The Double Redaction of the Deuteronomistic History*
(Sheffield: University of Sheffield Press, 1981). Still others within this second
group argue for multiple redactions before and after the exile. See H. Weippert,
"Die deuteronomistischen Beurteilungen der Konige von Israel und Juda und das
Problem der Redaktion der Konigsbucher," *Bib* 53 (1972): 301-39. Finally,
J. Van Seters, like Noth, proposes an exilic Dtr Hs. Unlike Noth, Van Seters'
historian does not use early tradition but composes an original version of the
reign of Saul and David. J. Van Seters, *In Search of History: Historiography in
the Ancient World and the Origins of Biblical History* (New Haven: Yale
University Press, 1983).

[18]Despite the characterization "Ark Narrative," this study recognizes the
important work on these chapters by P. Miller and J. J. M. Roberts who argue
that Yahweh and Yahweh's purpose are at the forefront of these traditions. See
Miller and Roberts, *The Hand of the Lord* (Baltimore and London: Johns
Hopkins University Press, 1977).

undercut these social elements invites exploration.[19] The following sociorhetorical exegesis of 1 Samuel 14:36-46 serves as an illustrative study.

Situated within the account of Saul's rejection as king (1 Sam.
13–15), 1 Samuel 14:36-46 constitutes one scene[20] in Saul's initiative
against the Philistines (chapters 13 and 14).[21] The stories in chapters 13
and 14 are derived primarily from narrative and annalistic sources on the
Philistine wars. Because the Philistine threat accounts for the commission
of Saul's leadership (1 Sam. 9:1–10:6),[22] these chapters constitute a turning point in the account of Saul's kingship. In the wake of the Philistine
threat, the actions of Saul incite the rejection of his kingship by Samuel
in chapter 13. The activity of Saul in chapter 14 reinforces this rejection.

---

[19]K. Burke maintains that "all communication is both sociological and
artistic." See K. Burke, *On Symbols and Society*, ed. Joseph R. Gusfield (Chicago
and London: University of Chicago Press, 1989) 44.

[20]On the difficulties of defining "scene," J. P. Fokkelman observes, "A scene
is a narrative text which to a high degree is understandable in itself and which
is characterized by the initiation, building up, and conclusion of an action (often
a conflict), which usually demonstrates unity of place and time, and brings together one or two and sometimes three protagonists. This definition is already in-
adequate and may not be applied to the texts unamended." See J. P. Fokkelman,
King David (II Samuel 9–20 and I Kings 1–2), Vol. 1, *Narrative Art and Poetry
in the Books of Samuel* (Assen: Van Gorcum, 1981) 9n.15.

[21]B. C. Birch argues against the unity of chaps. 13 and 14. He concludes that
they represent a collection of various materials that are stylistically diverse. See
Birch, *The Rise of the Israelite Monarchy: The Growth and Development of
1 Samuel 7–15* (Missoula: Scholars Press, 1976) 91. By contrast, V. P. Long and
J. M. Miller demonstrate the unity of chapters 13 and 14 on grounds of (a) thematic continuity, (b) correspondence of characters, (c) correspondence of setting,
and (d) material and verbal links. See Long, *The Reign and Rejection of King
Saul: A Case for Literary and Theological Coherence* (Atlanta: Scholars Press,
1989) 69, and J. M. Miller, "Saul's Rise to Power; Some Observations Concerning 1 Sam. 9:1–10:16; 10:26–11:15; and 13:2–14:46," *CBQ* 36 (1974): 161.

[22]B. Halpern, "The Uneasy Compromise: Israel Between League and
Monarchy," *Traditions in Transformation: Turning Points in Biblical Faith*, ed.
B. Halpern and J. D. Levenson (Winona Lake IN: Eisenbrauns, 1981) 65;
W. Richter, "Die *nagid* Formel: Ein Beitrag zur Erhellung des *nagid* Problems,"
BZ 9 (1965): 81; Long, *The Reign and Rejection of King Saul*, 52-54 and 63-64;
and Birch, *The Rise of the Israelite Monarchy*, 91-92.

In the opening of this chapter (1 Sam. 14:1-35),[23] Saul's son Jonathan and his armorbearer initiated a battle against the Philistines at Michmash. Jonathan acknowledged divine guidance before battle. When news that the enemy had been routed reached Saul, the king and his troops joined the fray. Though victory appeared to be Israel's, Saul made an oath to guarantee the triumph. He imposed a fast on the troops until sundown. Jonathan, not knowing of his father's oath, inadvertently ate some honey. These events set the stage for the subsequent story of judgment.

In 1 Samuel 14:36-46, Saul officiates as judge among this covenant people. He conducts a trial to identify and punish a suspected evildoer in the community. Two brief episodes narrate this drama[24] and structure its course.

> Episode I, vss. 36-42
> > Unit I. Preparation for Battle, vss. 36-37
> > Unit II. Preparation for a Trial, vss. 38-41
> > Unit III. A Trial and Indictment, vss. 41-42
> Episode II, vss. 43-46
> > Unit I. Confession and Sentence, vss. 43-44
> > Unit II. Community's Challenge to Saul, vs. 45
> > Unit III. Conclusion: Change in the Battle Plan, vs. 46

Saul's battle plan, his oath to punish an evildoer, and the subsequent trial determine the narrative progression in episode one (vss. 36-42). These three units create narrative tension which demands resolution. The sentencing of the criminal, the people's oath, and a change in the battle plan compose the second episode (vss. 43-46). Together, these units determine the outcome of the incumbent drama.

The story unfolds through the artistry of transpositions. The narrative action in the first episode is reversed or opposed in episode two. Saul's plan to battle the Philistines introduces the tale (vs. 36). The narrator's

---

[23]The narrative in vss. 1-46 can be labeled broadly as a "battle report" according to the general elements oulined by W. Richter, *Traditionsgeschichtliche Untersuchungen zum Richterbuch* (Bonn: Peter Hanstein, 1963) 263.

[24]"Episode" is understood here as "an action or incident standing out by itself but connected with a series of events." See C. L. Berhardt, *The New Century Handbook of English Literature* (New York: Appleton/Century/Crofts, 1967) 403-404.

conclusion reverses this war scheme (vs. 46). Saul's speech dominates episode one (vss. 36-42). In episode two (vss. 43-46), the people's speech determines the outcome of the tale. Saul's oath to indict an evildoer governs the storyline. Subsequently, the people's oath, which overturns Saul's judgment, resolves the plot.

The contrast in characters throughout this story collaborates with these reversals. Saul parades an array of power across these two brief episodes. He presides as military leader, judicial official, and cultic officer. By contrast, uncertainty surrounds the people's identity. Different translations of העם reflect this ambiguity.[25] Whether העם refers to "troops" versus the whole "people" fuels the debate. Spoken to and spoken about, the people initiate speech only once in this tale (vs. 45). Jonathan, Saul's son, is cast in a passive role. He speaks only once in response to an interrogation by Saul (vs. 43). Jonathan's activity in the previous story provides the point of controversy. Unaware of his father's oath, Jonathan ate some honey (1 Sam. 14:27). Accordingly, Saul's judicial activity condemns Jonathan to death. Yet, the people's intervention saves Jonathan's life. In this account, Jonathan's incrimination sets the king at cross purposes with the people.

Such dissonance throughout the narrative contributes to the growing dissension between Saul and the people. The fragile bond of allegiance between king and people erodes across this story. The king's judgment of a culprit evokes the people's judgment of this king. Rhetoric reveals and reinforces the social discord erupting across this scene.[26] How this

---

[25]H. W. Hertzberg, *I and II Samuel: A Commentary* (Philadelphia: Westminster Press, 1964) 108-109; W. Brueggemann, *First and Second Samuel*, Interpretation (Louisville: John Knox Press, 1990) 97-118; and H. P. Smith, *The Books of Samuel*, ICC (New York: Charles Scribner's Sons, 1899) 90-128, translate העם as "people." Ralph Klein, *I Samuel*, WBC 10 (Waco TX: Word Books, 1983) 130-43, and R. P. Gordon, *1 and 2 Samuel* (Exeter: Paternoster Press, 1986) 130-42, regard העם as the "army," "militia," or "troops." The translation "people" employed in this essay is based on the study by E. A. Speiser who shows that "עם was essentially a term denoting close family, that is, people in the sense of a larger, but fundamentally consanguineous body," See Speiser, "'People' and 'Nation' in Israel," *JBL* 79 (1960): 157-63.

[26]E. Said observes that representation in literature has always been related to literature's inherent social dimensions. Hence, Said calls for a sustained and

sociorhetorical interplay informs theological considerations invites the following sociorhetorical exegesis of this story.

Episode I, vss. 36-42

Three units make up this first episode. First, a battle proposal (vss. 36-37) warrants the arraignment of an evildoer. Second, the preparation for a trial (vss. 38-41) indicates a lot casting. Third, this cultic ordeal achieves an indictment (vss. 41-42).

Unit 1. Preparation for Battle, vss. 36-37

וַיֹּאמֶר שָׁאוּל

And Saul said,

נֵרְדָה אַחֲרֵי פְלִשְׁתִּים לַיְלָה

"Let us go down after the Philistines at night,

וְנָבֹזָה בָהֶם עַד־אוֹר הַבֹּקֶר

And let us plunder them until the light of morning,

וְלֹא־נַשְׁאֵר בָּהֶם אִישׁ

And let us not leave one of them."

וַיֹּאמְרוּ

And they said,

כָּל־הַטּוֹב בְּעֵינֶיךָ עֲשֵׂה

"All the good in your eyes, do!"

וַיֹּאמֶר הַכֹּהֵן

But the priest said,

נִקְרְבָה הֲלֹם אֶל־הָאֱלֹהִים:

"Let us consult God here." (vs. 36)

וַיִּשְׁאַל שָׁאוּל בֵּאלֹהִים

So Saul inquired of God,

הַאֵרֵד אַחֲרֵי פְלִשְׁתִּים

"Shall I go down after the Philistines?

הֲתִתְּנֵם בְּיַד יִשְׂרָאֵל

Will you give them into the hand of Israel?"

---

systematic examination of the interrelationship between the literary and the social features of narrative. See Said, "Opponents, Audiences, Constituencies and Community," *Politics of Interpretation*, ed. W. J. Mitchell (Chicago and London, University of Chicago Press, 1983) 5.

וְלֹא עָנָהוּ בַּיּוֹם הַהוּא:

But he (God) did not answer him on that day.   (vs. 37)

An array of direct discourse unfolds in this opening unit. The words of
Saul constitute the outer limits of these interactions. His recitations
border the responses of the priest and the people. His proposal for battle
initiates the conversation. "Let us go down. . . . " As leader, he also has
the last word. "Shall I go. . . . " The narrated report of God's silence
concludes these exchanges.

The proposal of Saul embodies the transitional status of his rule. Like
a monarch, he holds sufficient military authority to propose war. Like a
member of segmented society, his authority is subject to public approval.
The transitional nature of the new monarchic office is evident. Rhetoric
conveys the tentative character of his kingly authority as well as the
residual autonomy of the people. The grammatical forms of these introductory exchanges suggest these social relations. The cohortative speech
("Let us . . . ") of Saul aligns him with the people. The response of the
community in the form of an imperative ("do") attests to their collective
power. His interrogative address to God supposes the subservient status
of the king before the divine.

A speech by Saul not only commences the story but initiates a battle
plan.

וַיֹּאמֶר שָׁאוּל

And Saul said,

נֵרְדָה אַחֲרֵי פְלִשְׁתִּים לַיְלָה

"Let us go down after the Philistines at night,

וְנָבֹזָה בָהֶם עַד־אוֹר הַבֹּקֶר

And let us plunder them until the light of morning,

וְלֹא־נַשְׁאֵר בָּהֶם אִישׁ

And let us not leave one of them."

Saul's success in warfare depends upon his capacity to attract and maintain supporters.[27] Though Saul presides as military chief, he does not
order Israel to fight. Unlike the imperatives of a military commander, his

---

[27]M. Harris, *Cultural Materialism: The Struggle for a Science of Culture*
(New York: Random House, 1979) 92.

cohortative speech (נרדה נבזה נשאר) enlists the participation and approval of the people.[28] This diplomatic engagement of their cooperation ignores the degree of hardship therein. A threefold strategy specifies the military mission (נִרְדָה אַחֲרֵי פְלִשְׁתִּים), its method and length (הַבֹּקֶר עַד־אוֹר . . . לַיְלָה), and its scope (וְלֹא־נַשְׁאֵר בָּהֶם אִישׁ). In the previous battle, Saul's oath prevented the people from eating. His military tactics in the upcoming confrontation will prevent them from sleeping.[29]

The demands Saul imposes upon the people do not diminish their wholehearted support.

וַיֹּאמְרוּ

And they said,

כָּל־הַטּוֹב בְּעֵינֶיךָ עֲשֵׂה

"All the good in your eyes, do!"

The people ratify Saul's entire (כָּל) proposal. The expression "your eyes" metaphorically refers to his "opinion" or "judgment."[30] Hence, the endorsement of his complete (כָּל) battle plan accompanies the people's expression of their complete confidence in his leadership. "All the good in *your* eyes, do!"

Despite this vote of confidence, the royal authority of Saul is still subject to constraint. In some ancient Near Eastern societies, the authority of the monarch was absolute. The Sumerians asserted that kingship had descended from heaven.

When the crown of kingship was lowered from heaven
When the sceptor and the throne of kingship were lowered from heaven.[31]

---

[28]In contrast to the imperative form, the cohortative functions as a direct or indirect volitive to express a wish or request. See B. K. Waltke and M. O'Connor, *An Introduction to Biblical Hebrew Syntax* (Winowa Lake IN: Eisenbrauns, 1990) 573, and E. Kautzsch and A. E. Cowley, eds., *Gesenius' Hebrew Grammar*, 2nd English ed. (Oxford: Clarendon Press, 1910) 130.

[29]J. P. Fokkelman, *Narrative Art and Poetry in the Books of Samuel*, vol. 2, *The Crossing Fates* (Assen: Van Gorcum, 1986) 70.

[30]See also Jer. 7:11; Prov. 3:7; and Gen. 16:6.

[31]T. Jacobsen, *The Sumerian King List*, Assyrian Studies 11 (Chicago: University of Chicago, 1940) 58.

Divine authority empowered these kings. In Egypt, kingship counted as a function of the gods. The Pharaoh was considered an incarnation of the god Re.[32] By contrast, socioanthropological studies on Israel define a king's status as a vicegerent.[33] As liaison, the king carries out and oversees God's plan in the Israelite community. Thus far, Saul's military proposal lacks full authorization. Consultation with God is required. An injunction of the priest amends the agreement between Saul and the people.

וַיֹּאמֶר הַכֹּהֵן

But the priest said,

נִקְרְבָה הֲלֹם אֶל־הָאֱלֹהִים:

"Let us consult God here." (vs. 36)

A request for an oracle often preceded the initiation of battle in Israel. Before fighting Benjamin's sons, Israel consulted God at Bethel (Judg. 20:27). The whole community consulted God before the attack on the Canaanites (Judg. 1:1). David petitioned God prior to his battle against the Philistines (1 Sam. 23:2). For the covenant people, such consultations were common. By contrast, this injunction by the priest to the king is uncommon. "Let us consult God here." Nowhere else in Scripture does a priest instruct the king to consult God.[34] Instead, the king called upon the priest for the oracle. Before fighting the Amalekites, David ordered Abiathar the priest to bring the ephod and consult God (1 Sam. 30:8). In a previous battle, Saul himself commanded Ahijah to seek God's endorsement (1 Sam. 14:18-19). By contrast, in this account, the

---

[32]Frankfort, *Kingship and the Gods*, 238; and W. F. Edgerton, "The Government and the Governed in the Egyptian Empire," *JNES* 6 (1947): 152-60; and Ishida, *The Royal Dynasties in Ancient Israel*, 6.

[33]Mettinger, *King and Messiah*, 244; Whitelam, *The Just King*, 164; and W. M. Clark, "A Legal Background of the Yahwist's Use of 'Good and Evil' in Genesis 2–3," *JBL* 88 (1969): 269.

[34]For K. D. Budde, the priest's interference is so unacceptable that it warrants a textual change of the MT. Budde's emendation makes Saul call on the priest for an oracle. See Budde, *Die Bucher Samuel*, KHC 8 (Tubingen: J. C. B. Mohr, 1902) 100-101. Hertzberg, *I and II Samuel: A Commentary*, 116, also notes the uncommonness of the priest's injunction. He emends the text with לכהן in place of הכהן.

priest prompts Saul's consultation of Yahweh. The translation of the conjunction *waw* (ו) as "but" conveys the uncommonness of such an
interruption.[35]

Kingship in Israel was a regulated office. Samuel records the rights
and duties of the monarch in Israel (1 Sam. 10:25). Deuteronomy details
the nature and scope of the Israelite kingship (Deut. 17:14-20). The
priest's injunction in this story rehearses these limits on the Israelite
ruler. A king's authority must be exercised in consultation with the
divine.[36]

Unfortunately, the behavior of Saul manifests a pattern of declining
commitment to discover the will of God. In an earlier confrontation with
the Philistines, Saul conducted a battle on his own terms (1 Sam. 14:16-
24). Though he called to Ahijah the priest for an oracle, Saul broke off
the inquiry midstream. Eager to take advantage of the uprising in the Philistine camp, Saul abandoned the inquiry without waiting for an answer.
Instead, he bound the people to an oath to ensure the victory of that campaign. In addition to the rigors of battle, they must abide by a fast.

In the present story, Saul seeks a divine oracle only after the
promptings of the priest.

וַיִּשְׁאַל שָׁאוּל בֵּאלֹהִים

So Saul inquired of God,

הַאֵרֵד אַחֲרֵי פְלִשְׁתִּים

"Shall I go down after the Philistines?

הֲתִתְּנֵם בְּיַד יִשְׂרָאֵל

Will you give them into the hand of Israel?"

A two-part question sets forth the request for an oracle. The form of
Saul's inquiry subtly contrasts with his military proposal. The first-person
plural cohortative language (נֵרְדָה "Let us go down . . . "), which
enlisted the people's participation in the battle plan (vs.36), has been

[35]Against Hertzberg, *I and II Samuel: A Commentary*, 109, and S. Goldman,
Samuel: Hebrew Text and English Translation (London and Bournemouth:
Soncino Press, 1951) 82, who read "then." Klein, *I Samuel*, 31; P. K. McCarter,
I Samuel, AB 8 (Garden City NY: Doubleday, 1980) 244; and the NRSV, RSV,
NIV, and JB read "but," though no rationale is offered.
[36]Mettinger, *King and Messiah*, 61-80.

replaced by first-person speech (הַאֵרֵד "Shall I go down . . . "). The language of the request suggests a contract between two parties. "Shall I go . . . Will you give. . . . " Saul's petition for an oracle houses his own agenda. He seeks a permit for warfare and a guarantee of victory. The priest advised "let us consult God" (קרב, vs. 36). The narrator reports that "Saul inquired" (שׁאל, vs. 37) of God. Though, in appearance, קרב and שׁאל are synonymous, two different verbs might suggest differences in entreaties. The proposal by the priest (קרב) encourages an unqualified inquiry of the divine. Saul seeks something else. He seeks a guaranteed victory. A word play, "Saul sauled God" (וַיִּשְׁאַל שָׁאוּל, vs. 37), foreshadows the self-serving nature of Saul's request.

Rhetoric reveals the political program embedded in Saul's speech. The first question addresses a *condition* for battle: "Shall I go down after the Philistines?" The second question attends to the *outcome*: "Will you give them into the hand of Israel?"[37] The expression "into the hand of" metaphorically refers to the "control or power of."[38] Saul seeks to ensure Israel's control over the Philistines. Yet, the juxtaposition of the *condition* and the *outcome* of battle discloses his cunning. What God does for Israel ("Will you give them into Israel's hand . . . ") is bound up with what Saul himself does ("Shall I go . . . "). A military victory for Israel earns credit for Saul's military profile. A heightened military profile enhances Saul's political stature. Such strategy may conjure the allegiance of the people. But before God, it evokes only silence.

וְלֹא עָנָהוּ בַּיּוֹם הַהוּא:

But he [God] did not answer him on that day. (vs. 37)

---

[37]Traditionally, scholars tend to note only the "yes," "no" format of Saul's inquiry. See e.g. H. P. Smith, *The Books of Samuel*, 121; Goldman, *Samuel: Hebrew Text and English Translation*, 82; and Klein, *I Samuel*, 139. Here the juxtaposition of the two questions invites a different observation.

[38]See also Exod. 3:8; Isa. 41:20; and Gen. 16:6. In a brief study, J. J. Roberts examined the expression "the hand of Yahweh/Elohim" in light of extrabiblical parallels. He concluded that the expression was a common Near Eastern idiom for speaking of the power of the deity. See Roberts, "The Hand of Yahweh," *VT* 21 (1971): 244-52.

Divine silence signals a problem. In this story, the silence of God "on that day" threatens the battle plan of Saul "at night" (vs. 36). This disruption of the military campaign threatens the leadership of Saul. Further, the narrated report of God's silence conjures a discomforting recollection. In 1 Samuel 8:18, Samuel cautioned the people against the election of a king. A ruler would oppress them. Despite their cries for help, Samuel warned, "God will not answer on that day." Parallel language foreshadows the unsettling link between the warning by Samuel about a corrupt ruler and the narrated report of God's silence before Saul.[39]

The exchange of direct discourse across this first unit (vss. 36-37) has climaxed in divine silence. The lack of response by God not only threatens the military scheme of Saul, it alters the course of the story. Preparation for battle (vss. 36-37) gives way to preparation for a trial.

Unit 2. Preparation for a Trial, vss. 38-40

וַיֹּאמֶר שָׁאוּל

And Saul said,

גְּשׁוּ הֲלֹם כֹּל פִּנּוֹת הָעָם

"Come here all the leaders of the people,

וּדְעוּ

and know,

וּרְאוּ

and see,

בַּמָּה הָיְתָה הַחַטָּאת הַזֹּאת הַיּוֹם:

the sin that was committed this day. (vs. 38)

כִּי חַי־יְהוָה הַמּוֹשִׁיעַ אֶת־יִשְׂרָאֵל

If by the life of God, the one who delivered Israel,

כִּי אִם־יֶשְׁנוֹ בְּיוֹנָתָן בְּנִי

if even it is my son Jonathan,

כִּי מוֹת יָמוּת

indeed, he must die."

וְאֵין עֹנֵהוּ מִכָּל־הָעָם:

But there was no one answering him from any of the people.

---

[39]Apart from the present context, only one other instance records God's silence in response to a king's consultation before battle. When Saul inquired in 1 Sam. 28:6, the correlation between God's displeasure and God's silence was inescapable.

וַיֹּאמֶר אֶל־כָּל־יִשְׂרָאֵל

And he said to all Israel,

אַתֶּם תִּהְיוּ לְעֵבֶר אֶחָד

"You be over here.

וַאֲנִי וְיוֹנָתָן בְּנִי נִהְיֶה לְעֵבֶר אֶחָד

I and Jonathan, my son, we will be over there."

וַיֹּאמְרוּ הָעָם אֶל־שָׁאוּל

And the people said to Saul,

הַטּוֹב בְּעֵינֶיךָ עֲשֵׂה:

"The good in your eyes, do!"

Two exchanges between Saul and the people structure this unit. First, Saul issues an oath and a command. The people respond with silence. Second, Saul orders a lot casting (vs. 40). The people voice their approval. Narrator and characters join to conduct these interchanges.

וַיֹּאמֶר שָׁאוּל

And Saul said,

גֹּשׁוּ הֲלֹם כֹּל פִּנּוֹת הָעָם

"Come here all the leaders of the people,

וּדְעוּ

and know,

וּרְאוּ

and see,

בַּמָּה הָיְתָה הַחַטָּאת הַזֹּאת הַיּוֹם:

the sin that was committed this day." (vs. 38)

The words of Saul rupture the divine silence as well as initiate a conversation. In the wake of God's nonresponse, Saul declares the presence of sin as explanation. His interpretation harnesses any suspicions about his own credibility. Pursuit of an enemy in battle first requires pursuit of an evildoer among the people.

Saul begins by summoning the leaders of the people (פִּנּוֹת הָעָם)[40] to witness the identification and judgment of a suspected evildoer. These

---

[40]Literally, "corners" or "cornerstones" of the people. See Judg. 20:2; Isa. 19:13; and Zech. 10:4.

officials were the elders of the tribal lineages.[41] In segmentary society, such officials were called upon collectively to hear testimony about a crime, level judgments, and offer counsel to the community.[42] In Judges 20:2ff., for example, the elders heard the crime against the concubine of the Levite. Upon report of the story, they recommended steps to avenge this evil among the Benjaminites.

With the rise of monarchy, judicial authority is gradually transferred to the king. Despite the provisional status of kingship, Saul possesses sufficient judicial authority to preside at the upcoming trial. The enlistment of these elders will enhance his judicial stature.[43] Sociorhetorical interplay illustrates this dynamic. The form of Saul's address to these elders demonstrates his authority. With three imperatives (גְּשׁוּ, וּדְעוּ, וּרְאוּ), Saul commands these leaders of the people. At the same time, the content of his commands ("come," "see," "know") discloses his dependence upon them, as well as the role they will play at this hearing. As witnesses they will foster credibility and acceptance of Saul's judgments.[44] Further, their verification of his conviction of a sinner in the community is of far-reaching import. It will verify his interpretation of divine silence.

These elders are not the only witnesses whom Saul enlists. His recitation of an oath summons divine involvement.

כִּי חַי־יְהוָה הַמּוֹשִׁיעַ אֶת־יִשְׂרָאֵל

"If by the life of God, the one who delivered Israel,

---

[41]Wilson, "Israel's Judicial System in the Preexilic Period," 238-39; Whitelam, *The Just King*, 74; and A. F. Kirkpatrick, *The First and Second Books of Samuel* (Cambridge: Cambridge University Press, 1930) 114.

[42]Discussions of the judicial procedures among lineages in comparable settings can be found in P. Bohannan, *Justice and Judgment among the Tiv* (London: Oxford University Press, 1957); M. Gluckman, *The Judicial Process among the Barotse of Northern Rhodesia* (New Haven CT: Yale University, 1965); and P. H. Gulliver, *Social Control in an African Society* (London: Routledge and Kegan Paul, 1963).

[43]R. Wilson, "Enforcing the Covenant: The Mechanisms of Judicial Authority in Early Israel," *The Quest for the Kingdom of God: Studies in Honor of G. E. Mendenhall*, ed. H. B. Huffmon, F. A. Spina, and A. R. W. Green (Winona Lake IN: Eisenbrauns, 1983) 71.

[44]Wilson, "Israel's Preexilic Judicial System," 241-42.

כִּי אִם־יֶשְׁנוֹ בְּיוֹנָתָן בְּנִי

if even it is my son Jonathan,

כִּי מוֹת יָמוּת

indeed, he must die."

Oaths call on a deity to sanction the truth sworn by the speaker. The well-being and security in relationships, households, and society as a whole demand that people speak the truth.[45] People's confidence and trust in one another are secured or reinforced by oaths. The oath of Jonathan to David ensured the fugitive's safety (1 Sam. 20, 21, 23). The oath of Saul before the woman of Endor guaranteed her well-being (1 Sam. 28:10). In this story, divine silence has instigated doubt. The oath of Saul opposes the doubt and cultivates a renewed confidence in his word. With formulaic speech ("If by the life of God"), Saul calls on God to sanction his oath. Abigail swore "by the life of God" that David's enemies would be like Nabal (1 Sam. 25:23). On another occasion, Saul swore "by the life of God" to spare David's life (1 Sam. 19:6). Divine authority witnesses such pronouncements.

The particle כִּי delineates the three parts of Saul's recitation.[46] The asseveration, "if by the life of God," calls upon a divine witness. The protasis, "if even it is my son Jonathan," designates the authority and scope of Saul's word. The apodosis, "indeed, he must die," indicates the deadly consequence. The comprehensive nature of Saul's three-part oath overshadows the delay of his threefold battle proposal (vs. 36).

Jonathan, the son of Saul, represents the scope of the king's jurisdiction ("if even it is my son Jonathan"). Members of the royal household are subject to the judgment and punishment of the king. In the case of Jonathan, such justice may house a threat. The activities of Jonathan in the previous story contrast with activities of Saul in this account.[47] In

---

[45]See M. Pope, "Oaths," *IDB* (New York and Nashville: Abingdon Press, 1962) 575-77; J. Pedersen, *Israel: Its Life and Culture*, vols. 3-4, 2nd ed. (London: Oxford University Press, 1963) 450; and H. J. Boecker, *Law and the Administration of Justice* (Minneapolis: Augsburg Publishing House, 1980) 23-26.

[46]On the uses of the particle כִּי, see J. Muilenburg, "The Linguistic and Rhetorical Usages of the Particle *ki* in the Old Testament," *HUCA* 32 (1961): 135-60.

[47]P. Miscall, D. Jobling, D. Gunn, R. Polzin, and V. P. Long observe that

1 Samuel 14:1-15, Jonathan sought God's endorsement. He received a divine sanction and successfully defeated a Philistine installment. In the present story, Saul does not seek the counsel of God on his own initiative. Only after the promptings of the priest does Saul requests God's oracle and he receives no answer. Hence, his assault on the Philistines is delayed. Such contrasts between the king and his son cultivate alienation. Though the rhetoric of Saul highlights his kinship with this son ("Jonathan, my son"), the upcoming narrative reveals estrangement.

Finally, the oath of Saul closes with the imprecation, "indeed, he must die." The death sentence which concludes the oath threatens to put an end to Jonathan. Sociorhetorical interplay illustrates Jonathan's plight.

כִּי חַי־יְהוָה הַמּוֹשִׁיעַ אֶת־יִשְׂרָאֵל
"If by the *life* of God, the one who delivered Israel,

כִּי אִם־יֶשְׁנוֹ בְּיוֹנָתָן בְּנִי
if even it is my son Jonathan,

כִּי מוֹת יָמוּת
indeed, he must *die*."

The reference to *life* in the opening asseveration ("if by the life of God . . . ") contrasts with the punishment of *death* in the concluding curse ("he will die"). Positioned between these archetypal images, Jonathan's fate hovers between life and death. The upcoming trial will determine his destiny.

Saul has marshalled both human and divine seats of authority to bolster and endorse his own. The presence of the elders (פְּנוֹת הָעָם) advances his credibility. His invocation of God sanctions the truth of his speech. Ratification of his plan by God and the elders encourages the

---

Jonathan provides contrastive characterization with Saul throughout chapters 13 and 14 and thereby contributes to the rejection of Saul across these narratives. See Miscall, *1 Samuel, A Literary Reading* (Bloomington: Indiana University Press, 1986) 81-98; Jobling, *The Sense of Biblical Narrative* (Sheffield: JSOT Press, 1978) 8; Gunn, *The Fate of King Saul* (Sheffield: JSOT Press, 1980) 65-75; Polzin, *Samuel and the Deuteronomist* (San Francisco: Harper & Row Publishers, 1989) 137-39; and Long, *The Reign and Rejection of King Saul*, 70.

acceptance of his proposal by the people. These solicitations of support are warranted. The response of the people suggests concern about the advisability of Saul's course.

וְאֵין עֹנֵהוּ מִכָּל־הָעָם:

But there was no one answering him from any of the people.

Rhetoric foreshadows a shift in the social alignments in this tale. First, narrative contrasts forecast a change in public opinion. The silence of the community in response to the oath of Saul contrasts with their earlier support for his battle plan (vs. 36).

> And they [people] said, "All the good in your eyes, do!" (vs. 36)
> But there was no response from all/any of the people. (vs. 39)

Form and content together dramatize this estrangement. Direct discourse proclaims the people's approval of Saul's scheme. Alternatively, narrated discourse serves as a distancing rhetoric and reports their silence. Repetition of the same word כֹּל ("all" or "any") yields different meanings. Endorsement of everything (*all* the good . . .) Saul would do contrasts with the unanimous silence ("from *any* of the people") to his sworn proposition.

Second, narrative parallels suggests an alignment between God and the people. The nonresponse of the whole community parallels the nonresponse of the divine (vs. 37).[48]

> But he [God] did not answer him on that day. (vs. 37)
> But there was no answering from all the people. (vs. 39)

Narrated discourse crafts the form of these responses. The report of silence unites and illustrates their content. Divine silence before the king led Saul to an interpretation. A sinner must be identified and judged. The people's silence before Saul foreshadows another hearing. Whether Saul's oath constitutes an act of extreme religious fervor or a reckless wielding of authority awaits judgment.

---

[48]Miscall, *1 Samuel. A Literary Reading*, 138; Fokkelman, *The Crossing Fates*, 72; Klein, *I Samuel*, 139-40; and M. Sternberg, "The Bible's Art of Persuasion: Ideology, Rhetoric, and Poetics in Saul's Fall," *HUCA* 54 (1983): 47-48.

וַיֹּאמֶר אֶל־כָּל־יִשְׂרָאֵל

And he said to all Israel,

אַתֶּם תִּהְיוּ לְעֵבֶר אֶחָד

"You be over here.

וַאֲנִי וְיוֹנָתָן בְּנִי נִהְיֶה לְעֵבֶר אֶחָד

I and Jonathan, my son, we will be over there."

וַיֹּאמְרוּ הָעָם אֶל־שָׁאוּל

And the people said to Saul,

הַטּוֹב בְּעֵינֶיךָ עֲשֵׂה:

"The good in your eyes, do!"

In premonarchical Israel, God's judgments were procured by oracles or by lot casting.[49] Saul failed to procure an oracle for battle. That failure favors a lot casting in this instance. His directives, "You be over here. I and Jonathan, my son, we will be over there," prepare for the upcoming ordeal. The positioning of parties opposite each other indicates a lot casting. Though the exact procedure is uncertain, small stones marked with colors, signs, or letters were probably thrown between participants. The outcome could legislate land divisions, judicial decisions, or the selection of a militia.[50] Priests, military leaders, or elders among the clans conducted these consultations.[51] Joshua, Eleazar, and the heads of Israelite families divided Canaan by lots among the different Israelite tribes (Josh. 14–17). The elders selected men for the campaign against the Benjaminites by lot casting (Judg. 20:9ff.). Samuel oversaw the lot casting when Saul was elected king of Israel (1 Sam. 10:19ff.). In monarchical Israel, the judicial authority of the king eventually replaced these cultic practices. Wisdom (חכמה) would guide a king's judgments. When the woman of Tekoa asked for a judgment for her son, she recognized divine wisdom (חכמה) in David "to know all things on the earth" (2 Sam. 14:20). At another trial, all Israel acknowledged God's

---

[49]See Num. 26:52, 33:54, 36:2; Josh. 13:6, 7, 23:4, 1 Sam. 10:19.

[50]Mettinger, *King and Messiah*, 243; R. de Vaux, *Ancient Israel: Its Life and Institutions* (New York: McGraw-Hill, 1961) 158; C. Westermann, "Die Begriffe für Fragen und Suchen in Alten Testament," *KD* 6 (1960): 2-20; and F. D. Gealy, "Lots," *IDB* (New York and Nashville: Abingdon Press, 1962) 163-64.

[51]J. Lindblom, "Lot Casting in the Old Testament," *VT* 12 (1962): 164-78.

wisdom (חכמה) in Solomon to execute justice (1 Kgs. 3:28). This wisdom guaranteed the communication of God's judgment. "The king's legal decision had the same quality of inerrancy as is attached to oracular consultations and prophetic utterances."[52]

Saul's plan to cast lots follows his failure to obtain an oracle. The judicial wisdom recognized in later kings is not yet acknowledged in Saul.[53] Yet, some change in the judicial procedure from lineage society to monarchy is evident in this tale.[54] Typically, lots were cast equally among all suspect parties. For example, Joshua cast lots among all the tribes, clans, families and finally individuals to determine the guilty party (Josh. 7). By contrast, Saul orders the procedure to judge only between the people as a whole and his household.[55] The gradual shift from segmentary society to monarchy blurred lineage designations. The establishment of monarchy draws new lines in the social order. The royal household is set apart from the people. Rhetoric suggests this change in the social order. Saul's language reflects these new designations. The king's parallel directives segregate Saul and Jonathan from the people.

וַיֹּאמֶר אֶל־כָּל־יִשְׂרָאֵל

And he said to all Israel,

אַתֶּם תִּהְיוּ לְעֵבֶר אֶחָד

"You be over here.

וַאֲנִי וְיוֹנָתָן בְּנִי נִהְיֶה לְעֵבֶר אֶחָד

I and Jonathan, my son, we will be over there."

וַיֹּאמְרוּ הָעָם אֶל־שָׁאוּל

And the people said to Saul,

---

[52]Mettinger, *King and Messiah*, 244.

[53]In contrast to Saul's judicial ordeal, M. Noth (230-36) demonstrates that the legal decision of Solomon takes the place of the old sacral procedure of lot casting. See Noth, "Die Bewahrung von Solomos' gottlicher Weisheit," VTSup 3 (Leiden: Brill, 1955): 225-37.

[54]Against Birch, *The Rise of the Israelite Monarchy*, 87, who maintains that the earlier account of the people's sin (1 Sam. 14:32) and of Jonathan's sin (1 Sam. 14. 27) explains the unusual division for the lot casting. "The reader does not know whether Jonathan or the people will be designated for their sins," and thus the drama is heightened.

[55]See e.g. Josh. 7:10-26.

הַטּוֹב בְּעֵינֶיךָ עֲשֵׂה:

"The good in your eyes, do!"

The response of the people endorses the sacral ordeal. Lot casting compels the judgment of God. The people cannot refuse. But the answer by the people manifests a subdued approval. A literary nuance illustrates the reduction in public support.

"All that is good in your eyes, do!" (vs. 36)
"The good in your eyes, do!" (vs. 41)

In the opening of the story, the people proclaim their support for "all" (כֹּל) Saul proposed. Now they reduce their approval. This subtle change in the people's response foreshadows a gradual change in public opinion. As subsequent events will show, the people are unwilling to endorse "all" that Saul will do.

Unit 3. The Trial and Indictment, vss. 41-42

וַיֹּאמֶר שָׁאוּל אֶל־יְהוָה אֱלֹהֵי יִשְׂרָאֵל

And Saul said to the Lord, God of Israel,

הָבָה תָמִים[56]

"Give the right decision."

וַיִּלָּכֵד יוֹנָתָן וְשָׁאוּל וְהָעָם יָצָאוּ:

And Jonathan and Saul were taken but the people were saved.

---

[56]The phrase הבה תמים is often judged unintelligible. See S. R. Driver, *Notes on the Hebrew Text of the Books of Samuel* (Oxford: Clarendon Press, 1913) 117; H. P. Smith, *The Books of Samuel*, 122; E. Noort, "Eine weitere Kurz bemerkung zu I Samuel XIV. 41," *VT* 21 (1971), 112-13; and McCarter, *I Samuel*, 247-48, also see 30n.56. Lindblom, "Lot Casting in the Old Testament," 164-78, addresses the difficulty of this phrase. He translates הבה תמים as "give a true decision" with the observation that "from the sense 'complete, intact, blameless,' there is only a short step to the sense 'correct, true, reliable,'" 176. M. Tsevat, "Assyriological Notes on the First Book of Samuel," *Studies in the Bible*, ed. J. M. Grintz and J. Liver (Jerusalem: Kiryat Sepher L.T.D., 1964) 78, concurs with Lindblom's translation. Citing other Mesopotamian analogies, Tsevat explains הבה תמים as a prayer for a clear-cut answer. Other scholars who uphold the MY in vs. 41 include Hertzberg, *I and II Samuel*, 111; and H. J. Stoebe, *Das Erste Buch Samuelis*, KAT 8 (Gutersloh: Gerd Mohn, 1973) 266.

וַיֹּאמֶר שָׁאוּל

And Saul said,

הַפִּילוּ בֵּינִי וּבֵין יוֹנָתָן בְּנִי

"Cast between me and Jonathan, my son.

וַיִּלָּכֵד יוֹנָתָן:[57]

And Jonathan was taken.

A trial and a judgment conclude this first episode (vss. 36-42). Saul's directives in the preceding unit (vss. 38-40) anticipate this upcoming ordeal. When the lots are cast, the first round singles out Saul and his son. The second throw convicts Jonathan. Together, the narrator and the king report this judicial undertaking.

The two commands of Saul manage and direct the ordeal. The first imperative enlists God's participation.

וַיֹּאמֶר שָׁאוּל אֶל־יְהוָה אֱלֹהֵי יִשְׂרָאֵל

And Saul said to the Lord, God of Israel,

הָבָה תָמִים

"Give the right decision."

The form of Saul's speech to the divine contrasts with his earlier plea. In the opening of the story, Saul sought God's advice (vs. 37). With questions he petitioned the divine. The failure to win authorization by God for his war plan stirred anxiety in this king. His desperation in this predicament echoes in the form of his speech. In contrast to his earlier inquiry before God (vs. 37), he now commands a divine response. "Give the right decision."

---

[57]Some scholars object that vs. 42 in MT seems truncated and therefore read the longer version in the LXX. See Budde, *Die Bücher Samuel*, 102-103; and H. P. Smith, *The Books of Samuel*, 122. By contrast, others observe that a terse, economical style is characteristic of 1 and 2 Samuel. Those who read with MT include S. Pisano, *Additions or Omissions in the Books of Samuel* (Gottingen: Vanderhoeck und Ruprecht, 1984) 202; Driver, *Notes on the Hebrew Text of the Books of Samuel*, 118; Hertzberg, *I and II Samuel*, 111; and Stoebe, *Das Erste Buch Samuelis*, 266.

The second command of Saul specifies the nature of the procedure. He orders lots cast (הַפִּילוּ, vs. 42). Parallel structures of this two-part drama convey the orderliness of the procedure. The reported outcome follows the command of Saul at both intervals. Fixed verbs associated with the procedure narrate the results. One side is "taken" (לכד, vss. 41-42), while the other is "saved" (יצא, vs. 41).[58] The Hebrew verb לכד (to "capture," "take") indicates the offender (Josh. 7:14; 1 Sam. 10:20). Characteristic of acts of deliverance, יצא designates the one who escapes (Exod. 15:22, 21:2; Lev. 25:28-30).[59]

The outcome of lot casting was incontrovertible among the people. Rhetoric embodies the definitive character of these public results. The brevity and conciseness of the narrator's report match the decisiveness of the judgment. In the first round, "Jonathan and Saul were taken and the people were saved" (vs. 41). On the second throw, "Jonathan was taken" (vs. 42).

Though the longer reading of vss. 41-42 offered by LXX confirms this judgment, it also sets forth evidence of the mounting resistance of the people to the initiatives of Saul.

LXX[B]: καὶ εἶπεν Σαουλ Κύριε ὁ θεὸς Ισραηλ, τί ο̇τι οὐκ ἀπεκρίθης τῷ δούλῳ σου σήμερον; η ἐν ἐμοὶ ἢ ἐν Ιωναθαν τῷ υἱῷ μου ἡ ἀδικία, κύριε ὁ θεὸς Ισδραηλ, δὸς δήλους· καὶ ἐὰν τάδε ειπη, δος δη λαῷ σου Ισραηλ, δὸς δὴ ὁσιότητα. καὶ κληροῦται Ιωναθαν καὶ Σαουλ, καὶ ὁ λαὸς ἐξῆλθεν. (vs. 41)

The LXX allows the following retroversion < > of vs. 41.[60]

---

[58]Lindblom, "Lot Casting in the Old Testament," 177.

[59]This same technical vocabulary can be found in the account of Achan's trial (Josh. 7:16-18) and with Saul's own election (1 Sam. 10:19-21).

[60]The majority of scholars defend the originality of the longer version of vs. 41 in the LXX[B]. The apparent obscurity of הבה תמים, the abruptness of the MT, and the evidence of haplography (Israel[1] . . . Israel[2]) argue in favor of the longer reading. See J. Wellhausen, *Der Text der Bucher Samuelis* (Göttingen: Vanderhoeck und Ruprecht, 1871) 93-94; P. Dhorme, *Les Livres de Samuel*, Etudes Bibliques (Paris: J. Gabalda, 1910) 123-24; Driver, *Notes on the Hebrew Text*, 117-18; H. P. Smith, *The Books of Samuel*, 122; Noort, "Eine weitere Kurz-

ויאמר שאול

And Saul said,

יהוה אלהי ישראל

"Yahweh, God of Israel,

> למה לא עניַת את־עבדך היום

< Why have you not answered your servant today?

אם יש בי או ביונתן בני העון האלהי ישראל הבה אורים

If there is wrongdoing in me or my son Jonathan,
　　Lord God of Israel, give Urim.

ואם בעמך ישראל > [61]הבה תמים

But if in your people Israel, > give Thummim."

וילכד יונתן ושאול

And Jonathan and Saul were taken.

והעם יצאו:

But the people were saved. (vs. 41)

Saul opens the lot casting with a prayerful salutation. The interrogative form of his petition parallels his earlier request for an oracle (vs. 37). The content of his inquiry recalls the narrated report (vs. 37) of God's silence.

Narrator: But he (God) did not answer him on that day. (vs. 37)
Saul: "Why have you not answered *your servant* today?" (vs. 41)

Saul's claim as the servant of God amends the narrator's omission of this designation (vs.37). This characterization as "servant" conforms to the role of Israelite kings before God. Divine silence (vs. 37) portends an evaluation of this claim.

---

bemerkung zu I Samuel XIV.41," 112-13; McCarter, *I Samuel*, 247; and Klein, *I Samuel*, 132.

　　[61]On this verse and its retroversion, see A. Toeg, "A Textual Note on I Samuel XIV.41," *VT* 19 (1969): 493-98; Driver, *Notes on the Hebrew Text*, 117; and McCarter, *I Samuel*, 247.

Saul proceeds with the prosecution. Two agents, the Urim and Thummim, ascertain God's judgment.[62] This cultic apparatus places the whole community under investigation.

אם יש בי או ביונתן בני העון האלהי ישראל הבה אורים

> If there is wrongdoing in me or my son Jonathan,
> Lord God of Israel, give Urim.

ואם בעמך ישראל < הבה תמים

> But if in your people Israel, > give Thummim."

וילכד יונתן ושאול

And Jonathan and Saul were taken.

והעם יצאו:

But the people were saved.

Rhetoric attests to the judicial nature of the process. Parallel imperatives (הבה תמים . . . הבה אורים) dictate the equity of the procedure and contribute to the credibility of the outcome. While explanations of the Urim and Thummim remain guesswork, responsibility for this apparatus and their use in a cultic ordeal is clear. Management and interpretation of the Urim and Thummim fell within the scope of priestly duties (Deut. 33:8). Their employment indicated a cultic lot casting.[63] Eleazar the priest consults the Urim concerning Joshua's leadership of the community (Num. 27:21). Abiathar the priest consulted these oracular devices on behalf of David (1 Sam. 23:10-13). By contrast, the priest is seemingly absent from this cultic event. Saul's direct discourse never enlists priestly assistance. The priest who prompted Saul's inquiry in the opening of the story is never addressed here.

The narrator reports the outcome of the lot casting.

וילכד יונתן ושאול

And Jonathan and Saul were taken.

והעם יצאו:

But the people were saved.

---

[62]E. Robertson, "The Urim and Thummim: What Were They?" *VT* 14 (1964): 66-74; B. Johnson, "Urim and Thummim als Alphabet," *ASTI* 9 (1973): 23-29; and I. Mendelsohn, "Urim and Thummim," *IDB* (New York and Nashville: Abingdon Press, 1962) 739-40.

[63]Lindblom, "Lot Casting in the Old Testament," 170.

Characteristic verbs associated with this process (לכד יצא) narrate the results.[64] The lots implicate the royal household. A verdict, with its deadly consequence, threatens the king and his son.

Social anthropological studies suggest an advantage for Saul amidst these grievous straits. Kinship and family ties characterized segmentary society. With the rise of chiefs, a leader enhanced and secured his authority by deliberately dissociating himself from these kinship connections.[65] Saul's willingness to risk the life of his son may yield political benefits.

The alternate reading of the LXX continues in vs. 42.

LXX[B]: καὶ εἶπεν Σαουλ Βάλετε ἀνὰ μέσον ἐμοῦ καὶ ἀνὰ μέσον Ιωναθαν τοῦ υἱοῦ μου· ὃν ἂν κατακληρώσηται κύριος, ἀποθανέτω. καὶ εἶπεν ὁ λαὸς πρὸς Σαουλ Οὐκ ἔστιν τὸ ῥῆμα τοῦτο. καὶ κατεκράτησεν Σαουλ τοῦ λαου, καὶ βαλλουσιν ανὰ μεσον αυτοῦ καὶ ανα μεσον Ιωναθαν τοῦ υιοῦ αυτου, καὶ κατακληρουται Ιωναθαν.

The retroversion < > of vs. 42 in LXX reads as follows.[66]

ויאמר שאול

And Saul said,

> הפילו ביני ובין יונתן בני

< "Cast between me and between Jonathan, my son.

את אשר ילכד יהוה ימות

Whomever the Lord indicates, let him die."

ויאמר העם אל־שאול

But the people said to Saul,

---

[64]See discussion above, 64.

[65]Frick, *The Formation of the State in Ancient Israel*, 79; and Harris, *Cultural Materialism*, 92-100.

[66]Due to the abruptness and brevity of the MT, and on grounds of haplography (Jonathan, my son[1] . . . Jonathan, his son[2]), some scholars read with the LXX[B]. See Dhorme, *Les Livres de Samuel*, 124; Budde, *Die Bücher Samuel*, 102-103; H. P. Smith, *The Books of Samuel*, 122; McCarter, *I Samuel*, 244; and Klein, *I Samuel*, 131-32.

לא יהיה כדבר הזה

"This thing shall not be."

67< :ויחזק שאול בעם

But Saul prevailed against the people. ?

Despite desperate measures to enhance his authority, a growing opposition resists Saul's effort. When he repeats the death sentence harbored
in his oath, the people's objection replaces their earlier silence. "This
thing shall not be." In the opening of the story Saul enlisted the people's
cooperation and support. Now he overrides them. The verb חזק narrates
opposition. "But Saul prevailed against the people." An antagonism
erupting between the king and the people is embedded in the rhetorical
content.

ויאמר העם אל־שאול

But the people said to Saul,

לא יהיה כדבר הזה

"This thing shall not be."

< :ויחזק שאול בעם

But Saul prevailed against the people. >

Form and content of the narrator's report illustrate this social clash.
When the final lots are cast, the dreaded outcome is realized. Saul's
exercise of judicial authority has achieved an indictment. "Jonathan was
taken." Yet the report of the outcome of this phase of the ordeal differs
significantly from the report of the initial throw (vs. 41).

(vs. 41)	(vs. 42)
And Jonathan and Saul were taken.	And Jonathan was taken.
	. . . .
But the people were saved.	_____

Divine silence (vs. 37) has instigated this first episode (vss. 36-42).
Now the narrator's silence concerning Saul enshrines his fate. Though

---

[67]On this verse and its retroversion, see McCarter, *I Samuel*, 248; and H. P.
Smith, *The Books of Samuel*, 124.

Jonathan was "taken," the judgment upon Saul remains unknown.[68] The determination of Saul's destiny resides outside this sacral ordeal. The provisional status of the kingship of Saul makes him subject to the judgment of the people. In episode one, Saul presided as judge among the people. In the upcoming episode, Saul and his judicial undertakings will be judged by the people.

Episode II, vss. 43-46

The drama building across the first episode erects an ironic contrast to a preceding story (1 Sam. 14:1-16).[69] Jonathan, Saul's son, initiated a successful campaign against the Philistines. In the present story, the plan of Saul to battle the Philistines reaps a death sentence for Jonathan.

The drama of these circumstances warrants a rapid resolution. Accelerated narrative movement in episode two corresponds to the urgency of the crisis. Three units counter the events in the three divisions of episode one. First, Jonathan's confession and sentencing (vss. 43-44) raise questions about the reliability of Saul's lot casting (vss. 41-42). Second, the oath of the people (vs. 45) reverses the sworn death sentence by Saul (vs. 39). Third, the narrated conclusion (vs. 46) reports a reversal of Saul's battle plan (vs. 36).

Unit 1. Confession and Sentence, vss. 43-44

וַיֹּאמֶר שָׁאוּל אֶל־יוֹנָתָן

And Saul said to Jonathan,

הַגִּידָה לִּי מֶה עָשִׂיתָה

"Tell me what you did."

וַיַּגֶּד־לוֹ יוֹנָתָן וַיֹּאמֶר

And Jonathan revealed to him and he said,

טָעֹם טָעַמְתִּי בִּקְצֵה הַמַּטֶּה אֲשֶׁר־בְּיָדִי מְעַט דְּבַשׁ

"Indeed, I tasted with the tip of my stick in my hand a little honey,

---

[68]M. Sternberg observes that the presence and timing of gaps are a rare mastery of the narrative medium and encourages the reading of such silences. See Sternberg, *The Poetics of Biblical Narrative* (Bloomington: Indiana University Press, 1987) 230-35.

[69]D. Jobling, "Saul's Fall and Jonathan's Rise: Tradition and Redaction in I Samuel 14:1-46," *JBL* 95 (1970): 367-76.

and now I must surely die."

הִנְנִי אָמוּת:

And Saul said,

וַיֹּאמֶר שָׁאוּל

"May God do such and may (God) do again,

כֹּה־יַעֲשֶׂה אֱלֹהִים וְכֹה יוֹסִף

For you shall surely die, Jonathan." (vs. 44)

כִּי־מוֹת תָּמוּת יוֹנָתָן:

An exchange between Saul and Jonathan structures this unit. At Saul's request, Jonathan acknowledges his guilt. At Jonathan's admission of wrongdoing, Saul reiterates the death sentence. While Jonathan confesses the truth, Saul's speech provokes judgment.

In segmentary society and in chiefdoms, public support was necessary for a verdict to be upheld. "A typical way of soliciting communal support for a guilty verdict was to invite the defendant to confess his guilt. If he did so, there was little danger of his supporters or the society in general refusing to accept the decisions."[70] After the indictment by lots, Joshua solicited a confession of guilt from Achan. Following his acknowledgment of sin, the whole community participated in Achan's punishment (Josh. 7:1-26).

The growing dismay with Saul as judge in this tale could jeopardize the acceptance of his verdict. This judgment requires community approval. Saul invites Jonathan to confess his guilt.

And Saul said to Jonathan,

וַיֹּאמֶר שָׁאוּל אֶל־יוֹנָתָן

"Tell me what you did."

הַגִּידָה לִּי מֶה עָשִׂיתָה

And Jonathan revealed to him and he said,

וַיַּגֶּד־לוֹ יוֹנָתָן וַיֹּאמֶר

"Indeed, I tasted with the tip of my stick in my hand a little honey,

טָעֹם טָעַמְתִּי בִּקְצֵה הַמַּטֶּה אֲשֶׁר־בְּיָדִי מְעַט דְּבַשׁ

and now I must surely die."

הִנְנִי אָמוּת:

---

[70]Wilson, "Israel's Judicial System in the Preexilic Period," 236.

Saul compelled God's judgment by casting lots. Like Achan (Josh. 7:20), Jonathan's admission of guilt certifies the indictment. Jonathan acknowledges his misdeed which transgressed Saul's oath during the Battle at Michmash. Unlike the trial of Achan, the arraignment of Jonathan reveals the dubious nature of the deeds of Saul.[71] In contrast to the battle of Jericho, Michmash was not a holy war. Unlike the secret act of Achan, the deed of Jonathan was unwitting and public. Further, the act of Jonathan did not violate the *herem* of God. The oath of Saul perpetrated the transgression of Jonathan. Such differences raise questions about the appropriateness of the death sentence of Jonathan. Rhetoric discloses the unsettling disproportion between the crime and the punishment. The descriptions "tip of my stick" and "a little honey" not only qualify the minute size and limited scope of the deed, they narrate the incongruity between the deed and the vowed death sentence.[72] Judicial authority that acts on or ignores such disproportion invites a judgment of itself. Jonathan's confession of sin offers evidence for another trial. The judge and his machinations are about to be judged.

The oath of Saul to ensure a victory over the Philistines caused the sin of Jonathan. The oath of Saul to rout out an evildoer indicts Jonathan as sinner (vs.39). Amidst such straits, wisdom warrants a new course of action. Saul's sworn statements are not irrevocable. When the mother of Ephraim unwittingly cursed her own son, she converted it to a blessing (Judg. 17:1ff.).[73] Saul takes no such step.

In his final speech as judicial presider, Saul seals the fate of Jonathan and determines his own. He swears a third oath to carry out the death penalty.

וַיֹּאמֶר שָׁאוּל

And Saul said,

כֹּה־יַעֲשֶׂה אֱלֹהִים וְכֹה יוֹסִף

"May God do such and may (God) do again,

---

[71]The trials of Achan and Jonathan have been compared by Wilson, "Israel's Judicial System," 237-39; Whitelam, *The Just King*, 74; and Miscall, *I Samuel. A Literary Reading*, 96.

[72]V. P. Long, *The Reign and Rejection of King Saul*, 128.

[73]Gordon, *1 and 2 Samuel*, 56.

כִּי־מוֹת תָּמוּת יוֹנָתָן:
For you shall surely die, Jonathan." (vs. 44)

The sentencing has the impartiality of a judicial hearing. The endearing salutation "Jonathan, my son" (vss. 39, 40, 42) has been abbreviated to "Jonathan." This shift in rhetoric discloses a shift in social relations. Saul's abbreviation of "Jonathan, my son" to "Jonathan" effectively discontinues Saul's allusions to kinship ties with the identified sinner (vss. 39, 40, 42).

A chilling parallel from the book of Judges (Judg. 11:1-40) echoes in Saul's pronouncements.[74] The vow of Jephthah before battle (Judg. 11:30-13) cost him the life of his daughter. Similarly, the oath of Saul before God sacrifices the life of his own son. Upon learning that his daughter would die, Jephthah tore his clothes and cried aloud (Judg. 11:35). By contrast, Saul shows no sign of sorrow or regret. Instead, his speech reinforces the legitimacy of the sentence. Further, repetition of the verb עשׂה ("do") by Saul draws a shrewd connection between Jonathan's deed and God's involvement in its punishment.

"Tell to me what *you did*." (vs. 43)
"May *God do* such and may (God) do again" (vs. 44)

This senseless sacrifice of human life evokes the people's unequivocal retort.

Unit 2. The Community's Challenge to Saul, vs. 45

וַיֹּאמֶר הָעָם אֶל־שָׁאוּל
And the people said to Saul,

הֲיוֹנָתָן יָמוּת אֲשֶׁר עָשָׂה הַיְשׁוּעָה הַגְּדוֹלָה הַזֹּאת בְּיִשְׂרָאֵל
"Should Jonathan die,
    the one who made this great deliverance in Israel?

חָלִילָה חַי־יְהוָה
Far from it. By the life of Yahweh,

---

[74]Comparisons and contrasts of Jephthah's vow and Saul's oath have been noted by V. P. Long, *The Reign and Rejection of King Saul*, 124; Miscall, *1 Samuel. A Literary Reading*, 94, and D. Marcus, *Jephthah and His Vow* (Lubbock TX: Texas Tech Press, 1986) 29.

אִם־יִפֹּל מִשַּׂעֲרַת רֹאשׁוֹ אַרְצָה

not one of the hairs from his head shall fall to the ground,

כִּי־עִם־אֱלֹהִים עָשָׂה הַיּוֹם הַזֶּה

for God was with him in what he did this day."

וַיִּפְדּוּ הָעָם אֶת־יוֹנָתָן וְלֹא־מֵת:

And the people rescued Jonathan and he did not die. (vs. 45)

A rhetorical question and an oath set forth the reaction of the community. The rhetorical question of the people issues a countercharge to the pronouncements of Saul. Their oath challenges his sworn statement, as well as levels a reprisal. The narrator reports the forensic success of the people.

In response to the judgment and sentence of Jonathan by Saul, the people initiate speech.

הֲיוֹנָתָן יָמוּת אֲשֶׁר עָשָׂה הַיְשׁוּעָה הַגְּדוֹלָה הַזֹּאת בְּיִשְׂרָאֵל

"Should Jonathan die,
　　the one who made this great deliverance in Israel?

חָלִילָה חַי־יְהוָה

Far from it. By the life of Yahweh,

אִם־יִפֹּל מִשַּׂעֲרַת רֹאשׁוֹ אַרְצָה

not one of the hairs from his head shall fall to the ground,

כִּי־עִם־אֱלֹהִים עָשָׂה הַיּוֹם הַזֶּה

for God was with him in what he did this day."

Throughout the narrative, the people's speech manifests a gradual disenchantment with their king. In the opening of the story (vs. 36), they endorsed his complete battle plan. His vow to punish an evildoer elicited only their silence (vs. 39). The people objected to Saul's proclamation of the death penalty (vs. 42). Now they reject his judgment (vs. 45).

The public nature of this trial accorded the community a role in these proceedings. In segmentary society, no central ruling power authorized a sentence. The social pressure necessary to enforce a ruling resided in the society as a whole.[75] The Levite testified against the Benjaminites in the presence of the whole people (Judg. 20:1-4). Joshua conducted Achan's trial before the entire community (Josh. 7:16). Further, all Israel

---

[75]Wilson, "Israel's Preexilic Judicial System," 236-37.

concurred with the judgment and sentence by participating in the execution of Achan (Josh. 7:25). Remnants of this community authority surface in the trial of Jonathan by Saul. Without solicitation, the people issue an evaluation of the outcome.

A rhetorical question introduces the oration of the people. "Should Jonathan die . . . the one who made the great deliverance in Israel?" The inquiry exposes the contradiction in the judicial ruling of Saul. He sentences to death the one who has saved the life of Israel. His judgment is not only about to be challenged; the entire proceeding will be deemed a mistrial. Moreover, the oath of the people acknowledges Jonathan's "great deliverance of Israel." Their defense of Saul's son ironically parallels Saul's own description of God.

> (Saul) "For as Yahweh lives, the great deliverer of Israel. . . . " (vs. 39)
> (people) "Should Jonathan die, the one who made this great deliverance of Israel?" (vs. 45)

The activity of Jonathan among the people corresponds to the activity of God on their behalf. In one sworn statement, the people expose the questionable nature of the judge and his judgments. The sociorhetorical interplay magnifies Saul's alienation of the people. Rhetoric discloses this estrangement from Saul, as well as a shift in their allegiance to Jonathan. In the opening of the story, the community affirmed what Saul would do (עשה).

> "All that is good in your eyes, *do*!" (vs. 36)
> "The good in your eyes, *do*!" (vs. 40)

In their final speech, the people recount what Jonathan has done (עשה).

> "who *did* this great deliverance. . . . " (vs. 45)
> "for God was with him in what he *did* today." (vs. 45)

The single declaration by the people (vs. 45) contrasts with the profusion of speech by Saul throughout this story. Though Saul has presided as judge among the community, the sworn statement by the people opposes this judgment. The content of the oath of the people (vs. 45) counters the content of the two oaths of Saul (vss. 39-44). The narrator reports the outcome. "And the people rescued[76] Jonathan and he did not die."

---

[76]Budde, *Die Bücher Samuel*, 104, and Wellhausen, *Der Text der Bücher*

Unit 3. Conclusion, vs. 46

וַיַּעַל שָׁאוּל מֵאַחֲרֵי פְלִשְׁתִּים

And Saul broke off the pursuit of the Philistines

וּפְלִשְׁתִּים הָלְכוּ לִמְקוֹמָם:

and the Philistines returned to their place. (vs. 46)

The narrator offers a conclusion to the tale.[77] The form and content of this report convey a social dynamic of the outcome. The oath of Saul (vs. 39) silenced the people. The oath of the people (vs. 45) now silences Saul. The narrator announces the termination of Saul's battle plan.

> Saul broke off the pursuit of the Philistines and the Philistines returned home. (vs. 46)

Social anthropological studies disclose the foundation of judicial authority of kings and chieftains. Strategy and skills in battle coincide with their decision-making capacity.[78] Joshua successfully leads Israel to victory at Ai (Josh. 8:1-25) after his successful judgment and punishment of an evildoer (Josh. 7:16-26). The rhetorical boundaries of the present story confirm these sociological connections. In the opening of the story (vs. 36), Saul plots a bold assault against the Philistines; in the conclusion of the story he abandons his pursuit of the enemy (vs. 46).

וַיֹּאמֶר שָׁאוּל

And Saul said,

Samuelis, 95, once proposed that the people paid money or even substituted another person (Exod. 13:13, 15) to rescue Jonathan. Thus, they translate the verb here "ransomed." The text offers no such evidence. As Driver, *Notes on the Hebrew Text*, 91, observed, had "ransomed" been "the sense intended, . . . it would have been stated more circumstantially, instead of being left to the reader to infer it from a single word."

[77]S. Bar-Efrat observes the content of this conclusion is characteristic of the biblical narratives. Closures are frequently marked by a person's (or people's) departure. See Bar-Efrat, *Narrative Art in the Bible* (Sheffield: Almond Press, 1989) 130-31.

[78]Service, *Origins of the State and Civilization*, 74; and Flanagan, "Chiefs in Israel," 52.

נֵרְדָה אַחֲרֵי פְלִשְׁתִּים לַיְלָה
"Let us go down after the Philistines at night,

וְנָבְזָה בָהֶם עַד־אוֹר הַבֹּקֶר
And let us plunder them until the light of morning,

וְלֹא־נַשְׁאֵר בָּהֶם אִישׁ
And let us not leave one of them." (vs. 36)

וַיַּעַל שָׁאוּל מֵאַחֲרֵי פְלִשְׁתִּים
And Saul broke off the pursuit of the Philistines

וּפְלִשְׁתִּים הָלְכוּ לִמְקוֹמָם:
and the Philistines returned to their place. (vs. 46)

The boundaries of this episode reverse the war plan of Saul. This military retreat from the battle front follows the people's rejection of his judgment. The rejection of the decision of Saul and the concurrent rescue of Jonathan rest upon the people's understanding of God. The activity (deliverance) of Jonathan (vs. 45) mirrors divine activity. God is responsible for what Jonathan has done ("for God was with him in what he did today"). By contrast, the vows and lot casting of Saul compel God's judgment and punishment of Jonathan. The depiction of God by Saul stands over against the theology of the people.

Monarchical improvidence fosters this theological dilemma. As judge, Saul was to be the mediator of divine judgment. As king, Saul was to be the vicegerent of God.[79] Instead, Saul uses God to authorize himself. He swears by God, inquires of God, and interprets God. Yet, Saul plots a battle against the Philistines without consulting the divine. Only after the injunction of the priest, does Saul seeks divine consultation. When no answer from God is forthcoming, Saul quickly provides one. In the wake of divine silence, Saul orders an ordeal which will force God's response. Saul wields judicial authority by manipulating the divine. Such an audacious enterprise sets off a perilous chain of events. This loss of judicial credibility erodes Saul's military integrity. This decrease in military stature threatens kingly rule. The consequences of Saul's theological recklessness reach beyond this story. They portend the demise of his kingship.

---

[79] See esp., above, comments on 50-51 and 51n.33.

Wisdom Prompts a Hesitant King

A Sociorhetorical Exegesis of 2 Samuel 14:1-22

Clans composed the largest kinship group in early Israel.[1] It is uncertain whether clans existed as extended families or as lineages. The three or four generations which made up an extended family traced their descent from a common ancestor. Alternatively, lineages only used the language of kinship to describe their social connections.[2] Whether real or symbolic, notions of kinship governed the identities of clans in the biblical account. The segmentary genealogies in the Pentateuch indicate the prevalence of this kinship terminology (Gen. 35:22-26; 36; 46:8-27; Exod. 6:14-27; Num. 1–7; 26).

Clans also functioned as the primary social unit in premonarchic Israel.[3] The familial bonds of a clan assured members military protection

---

[1]On the social configuration of clans in Israel, see J. R. Porter, *The Extended Family in the Old Testament*, Occasional Papers in Social and Economic Administration 6 (London: Edutext, 1967); G. E. Mendenhall, "Social Organization in Early Israel," *Magnalia Dei: The Mighty Acts of God*, ed. F. M. Cross et al. (Garden City NY: Doubleday, 1976) 132-51; C. H. J. de Geus, *The Tribes of Israel* (Assen: Van Gorcum, 1976) 133-49; N. Gottwald, *Tribes of Yahweh* (Maryknoll NY: Orbis Books, 1979) 237-344; and L. Stager, "The Archaeology of the Family in Ancient Israel," *BASOR* 260 (1985): 1-35.

[2]For a general discussion of the structure of lineages, see R. Wilson, *Genealogy and History in the Biblical World* (New Haven and London: Yale University Press, 1977) 18-37.

[3]Gottwald, *The Tribes of Yahweh*, 287-88; de Geus, *The Tribes of Israel*,

(Judg. 7:23-25; 20:12-18). Land rights were delegated within this hereditary network (Josh. 15–19; Num. 26).[4] Further, residence in the clan guaranteed a family's economic security (Deut. 25:5-10; Josh. 22:6-8; Ruth 4.1-8). Any threat to these kinship ties posed a comprehensive threat to one's well-being.[5] The death of Zelophehad threatened the economic security of his daughters (Num. 27:1-11). Similarly, Naomi's future was jeopardized by the death of her husband and sons (Ruth 1:1-22). Judicial rulings, as well as natural causes, could inflict such peril. The judgment of a local court could cut one off from the protection and benefits of the clan. Death of a family head could sever a spouse or child from the security of this social framework.

The rise of a monarchy gradually obscured clans' identities. The national scope of the king's rule replaced the familial and local network of the clan. The mutual protection and military activity which had previously bound families together as a clan were now overseen by the monarch.[6] In the biblical accounts, David's military enterprises spanned the territorial outlines of the whole nation. He provided protection against the Philistines to the West (2 Sam. 5:17-25), the Moabites to the South (2 Sam. 8:2), the Aramaeans to the North (2 Sam. 10:15-19), and Ammonites to the East (2 Sam. 12:26-31).

The formation of the state altered the terms of the clan's self-governance. Kingship centralized duties formerly carried out by the clan. As a result, the monarch presided in matters of national interest, as well as in domestic concerns.[7] In the wake of a nationwide famine, David authorized the execution of Saul's descendants (2 Sam. 21:1-9). After the

---

137; and K. Whitelam, *The Just King: Monarchical Judicial Authority in Ancient Israel* (Sheffield: JSOT Press, 1979) 42-43.

[4]The references to "tribe" in these examples are territorial designations. For the problems on the definitions of a "tribe," see J. W. Rogerson, *Anthropology and the Old Testament* (Oxford: Blackwell, 1978) 86ff.

[5]On the duties and responsibilities of clans, see John M. Salmon, "Judicial Authority in Early Israel: A Historical Investigation of Old Testament Institutions" (Th.D. diss., Princeton Theological Seminary, 1968) 19-59.

[6]R. Wilson, "Israel's Judicial System in the Preexilic Period," *JQR* 74 (October, 1983): 233.

[7]For a discussion of factors responsible for this shift, see Frank Frick, *The Formation of the State in Ancient Israel* (Sheffield: Almond Press, 1985) 77ff.

death of Saul, David adjudicated in a domestic matter about the property
that belonged to Saul and his family (2 Sam. 9:9-10).

The social changes which resulted from the assimilation of the role
and function of clans under kingship are embedded in the biblical
narrative. The Succession Narrative (2 Sam. 9–20; 1 Kgs. 1–2) records
these social transitions.[8] Three units make up this literary corpus.[9] 2
Samuel 9–12 primarily concerns David and Bathsheba. Chapters 13–20
narrate the rebellion of Absalom. Finally, 1 Kings 1–2 recount Solomon's
succession to the throne of David.

The rhetorical integrity of 2 Samuel 9–20, 1 Kings 1–2 is widely
acclaimed.[10] An unbroken sequence of events attests to the unity and

---

[8]While general agreement exists on the boundaries of this narrative, the
question of genre is widely debated. Following the influential study by L. Rost,
Die Überlieferung von der Thronnachfolge Davids (Stuttgart: Kohlhammer,
1926); ET: *The Succession Throne of David* (Sheffield: Almond Press, 1982),
some scholars define these chapters as "history writing." See G. von Rad, "The
Beginnings of Historical Writing in Ancient Israel," in *The Problem of the
Hexateuch and Other Essays* (London: Oliver and Boyd, 1966) 166-204, and G.
Tucker, *Form Criticism of the Old Testament* (Philadelphia: Fortress Press, 1971)
36. R. N. Whybray, *The Succession Narrative*, SBT 2nd ser. 9 (London: SCM
Press, 1968) 56-95; and H. J. Hermission, "Weisheit und Geschichte," *Probleme
biblische Theologie*, ed. H. W. Wolff (Munich: Kaiser, 1971) 136-54, describe
the narrative as "wisdom" or "didactic literature." F. Langlamet, "Pour ou contre
Salomon? La redaction prosalomonienne de I Rois I-II," *RB* 83 (1976): 321-79,
481-528, considers the text to be originally anti-Solomonic (or Davidic) propa-
ganda which was then subjected to pro-Solomonic (or Davidic) redactions.
Literary studies, such as H. Hagan, "Deception as Motif and Theme in 2 Sam.
9–20; 1 Kgs. 1–2," *Bib* 60 (1979): 301-26, C. Conroy, *Absalom! Absalom!*
(Rome: Biblical Institute Press, 1978), and D. Gunn, *The Story of King David:
Genre and Interpretation* (Sheffield: JSOT, 1978), represent the narrative as
"story" or "literary fiction."

[9]Rost, *Die Überlieferung von der Thronnachfolge Davids*, 65-114, first identified "succession" as the major thematic interest of the narrative.

[10]In 1941, R. H. Pfeiffer, *Introduction to the Old Testament* (New York:
Harper Brothers, 1941) 357, wrote that the author of the succession narrative had
"created history as an art." More recently, Gunn, *The Story of King David*, 13,
observes that the high narrative art and skill of these chapters is a subject of
almost universal agreement among scholars. P. Ackroyd, "The Succession

coherence of these chapters.[11] The theme of succession to the throne persists throughout.[12] Precision and detail of the account craft a commendable narrative. For example, David and Bathsheba's bedroom scene (2 Sam. 11:1-5), as well as Amnon's sexual attack and victimization of his half-sister Tamar (2 Sam. 13:8-19) supply the intimate details. Reports of conversation contribute to the vividness of such stories. The narrator recounts what Amnon said to Tamar and what Nathan said to David. Even the contents of a letter which David wrote to Joab are reported (2 Sam. 11:15). Schematic arrangement of materials under patterns of "blessings" and "curses" has also been noted.[13] The wellspring of literary studies on these chapters attests to their celebrated status as fine narrative.[14]

Narrative (so-called)," *Int* 35 (1981): 383, describes this narrative as the "most vivid and readable in the Old Testament."

[11]It has long been accepted that the narrative contained in 2 Sam. 9–20 and 1 Kgs. 1–2 constitutes a coherent literary unit. See J. Wellhausen, *Einleitung in das Alte Testament* (Berlin: F. Bleek, 1878) 224-26; Rost, *Die Überlieferung von der Thronnachfolge Davids*, 3-5; von Rad, "The Beginnings of Historical Writing in Ancient Israel," 176-204; and G. Fohrer, *Introduction to the Old Testament*, trans. D. Green. (London: S.P.C.K., 1970) 222.

[12]The identification of the "succession" theme by Rost, *The Succession Throne of David*, 65-114, has reigned as the most influential factor in establishing and reinforcing the boundaries and literary integrity of this narrative. Recently, Gunn, *The Story of King David*, has challenged Rost's long-standing thesis on the basis of theme, genre, and scope of this narrative.

[13]R. A. Carlson, *David the Chosen King* (Uppsala: Almquist and Wiksells, 1964). Carlson also perceives this pattern permeating 2 Sam. 21–24 and therefore includes it in the orbit of his discussion.

[14]Along with the literary studies already cited in n. 8, above, see J. Blenkinsopp, "Theme and Motif in the Succession History (2 Sam. XI 2ff) and the Yahwist Corpus," *VTS* 15 (1966): 44-57; J. A. Wharton, "A Plausible Tale: Story and Theology in II Samuel 9–20, I Kings 1–2," *Int* 35 (1981): 341-54; P. K. McCarter, Jr., "Plots, True and False: The Succession Narrative as Court Apologetic," *Int* 35 (1981): 355-67; J. P. Fokkelman, *Narrative Art and Poetry in the Books of Samuel*, vol. 1, *King David (II Samuel 9-20 and I Kings 1-2)* (Assen: van Gorcum, 1981); G. W. Coats, "Parable, Fable, and Anecdote. Storytelling in the Succession Narrative," *Int* 35 (1981): 368-82; K. Sacon, "A Study of the Literary Structure of the Succession Narrative," *Studies in the*

A social drama unfolds across this refined literary terrain. A king assumes the authority and judicial responsibilities once held by clans. In the Absalom cycle, the narrator reports that people from various tribes now journey to King David for judicial decisions (2 Sam. 15:2). Confronted by a mourning widow, David overrules clan law on homicide (2 Sam. 14:1-21). In the wake of Nathan's report, David levels a judgment and sentence in a domestic crime on behalf of the supposed victim (2 Sam. 12:5-6).

The tensions of the transition from clan rule to kingship are etched in the literary artistry of this succession narrative. The form and content of these tales disclose the drama and dynamics of the social changes therein. A sociorhetorical exegesis of the following story will illustrate the interplay of these elements.

In 2 Samuel 14:1-22, King David overrules clan law on behalf of a supposed widow and her son. The story is part of the prologue (chaps. 13–14) to the tale of Absalom's rebellion and its sequel (chaps. 15–20). Previously, Absalom's sister Tamar had been raped by the king's son Amnon (2 Sam. 13:8-19). When no punishment was leveled upon the criminal, Absalom, his half-brother, avenged the deed by killing Amnon. Absalom avoided a sentence for his crime by escaping to Geshur. Chapter 14:1-22 narrates a plot by Joab, David's military commander, to secure Absalom's safe return. Joab enlists the assistance of a woman to accomplish the plan. The woman appears before the king as a widow. She reports that her son, like Absalom, has fled after killing his brother. The king promises the woman's son safety upon his return to the clan. Subsequently, the widow secures a visa and a vow of protection from the king for Absalom's return to Jerusalem. As such, the story conforms to the contours of a judicial parable. The requisites of deception, parallel circumstances, and the desired judgment constitute the essential elements.[15]

Period of David and Solomon and Other Essays (Tokyo: Yamakawa-Shuppansha, 1982) 27-54; and L. Perdue, "'Is There Anyone Left of the House of Saul . . . ?' Ambiguity and the Characterization of David in the Succession Narrative," *JSOT* 30 (1984): 67-84.

[15]U. Simon, "The Poor Man's Ewe-Lamb. An Example of a Juridical Parable," *Bib* 48 (1967): 207-42, demonstrates that the structure of 2 Sam. 14:1-22

The tale unfolds primarily through a rich and lengthy conversation between the woman and the king.[16] The components and the course of the conversation structure the tale.

Introduction to the Story, vss. 1-3
    Narrative Introduction to the Encounter, vs. 4a-c
        Unit I. An Appeal to Speak / Appeal Honored, vs. 4d
            Exchange 1, vss. 5-8
            Exchange 2, vss. 9-10
            Exchange 3, vs. 11
        Unit II. An Appeal to Speak / Appeal Honored, vs. 12
            The Woman's Speech, vss. 13-17
        Unit III. An Appeal to Speak / Appeal Honored, vs.18
            Final Exchange, vss. 19-20
Conclusion to the Story, vss. 21-22

In the introduction to the tale (vss. 1-4), Joab designs a meeting between the woman and the king. In the conclusion, Joab confirms his responsibility for the encounter. Narrated discourse about Joab followed by Joab's own direct discourse constitutes the form of these literary boundaries. As introduction and conclusion, these outer limits restrict Joab's involvement.

Three units structure the intervening conversation between the woman and the king.[17] An appeal to speak followed by a permission introduces and demarcates these three units. In unit I (vss. 5-11), the woman beseeches David and he inquires about her case. Three sets of exchanges follow (vss. 5-8, 9-10, 11). Each exchange concludes with a promise of assistance by the king (vss. 8, 10, 11c). In unit II (vss. 12-17), the woman makes a second appeal to speak to the king. He grants her

---

corresponds to the outline of a judicial parable. Similarly, Gunn, *The Story of King David*, 40-41, and H. Niehr, "Zur Gattung von Jes. 5:1-7," *BZ* 30 (1986): 99-104, identify the genre of this text as a judgment-eliciting parable.

[16]R. Alter, *The Art of Biblical Narrative* (New York: Basic Books, Inc., 1981) 63-87, notes the primacy of dialogue as a characteristic trait of the biblical narrative.

[17]Similarly, A. A. Anderson, *2 Samuel*, WBC 11 (Waco TX: Word Books, 1989) 185; and Fokkelman, *King David*, 130, delineate the structure of this passage on the basis of speech patterns.

request. Subsequently, the woman conducts an elaborate monologue. Longest of the three units, the woman's speech is of extraordinary significance. With metaphors and imagery, she skillfully establishes a connection between her fictitious scheme and the real dilemma of David and his son Absalom. In unit III (vss. 18-20), David requests the woman to speak by responding to his question. In the exchange that follows (vss. 19-20), the discussion shifts to David, the matter of his exiled son, and Joab's involvement.

A command by the king coupled with an appearance by Joab brings the story to a close. The ambiguity surrounding the king's sentiments for Absalom in the introduction of the story are resolved by the king's order in the conclusion (vs. 21).

The literary structure in conjunction with the development of characters illustrate and animate the social dynamics of the tale. The contrasting characterization of the king and the woman conforms to their contrasting social roles.[18] In the opening of the story, King David presides as judge in a case apparently divorced from his own affairs. By contrast, the unnamed widowed woman pleads a case upon which her own livelihood hinges. While David's kingship affords him ultimate authority, the woman's widowhood threatens her with destitution. The course and structure of the conversation challenge these appearances and reveal a different reality. The vulnerable widow actually dominates and directs the course of the conversation. Further, she skillfully determines its outcome. By contrast, the all-powerful king hesitates to exercise his authority. Literary irony discloses the pretense of these social roles and renders them mere facades.[19]

The warp and woof of these social and rhetorical features weave a surprising outcome. Joab devises a correspondence between a widowed woman and the king. Both parents have sons whose crime merits severe

---

[18]S. Bar-Efrat, *Narrative Art in the Bible* (Sheffield: Almond Press, 1989) 65-66, notes that in tales made up primarily of dialogue, "the person's style of speaking reveals social class."

[19]P. Duke, *Irony in the Fourth Gospel* (Atlanta: John Knox, 1985) 15, defines irony as "a leap from what seems to be to what is." In a more technical discussion, D. C. Muecke, *Irony* (Norfolk: Methuen, 1970) 25ff., differentiates between "verbal irony" which refers to the design of a narrative and "situational irony" where the anticipated occurrence is replaced surprisingly by another.

punishment. David's identification with the widow results in the return of Absalom.[20] But the woman's conversation with David achieves something more. Apart from her disguise, the woman's skill occasions other grounds for their association. Parallel rhetoric at the conclusion of the tale discloses this new kinship. The unexpected social dynamic of their conversation contributes to this development. This wise woman from Tekoa not only counsels the king on his responsibility concerning Absalom; she also invokes the king to rule wisely. Such interplay occasions the following sociorhetorical exegesis of this text.

Introduction, vss. 1-3

Narrated discourse opens the story and introduces two characters. The narrator introduces Joab by what he knows, says, and does. The narrator and Joab introduce the woman protagonist who will preside in the upcoming scene. By a series of commands, Joab fashions her role. She will appear before the king as a widow. Narrated discourse concludes this introduction and brings Joab's involvement to an abrupt halt.[21]

וַיֵּדַע יוֹאָב בֶּן־צְרֻיָה כִּי־לֵב הַמֶּלֶךְ עַל־אַבְשָׁלוֹם:

And Joab, son of Zeruiah, knew that the heart of the king
    was on/against Absalom. (vs. 1)

וַיִּשְׁלַח יוֹאָב תְּקוֹעָה

So Joab sent to Tekoa,

---

[20]However, the correspondence between David and the woman is not exact. Various incongruities have been noted between the woman's story and David's situation. Coats, "Parable, Fable, and Anecdote," 382, observes that while the death sentence threatened the woman's son, Absalom's life was not in danger. Whitelam, *The Just King*, 131, notes the lack of correspondence in the motives of the two fratricides. Absalom's crime was premeditated. The motive of the widow's son remains unknown. Hagan, "Deception as Motif and Theme," 331, suggests that the relationship here should be understood as "metaphorical rather than legal."

[21]Whitelam, *The Just King*, 130, contends that the abruptness with which Joab's direct speech ends (after כדבר הזה), indicates the corrupt nature of the text. "Joab's words ought to have been recorded here." By contrast, J. Mauchline, *1 and 2 Samuel* (London: Oliphants, 1971) 265, observes that the omission of Joab's instructions "does much to heighten the interest and suspense of the narrative."

וַיִּקַּח מִשָּׁם אִשָּׁה חֲכָמָה

and he fetched from there a wise woman,

וַיֹּאמֶר אֵלֶיהָ

and he said to her,

הִתְאַבְּלִי־נָא

"Observe mourning rites,

וְלִבְשִׁי־נָא בִגְדֵי־אֵבֶל

and dress in mourning garments

וְאַל־תָּסוּכִי שֶׁמֶן

but do not anoint yourself with oil.

וְהָיִית כְּאִשָּׁה זֶה יָמִים רַבִּים מִתְאַבֶּלֶת עַל־מֵת:

Be as a woman who for many days has been mourning on death. (vs. 2)

וּבָאת אֶל־הַמֶּלֶךְ

And go to the king,

וְדִבַּרְתְּ אֵלָיו כַּדָּבָר הַזֶּה

and speak to him concerning this matter."

וַיָּשֶׂם יוֹאָב אֶת־הַדְּבָרִים בְּפִיהָ:

And Joab put words into her mouth. (vs. 3)

David's son, Absalom, was in exile at Geshur. He had killed his half-brother Amnon, of whom David was especially fond. Though the actions of Absalom merit the anger of the king, his exile compounds the king's grief. The sorrow over the banishment of one son exacerbates the suffering of the king over the death of another.

וַיֵּדַע יוֹאָב בֶּן־צְרֻיָה כִּי־לֵב הַמֶּלֶךְ עַל־אַבְשָׁלוֹם:

And Joab, son of Zeruiah, knew that the heart of the king
   was on/against Absalom. (vs. 1)

David's social role as father and royal judge confounds his kingly sentiments. The royal sense of justice sets his heart *against* Absalom. The king's fatherly grief turns his heart *on* his exiled son. Rhetoric narrates the tension between these opposing social roles. The twofold meaning of the preposition עַל "on/against" conveys this ambiguity.[22]

---

[22]Fokkelman, *King David*, 126-27, McCarter, *II Samuel*, AB 9 (Garden City NY: Doubleday, 1984) 344, and Anderson, *II Samuel*, 187, translate the Hebrew

The narrator reports that Joab is privy to the king's dilemma. "And Joab, son of Zeruiah, knew that the heart of the king was on/against Absalom." Joab capitalizes on the complexity of these sentiments.

וַיִּשְׁלַח יוֹאָב תְּקוֹעָה

So Joab sent to Tekoa,

וַיִּקַּח מִשָּׁם אִשָּׁה חֲכָמָה

and he fetched from there a wise woman,

וַיֹּאמֶר אֵלֶיהָ

and he said to her,

הִתְאַבְּלִי־נָא

"Observe mourning rites,

וְלִבְשִׁי־נָא בִגְדֵי־אֵבֶל

and dress in mourning garments

וְאַל־תָּסוּכִי שֶׁמֶן

but do not anoint yourself with oil.

וְהָיִית כְּאִשָּׁה זֶה יָמִים רַבִּים מִתְאַבֶּלֶת עַל־מֵת:

Be as a woman who for many days has been mourning on death. (vs. 2)

וּבָאת אֶל־הַמֶּלֶךְ

And go to the king,

וְדִבַּרְתְּ אֵלָיו כַּדָּבָר הַזֶּה

and speak to him concerning this matter."

Rhetoric conveys the active scheming behind Joab's plot. Three in-dicative verbs (sent, fetched, said) narrate his initial machinations. Joab's imperatives to the woman (*observe, dress, do not anoint, be, go, speak*) dictate a disguise. The first four directives regulate her appearance.

observe *mourning* rites

dress in garments of *mourning*

do not anoint yourself

be as a woman who for many days has been *mourning* on death.

The disposition of *mourning* permeates her disguise. Anointing oneself with oil serves as the antithesis of one grieving. The negative admonition

---

עַל as "against." By contrast, J. Hoftijzer, "David and the Tekoite Woman," *VT* 20 (1970): 419, Walter Brueggemann, *First and Second Samuel*, Interpretation (Louisville: John Knox Press, 1990) 291, and R. Gordon, *1 & 2 Samuel* (Great Britain: Pater Noster Press, 1986) 266, translate עַל as "on" or "upon."

"do not anoint yourself with oil" reinforces this sad demeanor. The two subsequent commands ("go to the king" "and speak to him") prescribe her task. The woman from Tekoa will appear and act as a widow before the king.[23]

Compared to other societies, the plight of the widow in Israel was particularly pronounced. The legal codes of other ancient Near Eastern societies legislated on behalf of widows.[24] In the Code of Hammurabi, a widow was guaranteed a right to the marriage gift. Not even her own children could contest her inheritance.[25] The legal codes from Sumer also legislated in favor of the widow. Upon the death of her husband, a woman was exempt from her spouse's previous debts.[26] By contrast, Israelite widows were afforded no such benefits. Cut off from familial protection, the widow was an easy victim for the exactions of creditors (2 Kgs. 4:1-2). An Israelite woman might be spared this humiliation if she could take refuge in her father's house. After the death of her husbands Er and Onan, Tamar resided in her father's house (Gen. 38:11). The inheritance of a son or a relative might also rescue a woman from this destitution.[27] Naomi's social integrity is redeemed, in part, by the actions of her relative Boaz (Ruth 4:7-17).

Further, the plight of the widow was made public by the clothes she wore. In Genesis, descriptions of Tamar's dress (Gen. 38:14, 19) defined her precarious state. Accordingly, Joab attends to this important detail in this story: "And dress in garments of mourning" (v. 2).

Laws of protection offset the difficult status of widows in Israel.[28] Yet, the legal codes in the biblical texts identify widows, along with

---

[23]Fokkelman, *King David*, 128.

[24]H. E. von Waldow, "Social Responsibility and Social Structure in Early Israel," *CBQ* 32 (1970): 182-203; and Hans J. Boecker, *Law and the Administration of Justice in the Old Testament and Ancient East* (Minneapolis: Augsburg, 1980) 18ff.

[25]"The Code of Hammurabi," trans. T. Meeks, in *Ancient Near Eastern Texts*, ed. J. Pritchard (Princeton: Princeton University Press, 1955) 172.

[26]"The Laws Of Ur-Nammu," trans. J. J. Finkelstein, in *The Ancient Near East. Supplementary Texts and Pictures Relating to the Old Testament*, ed. J. Pritchard (Princeton: Princeton University Press, 1969) 87.

[27]Gottwald, *The Tribes of Yahweh*, 286ff.

[28]See Deut. 10:18; 14:29; 24:17; 26:12; and 27:19.

orphans and foreigners, as the most vulnerable members of society. Cut off from the privileges of the clan, they become subjects for charity.[29] The lamentable social status of widows governs Joab's rhetoric. His repetition of "mourning" (אבל) corresponds to and rehearses the tragedy of this state.

The narrator concludes the introduction by summarizing Joab's involvement.

וַיָּשֶׂם יוֹאָב אֶת־הַדְּבָרִים בְּפִיהָ׃

And Joab put words into her mouth. (vs. 3)

The formulaic expression "put words into someone's mouth" narrates Joab's activity.[30] In most cases, a superior usually instructs a subordinate. At the same time, the bearers of the words are persons of authority.[31] In the Book of Numbers, Balaam, a renowned seer, acknowledged God's words in his mouth (Num. 22:38, 23:5, 12, 16). Subsequently, this diviner confronted and instructed Balak, the king of Moab. In Ezra 8:17-18, "men of insight" and "leading men" were commissioned to speak the words "put into their mouths." However, the use of this formulaic expression does not indicate that instructions were literally dictated. God's promise to "be with [his] mouth" (Exod. 4:12) did not equip Moses with a script. Aaron was the speechmaker. Rather, the divine pronouncement authorized and endorsed Moses' authority in the community.

Similarly, Joab does not feed the woman her lines.[32] He merely authorizes her to speak. What she will say and how she will say it originate with the woman.[33] In the introduction, the narrator reveals the source

---

[29]See Boecker, *Law and the Administration of Justice in the Old Testament and Ancient East*, 53-134.

[30]See Num. 22:38; 23:5, 12, 16; Ezra 8:17; Deut. 31:19; Isa. 51:16; and 59:21.

[31]Claudia Camp, "The Wise Women of 2 Samuel: A Role Model for Women in Early Israel," *CBQ* 43 (1981): 18, and also her extended discussion on 17-18n.8.

[32]With S. Goldman, *Samuel: Hebrew Text and English Translation* (London and Bournemouth: Soncino Press, 1951) 266, who observes that "if the woman's task had been merely to repeat what she had learned by rote, Joab need not have gone out of his way to procure a wise woman for his purposes."

[33]With Camp, "The Wise Woman of 2 Samuel," 17-19, who argues for the

of her skill: "So Joab sent to Tekoa and he brought from there a wise woman." The counsel of wisdom will inspire the Tekoite woman's performance.[34] The woman herself will reveal the nature and source of this wisdom.

Narrative Introduction to the Encounter, vs.4

וַתֹּאמֶר [35] הָאִשָּׁה הַתְּקֹעִית אֶל־הַמֶּלֶךְ

And the Tekoite woman went to the king,

וַתִּפֹּל עַל־אַפֶּיהָ אַרְצָה

and she bowed her face to the ground,

וַתִּשְׁתָּחוּ

and she did homage to him.

The narrative description of the woman's behavior reinforces the authoritative stature of the king. Her approach, obeisance, speech, and homage before the king accord him sovereignty. At the same time, the literary features of this introduction undercut this social portrait. The narrative description subtly establishes the woman's importance in this story. Subject of four active verbs (*went, bowed, did homage, said*), she moves to the forefront of the account.

Unit I. Dialogue, vss. 4d-11

Unit I unfolds through direct speech. Three cycles of interchange between the woman and the king develop the plot. In exchange one (vss. 5-8), the disguised woman presents her legal case. In response, the king offers interest and vague assurance. In the second exchange (vss. 9-10) the woman offers to bear the consequences which the king might incur for a ruling on her behalf. Once again, David sidesteps the matter under

---

20 (1970): 419-44, esp. 444; Gordon, *I and II Samuel*, 267; and Goldman, *Samuel: Hebrew Text and English Translation*, 266. Against G. G. Nichol, "The Wisdom of Joab and the Wise Woman of Tekoa," *ST* 36 (1982): 97-104, who regards the story as an expression of Joab's wisdom; and Whybray, *The Succession Narrative*, 59, who attributes the woman's success to Joab.

[34]Camp, "The Wise Women of 2 Samuel," 14-29.

[35]Reading וַתָּבֹא "she went" with LXX, Syr., Vulg., Targ.[MSS], MT[MSS]. See McCarter, *I Samuel*, 338.

discussion. Instead, he promises her protection. In the third exchange (vs. 11), the woman prescribes what the king should do. In response, the king concedes to the requested judicial ruling. The widow's persistent initiative achieves the king's oath to rule on her son's behalf.

An Appeal to Speak / Appeal Honored, vss. 4d-5a

וַתֹּאמֶר

And she said,

הוֹשִׁעָה הַמֶּלֶךְ:

"Help, O King!" (vs. 4)

וַיֹּאמֶר־לָהּ הַמֶּלֶךְ

And the king said to her,

מַה־לָּךְ

"What's wrong?"

The growth of a kingdom gradually centralized authority. Like monarchs in other ancient Near Eastern societies, the Israelite king became directly responsible for maintaining justice and assuring all citizens access to the courts.[36] The protection and judgment on behalf of the least among the citizens were the foremost responsibility of the king.[37] In their legal inscriptions, Mesopotamian kings like Urukagina, Ur-Nammu, and Hammurabi boast of their virtue in this regard.[38] Even in nonlegal materials from Ugarit, Dan'el the king judges the case of the widow and the orphan.[39] Various accounts in the biblical texts concur with these portrayals. Ordinary citizens could plead their cases before the king. Absalom's criticism of David in 2 Samuel 15:3-4 indicates that various

---

[36]The notion of ancient Near Eastern kings' accessibility to all citizens is widely accepted and documented. For a brief summary of the evidence, see Whitelam, *The Just King*, 207-18.

[37]F. Charles Fensham, "Widow, Orphan, and the Poor in Ancient Near Eastern Legal and Wisdom Literature," *JNES* 21 (1962): 129-39.

[38]"Collections of Laws from Mesopotamia and Asia Minor," in *The Ancient Near East. Supplementary Texts and Pictures Relating to the Old Testament*, ed. Pritchard, 524; and "Collections of Laws from Mesopotamia and Asia Minor," in *Ancient Near Eastern Texts*, ed. Pritchard, 178 and 217.

[39]"Ugaritic Myths, Epics, and Legends," in *Ancient Near Eastern Texts*, ed. Pritchard, 151.

individuals came before the king for settlement of disputes. Further, the narrator's description in 2 Samuel 8:15 accords David this responsibility.[40] These narrative surroundings of the Tekoite woman's audience before King David establish the commonness of this scene.

Speech immediately hints at the speaker's social standing.[41] The form of the woman's address differs from the king's initial response. Her polite salutation ("Help, O King") suggests her dependent subservient status. By contrast, the hierarchical office of kingship appears to exempt David from such courtesies. His response is impersonal and abrupt ("What's wrong?"). The nature of her salutation, "Help, O King," acknowledges his idealized role as adjudicator. The widow appeals to David as the highest judge for הושעה "help."

Exchange 1, vss. 5-8

וַתֹּאמֶר

And she said,

אֲבָל אִשָּׁה־אַלְמָנָה אָנִי

"A mourning woman of widowhood am I,

וַיָּמָת אִישִׁי:

for dead is my husband. (vs. 5)

וּלְשִׁפְחָתְךָ שְׁנֵי בָנִים

To your servant were two sons.

וַיִּנָּצוּ שְׁנֵיהֶם בַּשָּׂדֶה

And the two of them were quarreling in the field.

וְאֵין מַצִּיל בֵּינֵיהֶם

And there was no one mediating between them.

וַיַּכּוֹ הָאֶחָד אֶת־הָאֶחָד

Then one struck the other,

וַיָּמֶת אֹתוֹ:

and he killed him. (vs. 6)

וְהִנֵּה קָמָה כָל־הַמִּשְׁפָּחָה עַל־שִׁפְחָתֶךָ

And Behold! The whole clan rose up against your servant.

---

[40]See James Montgomery, *The Books of Kings*, ICC (Edinburgh: T. & T. Clark, 1951) 109, for a survey of these parallels.

[41]Bar-Efrat, *Narrative Art in the Bible*, 66, notes the relationship between forms of speech and one's social role.

וַיֹּאמְרוּ

And they said,

תְּנִי אֶת־מַכֵּה אָחִיו

'Hand over the one who struck his brother

וּנְמִתֵהוּ בְּנֶפֶשׁ אָחִיו אֲשֶׁר הָרָג

so we can kill him for the life of his brother whom he killed.

וְנַשְׁמִידָה גַּם אֶת־הַיּוֹרֵשׁ

And also we will get rid of the one being heir.'

וְכִבּוּ אֶת־גַּחַלְתִּי אֲשֶׁר נִשְׁאָרָה[42]

And they will put out my one live coal which I have remaining,

לְבִלְתִּי שׂוֹם־לְאִישִׁי שֵׁם וּשְׁאֵרִית עַל־פְּנֵי הָאֲדָמָה׃

And not leave a name or descendant for my husband
on the face of the earth." (vs. 7)

וַיֹּאמֶר הַמֶּלֶךְ אֶל־הָאִשָּׁה

And the king said to the woman,

לְכִי לְבֵיתֵךְ

"Go to your house,

וַאֲנִי אֲצַוֶּה עָלָיִךְ׃

and I will give an order for you." (vs. 8)

The rhetorical features of her report illustrate her woeful social circumstances. Death has parted husband and wife. Grammar illustrates the separation.

אֲבָל אִשָּׁה־אַלְמָנָה אָנִי

"A mourning *woman* of widowhood am I,

וַיָּמָת אִישִׁי׃

for dead is my *husband*."

The identification of herself as a woman (אשה) at the opening of her statement stands apart from the mention of her husband (אשי) at the conclusion. Death (ימת) stands between them. The fivefold alliteration of the aleph (אבל, אשה, אלמנה, אני, אשי), injects her complaint with sighs of

---

[42]With Anderson, *2 Samuel*, 184, 4QSam seems to indicate השארתי "I have remaining," or נשארתי "which is my remaining one." See also E. C. Ulrich, "4QSam^c: A Fragmentary Manuscript of Samuel 14–15 from the Scribe of the *Serek Hay-yahad* (1QS)," *BASOR* 235 (1979): 10-11.

anguish.[43] The double identification of her social position ("A mourning woman of widowhood am I," "for dead is my husband") reinforces the urgency of her plea. Moreover, her speech juxtaposes a first-person reference to herself (אָנִי) and the reported death (יָמֹת). Her close proximity to death illustrates the life-endangering consequences for this widowed woman. Threatened by death, she turns to the king for life. The plot unfolds under the shadow of her widowhood. Rhetoric narrates her precarious social state.

וּלְשִׁפְחָתְךָ שְׁנֵי בָנִים

To your servant were two sons.

וַיִּנָּצוּ שְׁנֵיהֶם בַּשָּׂדֶה

And the two of them were quarreling in the field.

וְאֵין מַצִּיל בֵּינֵיהֶם

And there was no one mediating between them.

וַיַּכּוֹ הָאֶחָד אֶת־הָאֶחָד

Then one struck the other,

וַיָּמֶת אֹתוֹ:

and he killed him.

Speech reflects the widow's social standing. The woman's reference to herself as "your servant" (שִׁפְחָתְךָ) satisfies courtly courtesy.[44] With carefully balanced language she reports her tale. The two-part description of the circumstances (a quarrel, no mediator) matches the two-stage outcome ("one struck the other," "he killed him"). Antagonism harvests this violence. The changes in descriptive language across these five verbal statements track the course of this hostility and its consequences. Plural nouns and verbs in the opening pair of statements yield to singular forms in the concluding pair. The intervening statement ("There was no one . . . ") accounts for this change. With no one mediating between them, the two (שְׁנֵי, שְׁנֵיהֶם) who quarreled become (הָאֶחָד, הָאֶחָד) "the one" and "the other." Despite the drama of this initial description, the heart of her crisis lies beyond this tragic scene. The particle "Behold" (הִנֵּה) signals the critical moment.[45]

---

[43]Fokkelman, *King David*, 131.
[44]Conroy, *Absalom! Absalom!* 140.
[45]See T. Muraoka, *Emphatic Words and Structures in Biblical Hebrew*

וְהִנֵּה קָמָה כָל־הַמִּשְׁפָּחָה עַל־שִׁפְחָתֶךָ

And Behold! The whole clan rose up against your servant.

וַיֹּאמְרוּ

And they said,

תְּנִי אֶת־מַכֵּה אָחִיו

'Hand over the one who struck his brother

וּנְמִתֵהוּ בְּנֶפֶשׁ אָחִיו אֲשֶׁר הָרָג

so we can kill him for the life of his brother whom he killed.

וְנַשְׁמִידָה גַּם אֶת־הַיּוֹרֵשׁ

And also we will get rid of the one being heir.'

וְכִבּוּ אֶת־גַּחַלְתִּי אֲשֶׁר נִשְׁאָרָה

And they will put out my one live coal which I have remaining,

לְבִלְתִּי שׂוֹם־לְאִישִׁי שֵׁם וּשְׁאֵרִית עַל־פְּנֵי הָאֲדָמָה:

And not leave a name or descendant for my husband
    on the face of the earth." (vs. 7)

The judicial components of her circumstances govern the woman's speech. In pleading her own case before David, she must act as a witness as well as her own defense attorney. The form and content of her address verify this dual social role. The woman relates her story by quoting the clan.

> Hand over the one who struck his brother
> So we can kill him for the life of his brother whom he killed.

Her firsthand account qualifies her as a witness to the clan's deliberations. This shift to direct speech makes the clan's threat more immediate,[46] as well as contributes to the credibility of her tale.[47] In the case of

---

(Leiden: E. J. Brill, 1985) 137-40; and B. K. Waltke and M. O'Connor, *An Introduction to Biblical Hebrew Syntax* (Winona Lake IN: Eisenbrauns, 1990) 300, on the uses of הִנֵּה.

[46]A. F. Kirkpatrick, *The First and Second Books of Samuel* (London: Cambridge University Press, 1930) 350; and Bar-Efrat, *Narrative Art in the Bible*, 160.

[47]Against Bar-Efrat, *Narrative Art in the Bible*, 169, who concludes that the woman does not actually quote her clan but summarizes their deliberations. However, the shift from third-person to first-person speech argues in favor of a direct quotation.

her son's crime against his brother, the clan rules a homicide. Clan law punishes a death with a death. The biblical stories recall other instances of such practices. Gideon avenges his brothers' deaths by slaying their killers (Judg. 8:18-21). Even in stories concerning the early monarchy, accounts of this practice exist. Joab killed Abner in retaliation for Abner's slaying of Joab's brother Asahel (2 Sam. 2:18-23). Further, the legal codes in the biblical texts also verify the existence of this practice.[48]

In this story, the form of the woman's report represents the grounds for this ruling.

> *one who struck his brother*
> **so we can kill him**
> for the life of *his brother whom he killed.*

The criminal and his sentence (**so we can kill him**) are surrounded by his crime (*one who struck his brother, his brother whom he killed*). Repetition of "his brother" recalls the terms of kinship which have been violated. Such familial ties were the basis of clans. Disruption of these bonds was the clan's concern.[49]

Yet, such punishment was not always exacted for offenses within the family.[50] Customary law governed clans. By its nature, customary law was oral, local, and general.[51] In its generality, customary law changed in response to varying social conditions.[52] David did not inflict punish-

---

[48]The prohibition of murder is found in Exod. 20:13; the death sentence for murder occurs in Exod. 21:12 and Num. 35:31, 33.

[49]Salmon, "Judicial Authority in Early Israel," 46; and de Geus, *The Tribes of Israel,* 142.

[50]H. McKeating, "The Development of the Law on Homicide in Ancient Israel," *VT* 25 (1975): 50-51.

[51]Among the numerous studies on customary law, see Max Gluckman, *Politics, Law and Ritual in Tribal Society* (Oxford: Blackwell, 1965) 178-215; L. P. Mair, *An Introduction to Social Anthropology* (Oxford: Clarendon, 1972) 139-59; M. Barkun, *Law without Sanctions: Order in Primitive Societies and the World Community* (New Haven and London: Yale University Press, 1968); L. Pospisil, "Legal Levels and Multiplicity of Legal Systems in Human Society," *The Journal of Conflict Resolution* 11 (1967): 2-26; and S. F. Moor, *Law as Process: An Anthropological Approach* (London and Boston: Routledge and Kegan Paul, 1978) 13-24.

[52]I. Hamnett, *Chieftainship and Legitimacy. An anthropological study of*

ment on Amnon for his treatment of Tamar (2 Sam. 13:7-21). Neither did David punish Absalom for the murder of Amnon (2 Sam. 13:28-39).[53] Absalom banished himself for the deadly deed.

Moreover, a further disclosure by this witness undermines the clan's judicial integrity. The woman concludes her report of the clan's deliberations.

And also we will get rid of the one being heir.

The continuation of the woman's first-person report now raises questions about the clan's judgment. The clan's plan to punish the crime is also an occasion to destroy the family heir. A conflict of interest has disrupted the judicial process. Another agenda augments the clan's deliberations. The particle גם ("also") verifies the addendum. Destruction of the heir yields an inheritance for the clan (Num. 27:8-11).[54] The property of the widow's household would revert to other members of her husband's kin.[55] The motivation of the clan obscures their concerns for justice.[56] The clan's lawsuit against her son has become the woman's lawsuit against her clan. The antagonism that erupted between two brothers occasioned these hostilities. A word play, שפחה, משפחה (servant, clan), earmarks the

executive law in Lesotho (London: Routledge and Kegan Paul, 1975) 11.

[53]R. Wilson, "Israel's Preexilic Judicial System," _JQR_ 74 (1983): 243, explains the lack of action against Amnon and Absalom as a consequence of David's arbitrary and uneven judicial skills. By contrast, McKeating, "The Development of the Law on Homicide," 50, and E. Bellefontaine, "Customary Law and Chieftainship: Judicial Aspects of 2 Samuel 14:4-21," _JSOT_ 38 (1987): 54, understand these instances and other examples as evidence of the flexibility within customary law.

[54]E. W. Davies, "Inheritance Rights and the Hebrew Levirate Marriage," _VT_ 31 (1981): 138-44.

[55]For a discussion of family law and its ramifications for various members see A. Phillips, "Some Aspects of Family Law in Preexilic Israel," _VT_ 23 (1973): 349-61.

[56]Contra McKeating, "Vengeance Is Mine," _ExpTim_ 74 (1963): 239-45, who understands the extenuating circumstances as the only basis for the woman's appeal. Bellefontaine, "Customary Law and Chieftainship," 55, also recognizes this "conflict of interest" by which the vengeful kin would gain possession of family property upon the death of the heir.

new oppositions. Against customary law and against her own clan's ruling, the woman beseeches the king.[57]

With the skills of a lawyer, the woman details the ramifications.

They will put out my one live coal which I have remaining.
And not leave a name or descendant for my husband
   on the face of the earth.

The clan's two-stage destruction yields two outcomes. The death sentence by the clan, accompanied by their intent to destroy the heir, victimizes the woman and her husband. A chilling metaphor captures and conveys the social consequences for the woman.[58] "They will put out my one live coal which is remaining." The existence of the surviving son kindles the smoldering livelihood of this widow. The death of this offspring will snuff out her life.

But the devastation occasioned by the clan's ruling reaches beyond this widow. A second consequence compounds her grief. The loss of an heir means the loss of her husband's name and heritage. Israelites dreaded such extinction.[59] The woman who faces the plight of a widow now receives a further blow. Not only is her husband dead, but his name will also be obliterated. The woman returns to the matter of her deceased husband with which she opened her plea (vs. 5).

A mourning woman of widowhood am I
for he is dead, *my husband*. (vs. 5)

And not leave a name or descendant for *my husband*
on the face of the earth. (vs. 7)

This inclusio-like structure illustrates the all-encompassing nature of her grief.[60] The threatened loss of the husband's name and descendants inten-

---

[57]Bellafontaine, "Customary Law and Chieftainship," 55.

[58]Here, the metaphor functions in a "presentational" capacity. The imagery describes something (the woman's plight) in order to make its reality present. See P. Wheelwright, *Metaphor and Reality* (Bloomington: Indiana University Press, 1962) 70-91, on the functions of metaphor.

[59]Goldman, *Samuel: Hebrew Text and English Translation*, 267; and P. J. Budd, *Numbers*, WBC 5 (Waco TX: Word Books, 1984) 301.

[60]R. G. Moulton, *The Literary Study of the Bible* (Boston: D. C. Heath, 1899) 53-54, recognized this literary device and called it an "envelope figure." M.

sifies her initial sorrow over his death. The woman's reported loss is profound. The threefold repetition of "death" (מֵת) (vss. 5, 6, 7) rehearses her three privations.[61] Her speech erects a rhetorical edifice illustrating the crescendo-like momentum of her social travail.

Death of the Husband

A mourning woman of widowhood am I
for he is dead, my husband. (vs. 5)

Death of One Son

To your servant were two sons
And the two of them were quarreling in a field
And there was no one mediating between them.
Then one struck the other
And he killed him.

Threatened Death of Second Son

And Behold! The whole clan rose up against your servant
And they said,
"Hand over the one who struck his brother
So we can kill him for the life of his brother whom he killed.
And also we will get rid of the one being heir."
And they will put out the one live coal which is remaining
And not leave a name or a descendant for my husband
on the face of the earth." (vs. 7)

The incremental expansion in the form of her story coincides with the intensification of her loss. An increase of paratactic descriptions collaborates with an increase in her reported misfortunes.

The calamity amassing across her story camouflages her bold forensic skill. In bard-like fashion, she draws on the familiar.[62] Images from the

---

Kessler, "Inclusio in the Hebrew Bible," *Semitics* 6 (1978): 44-49, defined the functions of "inclusio." In this instance, the twofold mention of "husband" establishes a rhetorical boundary for the intervening material.

[61]Fokkelman, *King David*, 131.

[62]R. Culley, "An Approach to the Problem of Oral Tradition," *VT* 13 (1963): 113-25, identifies formulaic language, traditional phrases, and familiar story lines, as well as characters, as the stockpile upon which bards draw for their

Cain and Abel account ("two brothers," "in a field," "one struck the other") invade the listener's consciousness.[63] In that story, Cain was left to be a wanderer on the face of the earth. A similar fate awaits this widow. With no descendant of her husband "on the face of the earth" (vs. 7), she too will wander.[64] The pattern of the woman's story also corresponds to the pattern of the primeval tale. The fratricidal act sentences the criminal to a deadly fate. According to the clan's vendetta, punishment for a homicide required this outcome.[65] In the case of Cain, only a special intervention by God could save him. With high didactic skill, the woman's story subtly suggests a similar course of action for the king.

וַיֹּאמֶר הַמֶּלֶךְ אֶל־הָאִשָּׁה

And the king said to the woman,

לְכִי לְבֵיתֵךְ

"Go to your house,

וַאֲנִי אֲצַוֶּה עָלָיִךְ:

and I will give an order for you." (vs. 8)

The king promises the woman a ruling. An independent personal pronoun (אני) assures and emphasizes the exercise of his own royal authority.[66] The form of his command on behalf of this widow (עליך, vs. 8) appears to counter the clan's rule against her (על־שפחתך, vs. 7). However, his promise affords only vague protection. The content of his command remains unknown.

Exchange 2, vss.9-10

וַתֹּאמֶר הָאִשָּׁה הַתְּקוֹעִית אֶל־הַמֶּלֶךְ

And the Tekoite woman said to the king,

---

composition.

[63]These likenesses should not be mistaken for parallels. The clan's behavior and David's activity constitute the intended parallel of the woman's story. Against Blenkinsopp, "Theme and Motif in the Succession History," 51-52.

[64]See also Gunn, *The Story of King David*, 43; and Anderson, *2 Samuel*, 187.

[65]J. Blenkinsopp, "Jonathan's Sacrilege," *CBQ* 26 (1964): 449.

[66]Independent pronouns with finite verbs are often used for emphasis or to focus attention on the "first person" referent. See Muraoka, *Emphatic Words and Structures in Biblical Hebrew*, 58.

עָלַי אֲדֹנִי הַמֶּלֶךְ הֶעָוֹן וְעַל־בֵּית אָבִי
"On me (is) my Lord, the king's guilt, and on my father's house.

וְהַמֶּלֶךְ וְכִסְאוֹ נָקִי:
But the king and his throne are innocent." (vs. 9)

וַיֹּאמֶר הַמֶּלֶךְ
And the king said,

הַמְדַבֵּר אֵלַיִךְ וַהֲבֵאתוֹ[67] אֵלָי
"The one saying this to you, bring him to me.

וְלֹא־יֹסִיף עוֹד לָגַעַת בָּךְ:
And he will not bother you again." (vs. 10)

A variety of judicial options was available to kings.[68] A monarch could remit the entire case to local authority. A king could try the case himself and overrule clan law. The woman leads David toward the latter course of action by remedying an inherent complication.

וַתֹּאמֶר הָאִשָּׁה הַתְּקוֹעִית אֶל־הַמֶּלֶךְ
And the Tekoite woman said to the king,

עָלַי אֲדֹנִי הַמֶּלֶךְ הֶעָוֹן וְעַל־בֵּית אָבִי
"On me (is) my Lord, the king's guilt, and on my father's house.

וְהַמֶּלֶךְ וְכִסְאוֹ נָקִי:
But the king and his throne are innocent." (vs. 9)[69]

---

[67]וַהֲבֵאתוֹ is pointed as a 2nd masc. sg. I am reading here with most scholars who repoint it as a 2nd fem. sg. See Anderson, *2 Samuel*, 184; McCarter, *II Samuel*, 339; and Driver, *Notes on the Hebrew Text of the Books of Samuel*, 306.

[68]See G. C. Macholz, "Zur Geschichte der Justizorganisation in Juda," *ZAW* 84 (1972): 314-40; W. F. Leemans, "King Hammurabi as Judge," *Symbolae Ivridicae et Historicae Martino David Dedicatae* (Leiden: E. J. Brill, 1968) 110-20, has compiled a list of ancient Near Eastern texts which illustrate these options. Also K. Whitelam, *The Just King*, 132-34.

[69]The location and meaning of this verse are difficult. K. McCarter, *II Samuel*, 347-48, explains its problematic location as the result of a "Deuteronomistic expansion." K. N. Jung, "Court Etiquette in the Old Testament" (Ph.D. diss., Drew University, 1979) 42-52, cites this verse along with similar expressions (1 Sam. 25:24; Exod. 4:10; and Judg. 6:15) as examples of courtly language. J. Hoftijzer, "David and the Tekoite Woman," 428, understands the verse as a confession of guilt in the woman's plea for forgiveness for her son's deed.

Not only did one suffer for shedding blood; one could also be punished for preventing bloodshed. The blood of the murdered one must be atoned for. The typical formula of the talion law occurs in Exodus 21:23-25, Leviticus 24:18, 20, and Deuteronomy 19:21. Where there was innocent blood, there was always bloodguilt. In the book of Judges, God created a breach between Abimelech and the inhabitants of Shechem. "This was done in order that the violent murder of the seventy sons of Jerubbabel might recoil on Abimelech" who murdered them (Judg. 9:22-25). If the royal official overruled clan law on homicide, the issue of bloodguilt might still hold sway.[70] The woman's resort to direct first-person speech—"on me," "on my father's house"—confronts this drawback head on. An antonymic word pair, guilt and innocence (עֲוֹן, נָקִי), narrates the issue at hand.[71] Her willingness to shoulder the guilt (עֲוֹן) guarantees the king's innocence (נָקִי). The widow who sought refuge in the king now ensures his protection. Within this sphere of safety, David will act on behalf of the woman. However, the woman must act first.

וַיֹּאמֶר הַמֶּלֶךְ

And the king said,

הַמְדַבֵּר אֵלַיִךְ וַהֲבֵאתוֹ אֵלַי

"The one saying this to you, bring him to me.

וְלֹא־יֹסִיף עוֹד לָגַעַת בָּךְ:

And he will not bother you again." (vs. 10)

He orders her to bring to him the one speaking to her. Imperatives which are characteristic of a monarch conceal this king's hesitation. First, he ordered the woman to return home (vs. 8). Now he commands her to

---

Reading with McKeating, "The Development of the Law on Homicide in Ancient Israel," 52, who demonstrates that bloodguilt could attach itself to the one who has neglected or interfered with this exercise of vengeance (see 1 Kgs. 2:5-6, 31). The woman surmises this as the reason for David's vague ruling (vs. 8). Thus, she immediately proclaims her willingness to shoulder the potential guilt (vs. 9).

[70]H. McKeating, "The Development of the Law on Homicide in Ancient Israel," 58ff.

[71]Antonymic word pairs, like synonymous word pairs, act as a prop for the listener, and reiterate key ideas. See W. Watson, *Classical Hebrew Poetry* (Sheffield: JSOT, 1984) 140.

bring her opponent to him (vs. 10). The contradiction in orders sends the woman in different directions.

"*Go* to your house . . . " (vs. 8)
"*Bring* him to me . . . " (vs. 10)

The commands share a commonality. Each order strives to dismiss the litigant from the king's presence. The woman will not be dissuaded. The king's orders address only the circumstances of her plight. The widow requires a sworn ruling.

Exchange 3, vs. 11

וַתֹּאמֶר

And she said,

יִזְכָּר־נָא הַמֶּלֶךְ אֶת־יְהוָה אֱלֹהֶיךָ

"Let the king invoke the Lord, your God,

מֵהַרְבִּית גֹּאֵל הַדָּם לְשַׁחֵת

so that the avenger of blood will not increase destruction,

וְלֹא יַשְׁמִידוּ אֶת־בְּנִי

so that they will not destroy my son."

וַיֹּאמֶר

And he said,

חַי־יְהוָה

"By the life of God,

אִם־יִפֹּל מִשַּׂעֲרַת בְּנֵךְ אָרְצָה:

Not one hair from your son's head shall fall to the ground." (vs. 11)

In a desperate move which eclipses her subservient status, the woman affords the king direct guidance. She dictates to the monarch what he should do and why.

וַתֹּאמֶר

And she said,

יִזְכָּר־נָא הַמֶּלֶךְ אֶת־יְהוָה אֱלֹהֶיךָ

"Let the king invoke the Lord, your God,

מֵהַרְבִּית גֹּאֵל הַדָּם לְשַׁחֵת[72]

so that the avenger of blood will not increase destruction,

וְלֹא יַשְׁמִידוּ אֶת־בְּנִי

so that they will not destroy my son."

First, the woman requests that the king invoke God's name to confirm David's ruling. To invoke the Lord's name was tantamount to
uttering an oath. Now the woman strengthens the tenor of her entreaty by
employing the emphatic particle נָא.[73] The grounds for her request
accompany her plea. The clan will accomplish destruction by means of
the avenger of blood.

Social studies on the legal practices in the ancient Near East suggest
that the avenger of blood may have been a relative of the victim or an
officer in the community.[74] Joab's killing of Abner was an act of blood
revenge (2 Sam. 3:30) for Abner's murder of Joab's brother Asahel (2
Sam. 2:18-23).[75] Numbers 35:12 designates the next of kin as the גאל in

---

[72]The Hiph'il infinitive of רבה is often employed adverbially. See *Gesenius'
Hebrew Grammar*, 214 (§75ff), which cites Gen. 41:49, 22:17, Deut. 28:63 as
examples. With K. McCarter, *II Samuel*, 340, reading מהרבית) לשחת . . . מהרבות
being a scribal error for מהרבות), lit. "from destroying excessively."

[73]See *Gesenius' Hebrew Grammar*, 321; and B. K. Waltke and M. O'Conner
for a history of the discussions surrounding the function of the particle נָא.

[74]See M. Sulzberger, *The Ancient Hebrew Law* (London: Julius H. Greenstone, 1915) 54-56; F. C. Fensham, "A Few Aspects of the Legal Practices in
Samuel in Comparison with the Legal Material from the Ancient Near East,"
Studies on the Books of Samuel (Pretoria: University of South Africa Press, 1960)
18-26; R. de Vaux, *Ancient Israel* (London: Darton, Longham, and Todd, 1961)
11-12; D. A. Leggett, *The Levirate and Goel Institutions in the Old Testament
with Special Attention to the Book of Ruth* (Cherry Hill NJ: Mack Publishing Co.,
1974) 75-76; H. McKeating, "The Development of the Law on Homicide in
Ancient Israel," 50-53; A. Phillips, "Another Look at Murder," *JJS* 28 (1977):
111-14; and N. Gottwald, *The Tribes of Yahweh*, 263-67.

[75]H. McKeating, "The Development of the Law on Homicide," 51, also identifies Joab's deed as blood vengeance. However, McKeating also acknowledges
the irregularity of this act. In 1 Kgs. 2:5, David admonished Joab for avenging
blood which had been shed in battle.

such instances.[76] As representative of the people, this official acted in cases of murder. By shedding blood, the גאל fulfilled the responsibility of the clan.[77] A rhetorical feature of the text illustrates this social arrangement. A synonymous parallel in the woman's speech narrates this representation of the clan by the גאל.

> so that the avenger of blood will not increase destruction,
> so that they (clan) will not destroy my son

The persistent strategy of the woman extinguishes the reluctance of the monarch. David renders the desired ruling.

וַיֹּאמֶר

And he said,

חַי־יְהוָה

"By the life of God,

אִם־יִפֹּל מִשַּׂעֲרַת בְּנֵךְ אָרְצָה:

Not one hair from your son's head shall fall to the ground." (vs. 11)

David binds himself with an oath to act on the widow's behalf. An oath was an ancient and universal means of securing the truth.[78] Invocation of a deity sanctioned the validity of the oath. The common asseveration of David's oath, "by the life of God," acknowledged this divine witness.[79] Saul swore "by the life of God" in his oath to punish an evildoer (1 Sam.14:39). Abigail swore "by the life of God" before David that all his enemies would be like Nebal (1 Sam. 25:23).

The formula "not one hair from his head shall fall to the ground" guarantees comprehensive protection. The image conjures up a sense of utter safety for the widow's son, as well as for herself. In another story, the people employed this phrase to express their determination to rescue

---

[76]While the practice is attested to in these legal codes, very few narratives recount actual acts of blood vengeance by a גאל. The establishment of the cities of refuge (Exod. 21:12-14; Num. 35:9-34) may account for this low incidence.

[77]Phillips, "Another Look at Murder," 113; and de Vaux, *Ancient Israel*, 11.

[78]See M. Pope, "Oaths," *IDB* (New York and Nashville: Abingdon Press, 1962) 575-77; J. Pedersen, *Israel: Its Life and Culture*, vols. 3–4 (London: Oxford University Press, 1940) 450; and H. J. Boecker, *Law and Administration of Justice* (Minneapolis: Augsburg Publishing House, 1980) 23-26.

[79]Pope, "Oaths," 577.

Jonathan from King Saul's judicial ruling (1 Sam. 14:45).[80] In the present story, the expression narrates King David's determination to rescue another man from the judicial ruling of the people. Unbeknownst to David, the forthcoming application of this expression to Absalom assumes a different force. Upon Absalom's return to Jerusalem, he will conduct a revolt against his own father (2 Sam. 15–17). Ironically, Absalom's well-protected head of hair[81] will interfere with his own military advance and lead to his own demise (2 Sam. 18:9-15).[82] The king's so-called protection of "the hair of his head" when applied to Absalom will ensure the king's own protection. Hence, the woman leads David on a wise course.[83]

Three exchanges between the woman and the king have yielded an outcome. Each interchange concludes with a promise by the king. In the final exchange, David swears an oath of protection for the woman's son. This sworn statement not only ransoms the young lad's life; it paves the way for Absalom's return. The woman now appropriates her fiction to the reality at hand.

Unit II, vss. 12-17

With the exception of the woman's appeal to speak and the king's permission (vs. 12), unit II consists solely of the woman's monologue. She recasts her story in an open accusation of the king. Though she attends to David's dilemma concerning Absalom (vss. 13-14), she keeps

---

[80]This formula occurs in one other text. In 1 Kgs. 1:52, Solomon swears an oath to Adonijah. Once again, the expression accompanies a promise of protection.

[81]In another text, Absalom's hair invites the admiration of Israel (2 Sam. 14:25-26).

[82]J. Baldwin, *1 & 2 Samuel* (Leicester UK: InterVarsity Press, 1988) 256.

[83]Contra G. P. Ridout, "Prose Compositional Techniques in the Succession Narrative (2 Sam. 7, 9–20; 1 Kings 1–2)" (thesis, Graduate Theological Union, Berkeley CA, 1971) 137-38, who, because of Absalom's subsequent rebellion against David, describes the woman's accomplishment as therefore "empty of value"; and M. Sternberg, *The Poetics of Biblical Narrative* (Bloomington: Indiana University Press, 1987) 93, who contends that Absalom's return and subsequent revolt against David exposes the woman's rhetoric as "empty superlatives."

up her disguise (vss. 15-17).[84] With images, and allusions, she skillfully moves back and forth between David's reality and her fiction. Moreover, these two realms provide a common channel by which this wise woman moves toward a further goal. She will counsel David on his role as Israel's king.

וַתֹּאמֶר הָאִשָּׁה

And the woman said,

תְּדַבֶּר־נָא שִׁפְחָתְךָ אֶל־אֲדֹנִי הַמֶּלֶךְ דָּבָר

"Let your servant speak now a word to my Lord the king."

וַיֹּאמֶר

And he said,

דַּבֵּרִי:

"Speak!" (vs. 12)

וַתֹּאמֶר הָאִשָּׁה

And the woman said,

וְלָמָּה חָשַׁבְתָּה כָּזֹאת עַל־עַם אֱלֹהִים

"Why have you conspired like this against the people of God?

וּמִדַּבֵּר הַמֶּלֶךְ הַדָּבָר הַזֶּה כְּאָשֵׁם

For speaking thus, the king is guilty.

לְבִלְתִּי הָשִׁיב הַמֶּלֶךְ אֶת־נִדְּחוֹ:

For the king has not taken back the outcast. (vs. 13)

---

[84]The present position of vss. 15-17 has long been attributed to a scribal error. S. A. Cook, "Notes on the Composition of 2 Samuel," *AJSL* 16 (1899/1900): 158-59, and K. Budde, *Die Bücher Samuel*, KHC 8 (Tübingen: J. C. B. Mohr, 1902) 265ff., both argued that in vss. 12-14, the woman abandons her disguise and addresses the king's own situation. In vss. 15-17, she appears to take up her disguise again. Thus, vss. 15-17 must follow vs. 7. This emendation is supported today by Whitelam, *The Just King*, 130; and McCarter, *II Samuel*, 345-46. However, such an emendation ignores the woman's skill as well as the subtleties of her presentation. Between vss. 12-14 and 15-17, the woman moves back and forth between the two levels of the story. Further, there is no indication in vs. 12f that the widow gives up her disguise. Hence, the order of the received text is accepted and read here. See also Hoftijzer, "David and the Tekoite Woman," 438; Hertzberg, *I and II Samuel*, 332; Fokkelman, *King David*, 135-42; Gordon, *I and II Samuel*, 268; Baldwin, *1 & 2 Samuel*, 255; and Brueggemann, *First and Second Samuel*, 294-95.

כִּי־מוֹת נָמוּת

Surely we will die

וְכַמַּיִם הַנִּגָּרִים אַרְצָה אֲשֶׁר לֹא יֵאָסֵפוּ

Yes, as waters oozing away into the soil
    which can no more be gathered up.

וְלֹא־יִשָּׂא אֱלֹהִים נֶפֶשׁ וְחָשַׁב מַחֲשָׁבוֹת

But God does not take away life but conspires ways

לְבִלְתִּי יִדַּח מִמֶּנּוּ נִדָּח:

so that the one being estranged is not an outcast. (vs. 14)

וְעַתָּה אֲשֶׁר־בָּאתִי לְדַבֵּר אֶל־הַמֶּלֶךְ
אֲדֹנִי אֶת־הַדָּבָר הַזֶּה

Now, I came to the king, my Lord, to speak this word

כִּי יֵרְאֻנִי הָעָם

for the people made me afraid.

וַתֹּאמֶר שִׁפְחָתְךָ אֲדַבְּרָה־נָּא אֶל־הַמֶּלֶךְ

And so your servant thought, 'I will speak to the king.

אוּלַי יַעֲשֶׂה הַמֶּלֶךְ אֶת־דְּבַר אֲמָתוֹ

Perhaps the king will do this thing for his servant. (vs. 15)

כִּי יִשְׁמַע הַמֶּלֶךְ לְהַצִּיל אֶת־אֲמָתוֹ

For the king may determine to save his servant

מִכַּף הָאִישׁ לְהַשְׁמִיד אֹתִי וְאֶת־בְּנִי יַחַד

from the hand of the one who will cut off me and my son together

מִנַּחֲלַת אֱלֹהִים:

from the inheritance of God.' (vs. 16)

וַתֹּאמֶר שִׁפְחָתְךָ

And so your servant says,

יִהְיֶה־נָּא דְבַר־אֲדֹנִי הַמֶּלֶךְ לִמְנוּחָה

May the word of my Lord, the king, be final

כִּי כְּמַלְאַךְ הָאֱלֹהִים כֵּן אֲדֹנִי הַמֶּלֶךְ לִשְׁמֹעַ הַטּוֹב וְהָרָע

like a messenger of God is my Lord, the king,
    to judge good and evil.

וַיהוָה אֱלֹהֶיךָ יְהִי עִמָּךְ:

So may the Lord, your God, be with you. (vs. 17)

An Appeal to Speak / Appeal Honored, vs. 12

Despite her subservient posture before the king, the form of the woman's speech hints at her hidden authority.

וַתֹּאמֶר הָאִשָּׁה
And the woman said,

תְּדַבֶּר־נָא שִׁפְחָתְךָ אֶל־אֲדֹנִי הַמֶּלֶךְ דָּבָר
"Let your servant speak now a word to my Lord the king."

וַיֹּאמֶר
And he said,

דַּבֵּרִי:
"Speak!" (vs. 12)

An uncommon determination accompanies her courtly courtesies ("My Lord, the King," "your servant"). The particle נא, as well as her repetition of the root דבר ("word"), emphasize the significance of her upcoming word. Though she has gained the king's oath of protection, she still requires a further hearing. With aloofness characteristic of heirarchical authority, David grants her permission, "Speak." The woman responds with an inquiry.

The Woman's Speech, vss. 13-17

וְלָמָּה חָשַׁבְתָּה כָּזֹאת עַל־עַם אֱלֹהִים
"Why have you conspired like this against the people of God?

וּמִדַּבֵּר הַמֶּלֶךְ הַדָּבָר הַזֶּה כְּאָשֵׁם
For speaking thus, the king is guilty.

לְבִלְתִּי הָשִׁיב הַמֶּלֶךְ אֶת־נִדְחוֹ:
For the king has not taken back the outcast. (vs. 13)

כִּי־מוֹת נָמוּת
Surely we will die

וְכַמַּיִם הַנִּגָּרִים אַרְצָה אֲשֶׁר לֹא יֵאָסֵפוּ
Yes, as waters oozing away into the soil
    which can no more be gathered up.

וְלֹא־יִשָּׂא אֱלֹהִים נֶפֶשׁ וְחָשַׁב מַחֲשָׁבוֹת
But God does not take away life but conspires ways

לְבִלְתִּי יִדַּח מִמֶּנּוּ נִדָּח:
so that the one being estranged is not an outcast. (vs. 14)

Like an exponent of wisdom, the woman employs a rhetorical question and creates a tension that requires resolution. Wisdom traditions played a formative role in the development of this literary device.[85] Wisdom texts from the ancient Near East offer abundant evidence of the prevalence of rhetorical questions.[86] The woman's rhetorical question levels an accusation. David has conspired against the people of God. The preposition "against" (עַל) narrates the opposition. The parallel between the course of her destiny and Israel's fate begins to emerge. The clan's action "against" (עַל) this woman echoes in David's action "against" (עַל) the people.

> The whole clan rose up *against* your servant. (vs.7)
> you conspired like this *against* the people of God. (vs. 13)

Social anthropological studies on Israel define the king's role as a vicegerent.[87] Commissioned by God, the king was the mediator of divine law and adjudicator of divine justice for the people. Such an ideal of kingship prevailed in the ancient Near East.[88] In Mesopotamia, Lipit-Ishtar testified to his commissioning by the gods.

> Anu and Enlil called Lipit-Ishtar to the princeship of the land in order to establish justice in the land, to banish complaints, to turn back enmity and rebellion by the force of arms, to bring well-being to the Sumerians and Akkadians.[89]

---

[85]On the development and use of the rhetorical question, see R. Gordis, "A Rhetorical Use of Interrogative Questions in Biblical Hebrew," *AJSL* 49 (1932/ 1933): 212-17; M. Held, "Rhetorical Questions in Ugaritic and Biblical Hebrew," *ErIsr* 9 (1969): 71-79; and W. Watson, *Classical Hebrew Poetry*, 338-42.

[86]R. B. Y. Scott, "Folk Proverbs of the Ancient Near East," in *Studies in Ancient Israelite Wisdom*, ed. J. Crenshaw (New York: Ktav, 1976) 423, cites the prevalence of the rhetorical question, particularly within the Sumerian wisdom sayings. Job, a biblical wisdom text, is commonly noted for its use of rhetorical questions.

[87]T. N. D. Mettinger, *King and Messiah: The Civil and Sacral Legitimation of the Israelite Kings* (Lund: C. W. K. Gleerup, 1976) 244; and W. M. Clark, "A Legal Background of the Yahwist's Use of 'Good and Evil,'" *JBL* 88 (1967): 269; and Whitelam, *The Just King*, 164.

[88]For an elaboration of this ideal throughout ancient Near Eastern texts, see Whitelam, *The Just King*, 17-37.

[89]Pritchard, ed., *Ancient Near Eastern Texts*, 159.

In the Old Testament, Psalm 72 captured this ideal portrait.

> O God, endow this king with your own justice
> And give your righteousness to a king's son
>   that he may judge your people rightly. (Psalm 72:1-2a)

Similarly, a royal psalm expressed the monarch's understanding of his duty to establish justice on behalf of Yahweh.

> I sing of loyalty and justice
> I will raise a psalm of praise, O Lord. (Psalm 101:1)

The rhetorical features of the woman's presentation illustrate this social portrait of the king. The content of her speech levels an evaluation. The structure of her address erects an A-A^1 format which aligns the king and the deity.

וְלָמָּה חָשַׁבְתָּה כָּזֹאת עַל־עַם אֱלֹהִים

David
A
"Why have you *conspired* like this against the people of God?

וּמִדַּבֵּר הַמֶּלֶךְ הַדָּבָר הַזֶּה כְּאָשֵׁם

For speaking thus, the king is guilty.

לְבִלְתִּי הָשִׁיב הַמֶּלֶךְ אֶת־נִדְּחוֹ:

For the king has *not* taken back the *outcast*. (vs. 13)

כִּי־מוֹת נָמוּת

Surely we will die

וְכַמַּיִם הַנִּגָּרִים אַרְצָה אֲשֶׁר לֹא יֵאָסֵפוּ

Yes, as waters oozing away into the soil
  which can no more be gathered up.

וְלֹא־יִשָּׂא אֱלֹהִים נֶפֶשׁ וְחָשַׁב מַחֲשָׁבוֹת

God
A^1
But God does not take away life but *conspires* ways

לְבִלְתִּי יִדַּח מִמֶּנּוּ נִדָּח:

so that the one being estranged is *not* an *outcast*. (vs. 14)

Repetition of key words "conspire," "not," and "outcast" draws attention to God and David concurrently.[90] Yet, the content of the two descriptions (A and A^1) discloses a fundamental difference. David is reluctant to reinstate Absalom, the outcast. By contrast, God welcomes back the

---

[90]Fokkelman, *King David*, 137.

outcast. God's jurisdication is characterized by mercy.[91] David's rule is not. Further, the form of these portraits reinforces these differences. The one-line description of David's guilt has no counterpart in the disclosure about God. The literary dissonance between God's rule and David's reign reveals a social threat. The king has refused to address his own son's exile. Such equivocating governance endangers the well-being of all. What the king does on behalf of one of his subjects has ramifications for the life of all God's people.

The woman details the consequences. Her exclamation, "we will die," hovers between the descriptions of David's action and God's ways. The first person plural, "we," conjures several referents. The woman and her son, as well as the people of God, qualify as the victims. A metaphor illustrates the threat to their existence.[92]

> For surely we will die as waters oozing away into the earth
>   which can no more be gathered up.

The woman communicates the comprehensive nature of the threatened loss in a two-part description. The image, "as waters oozing away into the earth which can no more be gathered up," illustrates the crisis. Such idea patterns were characteristic of ancient Near Eastern folk wisdom.[93] Proverbs from these wisdom traditions "turned on the idea of identity, or equivalence."[94] "We will die" is equivalent to "the waters oozing away." Such equivalences clarified and intensified the experiences for the listener. In this case, the death of which the woman speaks is a death that leaves behind no traces of life. Hence, the woman exhibits her wisdom not only by her skillfull use of speech; she also employs forms of speech which identify her with wisdom traditions.

Further, the metaphor is reminiscent of her previous image of the flame (vs. 7). Each symbolizes a threat to existence. "The waters being

---

[91]Fokkelman, *King David*, 137; Hagan, "Deception as Motif and Theme in 2 Sam. 9–20; 1 Kgs. 1–2," 313; Goldman, *Samuel: Hebrew Text and English Translation*, 268.

[92]Fokkelman, *King David*, 137, notes that in narrative art, "metaphors are scarce and therefore particularly of significance."

[93]Scott, "Folk Proverbs of the Ancient Near East," 417-28; cited in Camp, "The Wise Woman of 2 Samuel," 20.

[94]Scott, "Folk Proverbs of the Ancient Near East," 419.

poured out" (vs. 14), coupled with the "flame being quenched" (vs. 7), threaten life with death. The archetypal depths of water, fire, life, and death join the woman's fiction to the reality at hand.

Amidst this confrontation with the king, the woman keeps up her disguise. The allusion to the reality of Absalom's exile, "one cast out" (vss. 12-14), collaborates with the fictitious plight of her own son. The adverb עַתָּה ("now") facilitates a transition between these two realms.[95]

וְעַתָּה אֲשֶׁר־בָּאתִי לְדַבֵּר אֶל־הַמֶּלֶךְ

אֲדֹנִי אֶת־הַדָּבָר הַזֶּה

Now, I came to the king, my Lord, to speak this word

כִּי יֵרְאֻנִי הָעָם

for the people made me afraid.

וַתֹּאמֶר שִׁפְחָתְךָ אֲדַבְּרָה־נָּא אֶל־הַמֶּלֶךְ

And so your servant thought, 'I will speak to the king.

אוּלַי יַעֲשֶׂה הַמֶּלֶךְ אֶת־דְּבַר אֲמָתוֹ׃

Perhaps the king will do this thing for his servant. (vs. 15)

כִּי יִשְׁמַע הַמֶּלֶךְ לְהַצִּיל אֶת־אֲמָתוֹ

For the king may determine to save his servant

מִכַּף הָאִישׁ לְהַשְׁמִיד אֹתִי וְאֶת־בְּנִי יַחַד

from the hand of the one who will cut off me and my son together

מִנַּחֲלַת אֱלֹהִים׃

from the inheritance of God.' (vs. 16)

The woman returns to her own story. Evidence of her lowly social status accompanies this retreat. Alternating references to herself as "your servant" (שִׁפְחָתֵךְ) and "his servant" (אֲמָתוֹ) reinforce her disguise. Though she continues her own story, she maintains a didactic role. She affords the king instruction on the nature of his office. The sociorhetorical features of her address highlight the bond between king and subject.

> *I* came to the *king*.
> *I* shall speak to the *king*.
> Perhaps the *king* will do this thing for his *servant*.
> For the *king* may see fit to save his *servant*.

---

[95]Contra McCarter, *II Samuel*, 346, who concludes that "now" (עתה) is "pointless" since he does not see the subtle connections between vss. 12-14 and 15-17.

Grammatical forms within her speech portray the interchange in the relationship. The king and his subordinate alternate as subject and object in her sentences. The content of these four statements reinforces the people's dependence upon the decisive rule of the monarch.

The woman prompts the king to act on behalf of his subjects' needs. A particle attests to her diplomacy. The force of "perhaps" (אוּלַי) conveys the woman's expression of hope while respecting the king's judicial freedom.[96]

The woman continues her pretext while pursuing a goal beyond the charade. She gives the king wise counsel without giving up her disguise. Cunningly, she cultivates a connection between her domestic problem, Absalom's exile, and Israel's fate. Her reference to "people" refers to her clan, as well as to the nation (vs. 7).[97] "Inheritance of God" denotes family property, as well as the community of Israel.[98] Gradually, the woman's presentation eclipses the concerns of her pretended circumstances and those of David's dilemma. Her language ("people of God," "inheritance of God") implies that covenant values are at stake.[99]

The woman summons David to a caliber of leadership inherent in the anointed office of kingship.

וַתֹּאמֶר שִׁפְחָתְךָ

And so your servant says,

---

[96]H. W. Wolff, *Obadiah and Jonah*, Augsburg Commentary (Minneapolis: Augsburg, 1977) 153, notes that "perhaps" plays a similar role in the book of Jonah. In Jonah 1:6, אוּלַי pays tribute to God's liberty of a final decision, as well as expresses hope.

[97]Gordon, *1 and 2 Samuel*, 268.

[98]Cf. 1 Kgs. 21:4 and 1 Sam. 26:19.

[99]C. Camp, "The Female Sage in Biblical Wisdom Literature," in *The Sage in Israel and the Ancient Near East*, ed. J. G. Gammie and L. Perdue (Winona Lake IN: Eisenbrauns, 1990) 189.

יְהִי־נָא דְּבַר־אֲדֹנִי הַמֶּלֶךְ לִמְנוּחָה[100]

May the word of my Lord, the king, be final

כִּי כְּמַלְאַךְ הָאֱלֹהִים כֵּן אֲדֹנִי הַמֶּלֶךְ
לִשְׁמֹעַ הַטּוֹב וְהָרָע[101]

like a messenger of God is my Lord, the king,
    to judge good and evil.

וַיהוָה אֱלֹהֶיךָ יְהִי עִמָּךְ:

So may the Lord, your God, be with you. (vs. 17)

Rhetoric houses a portrait of ideal kingship and the locus of its power. The content and form of the woman's speech sketch this social depiction. Not only are a monarch's judgments final; his rulings are all-encompassing. A merism, "to judge good and evil," illustrates the nature of this authority.[102]

Divine wisdom undergirds the exercise of a king's judicial authority. The allusions of the woman to this judicial wisdom are confirmed in a subsequent story.[103] Solomon prayed for the capacity to judge between "good and evil" (1 Kgs. 3:9). In response, God granted the gift of wisdom (1 Kgs. 3:12). Indirectly, the woman summons the king to draw upon this bestowal. "Like a messenger of God is my Lord the king to judge good and evil." Further, the artistry of her speech specifies the source of this wisdom. A simile, "like a messenger of God," acknowledges David's kinship with the divine.[104] On another occasion, Mephibosheth acknowl-

---

[100]With McCarter, *II Samuel*, 339, and Hoftijzer, "David and the Tekoite Woman," 439-40, למנוחה = literally, "a resting, a resolution," thus "final." Hence, the woman suggests by למנוחה that the finality of the king's word will put the matter to rest.

[101]לשמע with הטוב והרע or משפט = "to hear" in a judicial sense or "to judge" (see 1 Kgs. 3:9). See Mettinger, *Solomonic State Officials*, 126, 241.

[102]S. Geller, *Parallelism in Early Biblical Poetry* (Ann Arbor: Scholars Press, 1979) 35, defines "merismus" as "the statement of extremes, which may imply everything that is between." For an extended discussion of this literary device, see A. M. Honeyman, "Merismus in Biblical Hebrew," *JBL* 71 (1952): 11-18.

[103]Mettinger, *Solomonic State Officials*, 242.

[104]Hoftijzer, "David and the Tekoite Woman," 440; A. R. Johnson, *Sacral Kingship in Ancient Israel* (Cardiff: University of Wales, 1967) 16; S. Talmon, *King, Cult, and Calendar in Ancient Israel* (Jerusalem: Magnes Press, 1986) 37;

edged David's capacity to judge what was "right" because the king "is
like a messenger of God" (2 Sam. 19:27). Instilled with God's wisdom,
the king is the mediator of God's judgments. A concluding doxology reinforces God's patronage of the king's power. "So may God be with
you." Under the auspices of the woman's blessing, the monarch will act.

Unit III, vss. 18-20

Unit three (vss. 18-20) unfolds in the course of two exchanges between the woman and the king. The woman's tale of her domestic problem has instigated the king's own self-scrutiny. David questions the
woman regarding the origin of this scheme. The woman responds with
a solemn oath and reveals Joab's involvement. She also affords the king
a final instruction.

וַיַּעַן הַמֶּלֶךְ וַיֹּאמֶר אֶל־הָאִשָּׁה

And the king spoke, and he said to the woman,

אַל־נָא תְכַחֲדִי מִמֶּנִּי דָּבָר אֲשֶׁר אָנֹכִי שֹׁאֵל אֹתָךְ

"Do not withhold from me the word which I am asking you."

וַתֹּאמֶר הָאִשָּׁה

And the woman said,

יְדַבֶּר־נָא אֲדֹנִי הַמֶּלֶךְ:

"Speak now, my Lord, the king." (vs. 18)

וַיֹּאמֶר הַמֶּלֶךְ

And the king said,

הֲיַד יוֹאָב אִתָּךְ בְּכָל־זֹאת

"Was the hand of Joab with you in all this?"

וַתַּעַן הָאִשָּׁה וַתֹּאמֶר

And the woman answered, and said,

חֵי־נַפְשְׁךָ אֲדֹנִי הַמֶּלֶךְ

"By the life of my Lord, the king,

אִם־אִשׁ לְהֵמִין וּלְהַשְׂמִיל מִכֹּל אֲשֶׁר־דִּבֶּר אֲדֹנִי הַמֶּלֶךְ

One cannot turn right or left from what my Lord, the king, says.

כִּי־עַבְדְּךָ יוֹאָב הוּא צִוָּנִי

Indeed, your servant Joab instructed me.

וְהוּא שָׂם בְּפִי שִׁפְחָתְךָ אֵת כָּל־הַדְּבָרִים הָאֵלֶּה:

He put all these words into your servant's mouth. (vs. 19)

---

and Whitelam, *The Just King*, 135.

לְבַעֲבוּר סַבֵּב[105] אֶת־פְּנֵי הַדָּבָר
In order to change the circumstances of the matter,

עָשָׂה עַבְדְּךָ יוֹאָב אֶת־הַדָּבָר הַזֶּה
Your servant Joab did this thing.

וַאדֹנִי חָכָם כְּחָכְמַת מַלְאַךְ הָאֱלֹהִים
And my Lord is wise like the wisdom of a messenger of God,

לָדַעַת אֶת־כָּל־אֲשֶׁר בָּאָרֶץ:
to know all that is on the earth." (vs. 20)

An Appeal to Speak / Appeal Honored, vs. 18

וַיַּעַן הַמֶּלֶךְ וַיֹּאמֶר אֶל־הָאִשָּׁה
And the king spoke, and he said to the woman,

אַל־נָא תְכַחֲדִי מִמֶּנִּי דָּבָר אֲשֶׁר אָנֹכִי שֹׁאֵל אֹתָךְ
"Do not withhold from me the word which I am asking you."

וַתֹּאמֶר הָאִשָּׁה
And the woman said,

יְדַבֶּר־נָא אֲדֹנִי הַמֶּלֶךְ:
"Speak now, my Lord, the king." (vs. 18)

For the first time in the story, the king initiates an exchange. The nature of his speech suggests David suspects the ruse. His use of "withhold" (כחד) conveys his expectations. The king anticipates the woman's resistance to his question. With emphatic speech (על־נא), he commands the woman to speak the truth. The woman matches the king's emphatic tone (ידבר־נא) and invites his inquiry. The monarch's question displays his own latent alertness. He not only perceives a scheme; he also suspects Joab's involvement.

Final Exchange, vss. 19-20

וַיֹּאמֶר הַמֶּלֶךְ
And the king said,

הֲיַד יוֹאָב אִתָּךְ בְּכָל־זֹאת
"Was the hand of Joab with you in all this?"

---

[105]The qal of סבב "to turn" becomes "to change, transform" in the piel infinitive construct here. See BDB, 686.

The woman's response is immediate and direct. Her straightforward answer verifies her uprightness.

וַתַּעַן הָאִשָּׁה וַתֹּאמֶר

And the woman answered, and said,

חֵי־נַפְשְׁךָ אֲדֹנִי הַמֶּלֶךְ

"By the life of my Lord, the king,

אִם־אִשׁ לְהֵמִין וּלְהַשְׂמִיל מִכֹּל אֲשֶׁר־דִּבֶּר אֲדֹנִי הַמֶּלֶךְ

One cannot turn right or left from what my Lord, the king, says.

כִּי־עַבְדְּךָ יוֹאָב הוּא צִוָּנִי

Indeed, your servant Joab instructed me.

וְהוּא שָׂם בְּפִי שִׁפְחָתְךָ אֵת כָּל־הַדְּבָרִים הָאֵלֶּה:

He put all these words into your servant's mouth. (vs. 19)

לְבַעֲבוּר סַבֵּב אֶת־פְּנֵי הַדָּבָר

In order to change the circumstances of the matter,

עָשָׂה עַבְדְּךָ יוֹאָב אֶת־הַדָּבָר הַזֶּה

Your servant Joab did this thing.

וַאדֹנִי חָכָם כְּחָכְמַת מַלְאַךְ הָאֱלֹהִים

And my Lord is wise like the wisdom of a messenger of God,

לָדַעַת אֶת־כָּל־אֲשֶׁר בָּאָרֶץ:

to know all that is on the earth." (vs. 20)

With her own sworn statement, she matches the king's previous oath (vs. 11). Swearing by "the life of the king" acknowledges his authority. Such pronouncements were tantamount to swearing by "the life of God."[106] Oaths recognized God's power over life and death. The woman's sworn statement, "By the life of my Lord, the King," recognizes David's same power.[107] A merism ("right to left") illustrates the boundless terrain of such jurisdiction. Once again, the woman instructs the king on his kinship with the divine.

Further, the woman's oath verifies the truth of her upcoming disclosure. Joab is responsible. "Indeed, your servant Joab instructed me.

---

[106]See M. R. Lehmann, "Biblical Oaths," *ZAW* 81 (1969): 83-86; cited in Mettinger, *Solomonic State Officials*, 133. Oaths by "the life of God" and "the life of the King" illustrate this equivalence. See 1 Sam. 25:26; 2 Sam. 15:21; and 1 Sam. 20:3.

[107]P. A. H. de Boer, "Vive de roi," *VT* 5 (1955) 230ff.

. . . " The ruse has ended. There is no widow to save. Her disclosure of Joab's role is, at the same time, an acknowledgement of her own disguise.

The form of the woman's speech redirects the focus of the king's inquiry.

חֵי־נַפְשְׁךָ אֲדֹנִי הַמֶּלֶךְ

"By the life of my Lord, the king,

אִם־אִשׁ לְהֵמִין וּלְהַשְׂמִיל מִכֹּל אֲשֶׁר־דִּבֶּר אֲדֹנִי הַמֶּלֶךְ

One cannot turn right or left from what my Lord, the king, says.

כִּי־עַבְדְּךָ יוֹאָב הוּא צִוָּנִי

Indeed, your servant Joab instructed me.

וְהוּא שָׂם בְּפִי שִׁפְחָתְךָ אֵת כָּל־הַדְּבָרִים הָאֵלֶּה:

He put all these words into your servant's mouth. (vs. 19)

לְבַעֲבוּר סַבֵּב אֶת־פְּנֵי הַדָּבָר

In order to change the circumstances of the matter,

עָשָׂה עַבְדְּךָ יוֹאָב אֶת־הַדָּבָר הַזֶּה

Your servant Joab did this thing.

וַאדֹנִי חָכָם כְּחָכְמַת מַלְאַךְ הָאֱלֹהִים

And my Lord is wise like the wisdom of a messenger of God,

לָדַעַת אֶת־כָּל־אֲשֶׁר בָּאָרֶץ:

to know all that is on the earth." (vs. 20)

The chiastic-like structure of her response[108] spotlights the purpose rather than the person behind the plot. She attends to this central focus by first underscoring her own authority. The formula, "he put all these words into my mouth," confirms the woman's authorization for the task.[109] Her artistically wrought ambiguity ("in order to change the circumstances of the matter") invites a twofold reflection. The scheme of

---

[108]On types and functions of chiasms, see A. R. Ceresko, "The Chiastic Word Pattern in Hebrew," *CBQ* 38 (1976): 303-11, and "The Function of Chiasmus in Hebrew Poetry," *CBQ* 40 (1978): 1-10; also F. I. Andersen, *The Sentence in Biblical Hebrew* (The Hague: Mouton, 1974) 119-40. On the study of chiastic structures in the Succession Narrative, see Ridout, "Prose Compositional Techniques," 47-74; and Conroy, *Absalom! Absalom!* 143-45.

[109]See discussion on 88-89, above.

Joab sought "to change" the fate of Absalom. The wise counsel of the woman endeavors "to change" the manner in which the king ruled.

In her previous speech (vss. 12-17), the woman acknowledged the king's authority. By assigning him judgment between "good and evil," she hinted at his charism.

like a messenger of God is my Lord the king
to judge between good and evil. (vs. 17)

In the present recitation, her concluding remarks detail those inferences.

My Lord the king is wise
like the wisdom of a messenger of God. (vs. 20)

The woman names the endowment. Wisdom is bestowed upon the king. Once again, the image "messenger of God" reminds the king of his associatiom with the divine. The implications of this kinship are drawn out further. She affords the king omniscient-like governance: "to know all that is on the earth."

In the opening of her response, the woman's oath ("By your life my Lord, the king . . . ") paid tribute to the authority of the monarch. At the conclusion of her answer, the acclamation of the king's wisdom qualifies this power. The wisdom guiding the king's authority is "like the wisdom of a messenger of God" (v. 20).

Such counsel on the part of the wise woman moves the king to an unequivocating judgment.[110]

---

[110]Despite the woman's accurate sketch of the ideal of kingship in Israel, as well as her high didactic skill in moving the king to a decision, some scholars discount her speech as mere flattery. Bar-Efrat, *Narrative Art in the Bible*, 58, characterizes the woman as "fawning" to obtain the king's good will and to protect herself. Sternberg, "The Bible's Art of Persuasion," 93, disqualifies the woman's rhetoric as "empty superlatives." Hoftijzer, "David and the Tekoite Woman," 440, and McCarter, *II Samuel*, 347, offer similar evaluations. Fokkelman, *King David*, 141n.24, evaluates these kinds of interpretations as "gravely depressing" and "sexist." His literary analysis of the woman's speeches concludes otherwise: "She is truly a wise woman," 41.

Conclusion, vss. 21-22

וַיֹּאמֶר הַמֶּלֶךְ אֶל־יוֹאָב

And the king said to Joab,

הִנֵּה־נָא עָשִׂיתִי אֶת־הַדָּבָר הַזֶּה

"Behold I will do this thing.

וְלֵךְ הָשֵׁב אֶת־הַנַּעַר אֶת־אַבְשָׁלוֹם:

Go, bring back the young man, Absalom." (vs. 21)

וַיִּפֹּל יוֹאָב אֶל־פָּנָיו אַרְצָה

And Joab bowed his face to the ground

וַיִּשְׁתָּחוּ

And he honored him

וַיְבָרֶךְ אֶת־הַמֶּלֶךְ

And he blessed the king.

וַיֹּאמֶר יוֹאָב

And Joab said,

הַיּוֹם יָדַע עַבְדְּךָ כִּי־מָצָאתִי חֵן בְּעֵינֶיךָ אֲדֹנִי הַמֶּלֶךְ

Today, your servant knows that I have found favor in your eyes,
    my Lord, the king.

אֲשֶׁר־עָשָׂה הַמֶּלֶךְ אֶת־דְּבַר עַבְדֶּן

because the king granted the request of your servant. (vs. 22)

In the conclusion, Joab abruptly replaces the woman and is the addressee of the king's final remarks. Joab's act of homage here (vs. 22) corresponds to the woman's act of prostration (vs. 4) at the opening of the story. Joab's blessing on the king (vs. 22) parallels the woman's blessing of the king (vs. 17).

This reintroduction of Joab signals a resolution to the plot. The story which opens with Joab now concludes with his return. Joab's commands to the woman at the opening of the story have occasioned David's command to Joab at the conclusion. Absalom's fate is reversed. The content of the king's order corresponds with Joab's scheme. Absalom will return.

The sociorhetorical interplay across this tale discloses a further outcome. The contrasting characterization of David and the woman represents the prevailing social categories in this story: king over subject, named over unnamed, powerful over powerless, male over female. Yet, rhetoric reveals a curious dynamic amidst these social differences. The nameless woman assertively directed the conversation and determined its course. By contrast, David hesitated to make a judicial ruling despite his monarchical stature. The woman prodded the king three times (vss. 4ff., 9, 11) for a ruling which was within his judicial power. The king questioned the woman only once to uncover the origin and motive behind her words (vs. 19). Further, the woman subject instructed a monarch on the nature, scope, and locus of his authority. The king heeded the woman's counsel and ordered Absalom's return.

In David's concluding speech, rhetoric continues to undermine prevailing social categories. The king's words to Joab replicate the wise woman's plea.

(Woman)   "Perhaps, he will do this thing. . . . " (vs. 15)
(King)   "Behold, I will do this thing. . . . " (vs. 21)

The social distance between the woman and the king is suspect. Wisdom invites a redefinition of their relationship. The woman showed herself wise in her ability to keep up her disguise. As an inferior, she boldly confronted a superior. She skillfully employed idioms, patterns of speech, and tactics characteristic of folk wisdom. Further, she manifested supreme forensic skill. She spoke the right word at the right time. She infused her words with a surplus of meaning. As a result, she changed the course of events and she changed the heart of a king. But her goal was not limited to the fate of Absalom. The concerns voiced by the woman showed her to be "an active tradent of covenant values"[111] (land, inheritance). David's decision acknowledged her authority.

The investiture of David as Israel's king made him the viceroy of God. A charism equipped him for this task. The woman specified and detailed the nature of this asset. The subsequent story of Solomon's request for wisdom in 1 Kings 3:1-14, confirms its character. Divine wisdom informs kingship in Israel. A wise king mediates God's judgments to the people. In this story, a wise woman mediates God's wisdom to the king. The fate of the people, Israel, hung in the balance. The authority, instruction, and insight of this wise woman have induced the king to rule wisely. Wisdom disqualifies social differences and constitutes their kinship.

---

[111]Camp, "The Female Sage in Biblical Wisdom Literature," 189. On this point, Camp proceeds to caution against any arbitrary division between "so-called secular wisdom tradition and religious Yahwism," 189.

The Underside
of Monarchic Rule

A Sociorhetorical Exegesis
of 1 Kings 3:16-28

The story of Israel's statehood unfolded under the banner of kingship. Changes in the social configurations of the state wrought changes in the shape of the royal office.[1] As local autonomy decreased, the authority of centralized leadership increased. Saul, the first monarch, relied on the elders of the clans for the endorsement and support of his decisions (1 Sam. 14:38-39). In subsequent years, the authority of these local ruling bodies receded.[2] By the time of Solomon, the king initiated building

---

[1]Besides the scant biblical evidence, theorists have used comparative anthropological studies, as well as archaeological evidence to elaborate the nature of these changes. See M. Fried, *The Evolution of a Political Society—An Essay in Political Anthropology* (New York: Random House, 1967); A. Malamat, "Organs of Statecraft in the Israelite Monarchy," *BAR* 3 (1970): 163-98; R. Cohen and R. Elman, eds., *Origins of the State. The Anthropology of Political Evolution* (Philadelphia: ISHI Publications, 1978); H. Tadmor, "Traditional Institutions and the Monarchy: Social and Political Tensions in the Time of David and Solomon," *Studies in the Period of David and Solomon*, ed.T. Ishida (Tokyo: Yamakawa-Shuppansha, 1982) 239-57; and F. Frick, *The Formation of the State in Ancient Israel: A Survey of Models and Theories* (Decatur GA: Almond Press, 1985).

[2]On the relationship between elders and centralized government, see J. L. McKenzie, "Elders in the Old Testament," *Studia Biblica et Orientalia* 10 (1959): 388-406; H. Tadmor, "The People and the Kingship in Ancient Israel: The Role of the Political Institutions in the Biblical Period," *Journal of World History* 11 (1968): 46-68; H. Reviv, "Structure of Society," *The Age of the Monarchies: Culture and Society—The World History of the Jewish People*, ed.

projects (1 Kgs. 9:10-19), established trade routes (1 Kgs. 10:1-13), and issued judicial rulings (1 Kgs. 3:16-28) without recourse to local authorities.

The size of the nation also altered the king's role. The country grew from a one-nation state under Saul to a multinational empire under David.[3] Numerous military campaigns made this expansion possible. King David became the military warrior par excellence.[4] The increased scope of the empire, which resulted from this military prowess, increased the monarch's responsibilities. Appointees of the king gradually absorbed the growing duties of the royal office.[5] By the time of Solomon's reign, a royal class of couriers and officers surrounded the king.[6] Benaiah, David's bodyguard, was appointed the commander of Solomon's army (1 Kgs. 2:35). Solomon made Elihoreph and Ahijah his scribes (1 Kgs. 4:3). Adoniram was in charge of collecting the tribute to the king (1 Kgs. 4:6). When Solomon divided his kingdom along more equitable demographic and socioeconomic lines,[7] governors were appointed for each of the

---

A. Malamat (Jerusalem: Masada Press, 1979); H. Tadmor, "Traditional Institutions," 240-42; and H. Reviv, *The Elders in Ancient Israel—A Study of a Biblical Institution* (Jerusalem: Magnes Press, 1989) 35-136.

[3]J. H. Hayes and J. Maxwell Miller, eds., *Israelite and Judaean History* (Philadelphia: Trinity Press International, 1977) 349, characterize David's reign as an "imperialistic expansion."

[4]K. Whitelam, *The Just King—Monarchical Judicial Authority in Ancient Israel* (Sheffield: JSOT Press, 1979) 166.

[5]See B. Mazar, "The Military Elite of David," *VT* 13 (1963): 310-20; T. N. D. Mettinger, *Solomonic State Officials—A Study of the Civil Government Officials of the Israelite Monarchy* (Lund: C. W. K. Gleerup, 1971); E. W. Heaton, *Solomon's New Men—The Emergence of Ancient Israel as a National State* (New York: Pica Press, 1974) 47-60; and N. Gottwald, *The Hebrew Bible—A Socioliterary Introduction* (Philadelphia: Fortress Press, 1985) 323-24.

[6]B. Halpern, *The Constitution of Monarchy in Israel* (Ann Arbor MI: Scholars Press, 1981) 244-45.

[7]See G. E. Wright, "The Provinces of Solomon (1 Kings 4:7-19)," *ErIs* 8 (1967): 58-68, who argues that the divisions addressed economic concerns; and Mettinger, *Solomonic State Officials*, 112-21, who emphasizes political and territorial factors behind the divisions. N. Gottwald, *Tribes of Yahweh* (Maryknoll NY: Orbis, 1979) 368-70, argues for a combination of both economic and territorial factors influencing the divisions.

districts (1 Kgs. 4:7-8). Azariah, chief of district governors, oversaw these local rulers (1 Kgs. 4:5).[8] Ahishar served as Solomon's steward (1 Kgs. 4:6). Finally, Solomon's appointment of Zadok (1 Kgs. 4:4), Abiathar (1 Kgs. 4:4), and Azariah (1 Kgs. 4:2) expanded the priesthood.

Such specialization redefined the royal office. Over time, the king's direct involvement in military and domestic activities diminished.[9] Instead, he became the figurehead of an established hierarchical social order, as well as the locus of all authority.

The Deuteronomistic History recounts these various stages in the social evolution of kingship. 1 Samuel 8–15 sets forth the variegated portrait of Saul's tenure as king.[10] The court history (2 Sam. 9–20, 1 Kgs. 1–2) represents the advances in kingship under David.[11] 1 Kings, which recounts Solomon's reign, represents kingship as a secure and fully established office.

1 Kings opens with a report of the transfer of kingship from David to Solomon (1 Kgs. 1–2). These chapters mark the passing from one epoch to another.[12] The Solomonic Narrative, which follows in 1 Kings

---

[8]The configuration of Egypt's administrative system was thought to have influenced Solomon's organization of his kingdom into districts. See D. B. Redford, "Studies in the Relations between Palestine and Egypt during the First Millennium B.C.," *Studies in the Ancient Palestinian World*, ed. J. W. Weavers and D. B. Redford (Toronto: University of Toronto Press, 1972) 153ff.; and G. W. Ahlstrom, *Royal Administration and National Religion in Ancient Palestine* (Leiden: E. J. Brill, 1982) 32-33.

[9]S. Tadmor, *King, Cult, and Calendar in Ancient Israel* (Jerusalem: Magnes Press, 1986) 32, notes that consequently, Solomon's reign was marked by a "total loss of close relationship between people and king."

[10]See chap. 4, pp. 39-76.

[11]See chap. 5, pp. 77-121.

[12]L. Rost, *Die Uberlieferung von der Thronnachfolge David* (Stuttgart: W. Kohlhammer, 1926) 86-87, first proposed that 1 Kings 1–2 formed the conclusion to the Succession Narrative. Because of the literary disunity in this complex, other theories were offered. M. Noth, *Konige—1 Teilband* (Neukirchen Verlag: Neukirchen-Vluyn, 1968) 8-9, viewed 2:5-9, 13-35, and 36-46 as a series of appendices. T. N. D. Mettinger, *King and Messiah: The Civil and Sacral Legitimation of the Israelite Kings* (Lund: C.W.K. Gleerup, 1976) 28, argued that the Succession Narrative was inconsonant with the political murders in chaps. 1

3–11, celebrates the glorious reign of this king.[13] Chapters 3–9:25 offer an overview of Solomon's administration and domestic affairs. Chapters 9:26–10:29 present a picture of Solomon's international dealings. The final chapter (chapter 11) of the Solomonic Narrative suggests the king's shortcomings, describes his adversaries, and summarizes his reign. The characteristic regnal formula (11:41-43) concludes this narrative.

In the biblical story, Solomon's reign represents a novum in Israelite kingship.[14] His rule marked the culmination of years of transition and change. An idealized depiction of this king and his kingdom illustrates and celebrates this climax.[15] The images of wealth, power, and fame

---

and 2. Recently, A. Frisch, "Structure and Its Significance: The Narrative of Solomon's Reign (1 Kgs. 1–12:24)," *JSOT* 51 (1991): 3-14, and K. I. Parker, "Repetition as a Structuring Device in 1 Kings 1–11," *JSOT* 42 (1988): 19-27, argue in favor of the unity of chaps. 1–11 based upon patterns of symmetry. Wherever chaps. 1 and 2 are located, they do form the conclusion of David's reign and the introduction to the Solomonic era.

[13]Chaps. 3–11 are made up of a variety of materials (lists, dream accounts, reports of diplomatic relations, etc.). Though source-critical studies on these chapters are inconclusive, many scholars recognize "the book of the acts of Solomon" (1 Kgs. 11:41) as one of the potential sources for these materials. See J. Montgomery and H. S. Gehman, *The Book of Kings*, ICC (Edinburgh: T.&T. Clark, 1951) 32; J. Gray, *I & II Kings. A Commentary* (London: SCM Press LTD, 1964) 29; J. Liver, "The Book of the Acts of Solomon," *Bib* 48 (1967): 75-101; and S. DeVries, *I Kings*, WBC (Waco TX: Word Books, 1985) xlix.

[14]Other scholars have detected the uniqueness of Solomon's kingship. G. von Rad, *The Problem of the Hexateuch and Other Essays* (New York: McGraw Hill, 1966) 69-74, referred to the era of this king as "Solomonic Enlightenment." F. Cross, *Canaanite Myth and Hebrew Epic* (Cambridge: Harvard University Press, 1973) 239-41, speaks about Solomon's reign as a "departure" from the ways of previous kings. Most recently, W. Brueggemann, "The Social Significance of Solomon as a Patron of Wisdom," *The Sage in Israel and the Ancient Near East*, ed. J. Gammie and L. Perdue (Winona Lake IN: Eisenbrauns, 1990) 120, designates Solomon's reign as a "novum" and "a sociocultural mutation."

[15]G. E. Mendenhall, "The Shady Side of Wisdom: The Date and Purpose of Genesis 3," *A Light Unto My Path: Old Testament Studies in Honor of Jacob M. Myers*, ed. H. N. Bream, R. D. Heim, and C. A. Moore (Philadelphia: Temple University, 1974) 324, noted that the Solomonic Narrative promoted the idea of kingship in Israel. Whitelam, *The Just King—Monarchical Judicial Authority in*

which prevail across the Solomonic Narrative invite the designation "ideological stories." These ideological stories shape the contours of chapters 3–11 and promote the interest, idea, and value system of a kingship.[16]

The king and his kingdom are depicted as models of political and material success. Solomon's reign was immune to the rebellions that plagued other kings.[17] No murder or intrigue marred his royal tenure.[18] In the wake of an abrupt respite from war, Solomon received tribute and homage from neighboring nations (1 Kgs. 10:23-25). International fame accompanied his mercantile endeavors (1 Kgs. 10:6-9). Ambitious building projects conceived by but forbidden to David were completed and celebrated under Solomon's suzerainty (1 Kgs. 5–8). Though Solomon assumed priestly functions (1 Kgs. 8:14-64), no account of resistance by traditionally minded Israelites is recorded.[19] Cultic actions which caused a rupture between Saul and Samuel (1 Sam. 13:10-14) go uncontested when performed by Solomon. Even his international difficulties with Edom and Damascus (1 Kgs. 11:14-25), and his internal problems in the North (1 Kgs. 11:26-40) receive only brief remarks.[20]

Ancient Israel, 162, and S. Lasine, "The Riddle of Solomon's Judgment," *JSOT* 45 (1989): 77-78, view these chapters as ideological literature.

[16]H. Mottu, "Jeremiah vs. Hananiah: Ideology and Truth in Old Testament Prophecy," *The Bible and Liberation*, ed. N. Gottwald (Maryknoll NY: Orbis, 1983) 239, defined ideology as a one dimensional representation which assigns universal validity to an idea, interest, person, or value system.

[17]Absalom threatened David's kingship. Sheba ben Bichri challenged the very legitimacy of David's rule over the ten tribes of Israel. Jeroboam's revolt followed Solomon's reign but never threatened his rule. On rebellions against Israelite kings, see H. Tadmor, "Traditional Institutions and the Monarchy," 245-46, and M. A. Cohen, "The Rebellions During the Reign of David: An Inquiry into the Social Dynamics in Ancient Israel," *Studies in Jewish Bibliography, History, and Literature in Honor of I. E. Kiev*, ed. C. Berlin (New York: Ktav Publishers, 1971) 91-112.

[18]Though a domestic rebellion (1 Kgs. 1:11-12) accompanies Solomon's appointment as king, this account resides outside the literary confines of the Solomonic Narrative (1 Kgs. 3–11).

[19]Hayes and Miller, *Israelite and Judean History*, 369.

[20]N. Gottwald, *Hebrew Bible—A Socioliterary Introduction*, 313, notes

Further, they are located at the end of the narrative followed by a regnal resume which accords high praise to Solomon (1 Kgs. 11:41-43).

As king, Solomon was the recipient of praise and gifts from God (1 Kgs. 3:10-13). As the controlling force behind his wealthy empire, he was the recipient of praise and gifts from people (1 Kgs. 10:23-25). Moreover, Solomon's kingship was legitimized and endorsed by a new epistemology.[21] Wisdom, which prescribed codes of behavior, defined patterns in existence, and offered explanations to ultimate questions, permeated this king's identity and reign.[22] Wisdom provided divine approval for Solomon's kingship which otherwise lacked authorization.[23] References to his wisdom dominate throughout the course of this story. Solomon's wealth, fame, and popularity are evidence of his wise rule. The social depiction of Solomon as "wise" suggests kingship has "arrived" under this ruler. The idealized portrait of the king as "wise" captures and endorses the culmination of kingship in Israel's story.

The literary character of the Solomonic Narrative collaborates with this idealized social depiction.[24] The exhortative tone of these chapters

---

further that Solomon is exonerated from blame when these conflicts are "bluntly blamed on religious corruption owing to the influence of Solomon's foreign wives (1 Kgs. 11:1-13)."

[21]Brueggemann, "The Social Significance of Solomon as a Patron of Wisdom," 121-22.

[22]Although the relation between Solomon and wisdom is indisputable, the nature of that relation remains contested. See R. B. Y. Scott, "Solomon and the Beginnings of Wisdom in Israel," *Wisdom in Israel and in the Ancient Near East*, VTSup 3 (Leiden: Brill, 1955) 262-79; and J. L. Crenshaw, *Old Testament Wisdom* (Atlanta: John Knox, 1981) 42-54, for a discussion of these difficulties.

[23]Because Solomon ascended the throne without the traditional charismatic designation which characterized Saul and David's election, God's gift of wisdom provided Solomon's kingship with divine sanction. See Hayes and Miller, *Israelite and Judean History*, 365-66.

[24]For a discussion of the literary features of the Solomonic Narrative, see B. Porten, "Structure and Theme of the Solomonic Narrative (1 Kings 3–11)," *HUCA* 38 (1967): 93-128; B. O. Long, *I Kings with an Introduction to Historical Literature*, FOTL (Grand Rapids: Eerdmans, 1984) 14-32; G. Savran, "1 and 2 Kings," *The Literary Guide to the Bible*, ed. R. Alter and F. Kermode (Cambridge: Belknap Press of Harvard University Press, 1987) 155-58.

reinforces the one-dimensional portrait of Solomon as the epitome of kingship. The dominant lietmotif, wisdom, legitimizes Solomon's political and economic success.[25] Finally, the lack of narrative drama across these chapters[26] underscores the secure and placid era heralded by Solomon's reign. Only one story interrupts this dramaless literary terrain to introduce significant tension.

In 1 Kings 3:16-28, a trial concerning the maternal rights over a child puts Solomon and his judicial wisdom to the test.[27] Two women stand before the king and request a judgment.[28] After the women present their cases, the king issues an order. When the order discloses the true mother, the monarch levels a judgment.

Two brief episodes[29] make up this judicial scene.[30] The progression of direct speech structures its design.

Episode I, vss. 16-22. The Dispute
    First Woman's Speech, vss. 17-21
    Second Woman's Speech, vs. 22a

---

[25]Porten, "Structure and Theme of the Solomonic Narrative (1 Kings 3–11)," 124; and B. O. Long, *I Kings with an Introduction to Historical Literature*, 59.

[26]Savran, "1 and 2 Kings," 155.

[27]It has long been recognized that a variety of parallel stories in ancient folk literature exists where an endangered child is saved by its mother. See H. Gressmann, "Das Salomonische Urteil," *Deutsche Rundschau* 130 (1907): 212; Noth, *Konige—1 Teilband*, 47; and Montgomery and Gehman, *The Book of Kings*, 108-109.

[28]Various genres have been proposed for these verses. DeVries, *I Kings*, 57, and K. A. Deurloo, "The King's Wisdom in Judgment—Narration as Example (I Kings iii)," *New Avenues in the Study of the Old Testament*, ed. A. S. Van der Woude (Leiden: E. J. Brill, 1989) 16, suggest "anecdote." Long, *I Kings with an Introduction to Historical Literature*, 70, and Gray, *I & II Kings. A Commentary*, 128, propose "saga" or "story." A. Jolles, *Einfache Formen* (Tubingen: Max Niemeyer, 1958) 132-33, and Lasine, "The Riddle of Solomon's Judgment," 62, describe the story as a "law court riddle."

[29]For a definition of "episode," see chap. 4, n. 24, above.

[30]So also Long, *I Kings with an Introduction to Historical Literature*, 67-68; DeVries, *I Kings*, 57; and W. A. M. Beuken, "No Wise King Without a Wise Woman (I Kings III 16-28)," *New Avenues in the Study of the Old Testament*, ed. A. S. Van der Woude (Leiden: E. J. Brill, 1989) 3-4.

First Woman's Speech, vs. 22b
Narrative Summary and Transition, vs. 22c

Episode II, vss. 23-28
    The King's Speech, vss. 23-25
Narrated Discourse, vs. 26a
    The First Woman's Speech, vs. 26b
    The Other Woman's Speech, vs. 26c
    The King's Speech, vs. 27
Narrative Conclusion—Israel's Response, vs. 28

In episode one (vss. 16-22), the alternating speech between the woman plaintiff and the woman defendant sets forth the dispute. In episode two, (vss. 23-28), a series of interchanges between the king and the women yields a judgment. A narrative summary (vs. 22c) demarcates the two units. Narrative boundaries (vss. 16 and 28) enclose the whole scene. In the opening of the story, the narrative description (vs. 16) introduces the two women. At the conclusion of the tale, the narrative epilogue (vs. 28) reports Israel's acknowledgment of God's wisdom in the king.

Recognition of Solomon's wisdom ties this story to the preceding narrative. In Solomon's dream at Gibeon (1 Kgs. 3:1-15), God promised the king the gift of wisdom. In the subsequent tale, Israel's recognition of Solomon's wisdom illustrates and confirms the fulfillment of God's promise.[31]

Yet, the depiction of the wise king in this tale subtly distinguishes itself from the portrait of a wise Solomon in the surrounding literary corpus. Three other texts in the Solomonic Narrative draw attention to the king's sapiential charism. In the dream at Gibeon (1 Kgs. 3:1-15), God promises wisdom to Solomon in conjunction with a promise of wealth

---

[31]C. F. Keil and F. Delitzsch, *Biblical Commentary on the Old Testament* (Grand Rapids: Wm. B. Eerdmans Publishing Company, 1962) 43; J. Robinson, *The First Book of Kings* (Cambridge MA: Harvard University Press, 1972) 54; E. Wurthwein, *Die Bucher der Konige 1 Konige 1–16* (Göttingen: Vanderhoeck und Ruprecht, 1977) 38; Noth, *Konige—1 Teilband*, 53; Nelsen, 37; Long, *I Kings with an Introduction to Historical Literature*, 70; Beuken, "No Wise King Without a Wise Woman (I Kings III 16-28)," 1; and Deurloo, "The King's Wisdom in Judgment—Narration as Example (I Kings iii)," 16.

and fame (1 Kgs. 3:12-13).[32] In the narrator's summary in 1 Kings 4:31-35 [MT 5:9-14], Solomon's wisdom elevates him above all other powerful leaders, as well as makes him the recipient of their gifts. In the final citation (1 Kgs. 10:1-13), the Queen of Sheba ties Solomon's wisdom to his successful mercantile and materialistic enterprises.

Only in this tale of the king's judgment before the two women is Solomon's wisdom associated with the preservation of human life. Moreover, only in this tale is the king's wisdom specifically qualified as "the wisdom of God" (1 Kgs. 3:28).[33]

Further, this tale of two women before the king distinguishes itself from its literary surroundings. The story is enclosed on all sides by elaborate narrative. There is nothing of the "prolix theologizing of 1 Kings 3:4-14 or archivelike succinctness of 1 Kings 4:1-6"[34] within its boundaries. Unlike its narrative environs, this tale tells itself in a profusion of direct speech.

This literary distinctiveness coincides with a distinct social portrait of the king. This is the only story in the Solomonic Narrative where the king interacts directly with his subjects.[35] The nature of these exchanges challenges the idealized portrait of Solomon in the surrounding Solomonic Narrative. Literary patterns, repetitions, and artistic progressions will sketch a different depiction of this king. The interplay between the social and rhetorical features in the story will expose the underside of royal ideology. The portrait of Solomon in this tale will clash with the magnanimous monarch who presides in the surrounding Solomonic Narrative. The following sociorhetorical exegesis will propose a theological explanation for this dissonance.

Episode I, vss. 16-22

A conflict between two women structures the first episode. By means of three consecutive speeches, the women present their case before the king. Narrated discourse surrounds their exchanges. The opening descrip-

---

[32]On this text, see the study by Helen A. Kenik, *Design for Kingship* (Chico CA: Scholars Press, 1983).

[33]This expression, חכמת אלהים, does not occur anywhere else in the O.T.

[34]Long, *I Kings with an Introduction to Historical Literature*, 68.

[35]Savran, "1 and 2 Kings," 155.

tion introduces the two women (vs. 16). The conclusion summarizes their activity before the king (vs. 22c).

Introduction, vs. 16

A brief introduction positions two women prostitutes before a king. The social identities, "women prostitutes" and "a king," highlight their difference. Parallel language with the preceding story lobbies in favor of their kinship.

אָז תָּבֹאנָה שְׁתַּיִם נָשִׁים זֹנוֹת אֶל־הַמֶּלֶךְ וַתַּעֲמֹדְנָה לְפָנָיו:

Then two women prostitutes came to the king
    and stood before him. (vs. 16)

The particle אָז ("then") introduces the story of the two women before the king. This temporal particle establishes the connection between this story and the preceding account.[36] In a dream at Gibeon (1 Kgs. 15:1-16), God promised Solomon the gift of wisdom (1 Kgs. 3:12). The tale of two women before the king mediates between this promise and its fulfillment. But the strategic placement of this particle accomplishes something more. Besides establishing the broad link between two stories, the particle אָז engages a more immediate connection between two verses. At the conclusion of the preceding story (vs. 15), Solomon traveled to Jerusalem to offer sacrifices before the Lord.

And Solomon . . . *came* to Jerusalem and he *stood before*
    the ark of the Lord's covenant. . . . (vs. 15)

In the opening of the subsequent tale (vs. 16), two women approach the king to request a judgment.

Then (אָז) two woman prostitutes *came* to the king
    and they *stood before* him. (vs. 16)

---

[36]See I. Rabinowitz, "'AZ Followed by the Imperfect Verb Form in Preterite Contexts: A Redactional Device in Biblical Hebrew," *VT* 34 (1984): 54; DeVries, *I Kings*, 57; Beuken, "No Wise King Without a Wise Woman (I Kings III 16-28)," 8; and Deurloo, "The King's Wisdom in Judgment—Narration as Example (I Kings iii)," 16.

Social identities separate the king from these two women subjects. Narrative description undercuts these social differences and embodies a basis for their alignment. The continuity in description between the king and the women ("came," "stood," "before") discloses a continuity in status. Each is subject before a higher authority. As the women come and stand subordinate before the king, so the king comes and stands subordinate before God.

In this introduction, narrative description further specifies the women's status. The women are introduced as "prostitutes" (זֹנָה). Prostitution was a well attested institution in Israel.[37] Tamar disguised herself as a prostitute in order to summon Judah, her father-in-law, to responsibility (Gen. 38). In another story, Rahab, a prostitute, provided refuge for Israelite spies (Josh. 2). After Rahab and her family were spared destruction, they "settled permanently among the Israelites" (Josh. 6:25). In Leviticus 21:7, 14, priests were prohibited from marrying a harlot. Implicitly, the law recognized the practice by others in Israel.

Thus, the designation of the women as "prostitutes" is an identity, not a judgment.[38] As an identity, "prostitute" does connote the subordinate nature of these women's social position. The prostitute and her offspring lacked kinship and legal status within the community.[39] Without male protectors, prostitutes were, at best, "functional widows."[40] Because no legal statutes legislated on their behalf, prostitutes and their orphan chil-

---

[37]P. Bird, "The Harlot as Heroine: Narrative Art and Social Presupposition in Three Old Testament Texts," *Semeia* 46 (1989): 132.

[38]P. Trible, *God and the Rhetoric of Sexuality* (Philadelphia: Fortress Press, 1978) 31.

[39]For a general discussion of what is known about prostitution in the Ancient Near East, see G. Lerner, "The Origin of Prostitution in Ancient Mesopotamia," *Signs: Journal of Women in Culture and Society* 11 (1986): 236-54; J. Gagon, "Prostitution," *International Encyclopedia of the Social Sciences*, ed. D. Silk (New York: Macmillan and the Free Press, 1968) 592-98; and D. Setel, "Prophets and Pornography: Female Sexual Imagery in Hosea," *Feminist Interpretation of the Bible*, ed. Letty M. Russell (Philadelphia: Westminster Press, 1985) 86-95.

[40]C. Fontaine, "The Bearing of Wisdom on the Shape of 2 Samuel 11–12 and 1 Kings 3," *JSOT* 34 (1986): 67.

dren were a kind of "resident alien."[41] The story of Jephthah in the book
of Judges is illustrative. As the offspring of a prostitute, Jephthah was
initially denied kinship and inheritance within the community (Judg.
11:1).

Ranked among the poor, prostitutes and their children must speak and
fend for themselves. The rhetorical features of this story reinforce this
social depiction. Though the narrator introduces them (vs. 16), these self-
reliant women tell their own tale.[42]

Three Speeches vss. 17-22ab

By means of three speeches, the women set forth their dispute before
the king. In the first presentation, one woman argues her case and
assumes the role of plaintiff (vss. 17-21). In the second address, the other
woman speaks as a defendant and denies the charges (vs. 22a). In the
concluding response, the first woman plaintiff levels a countercharge
which results in an impasse (vs. 22b).

Speech One, vss. 17-21

In a three-phrased presentation (vss. 17-21), the first woman sets
forth the unresolvable circumstances. First, she outlines a context (vss.
17-18). Plural forms of speech dominate this description. Second, she
narrates the details of a crime (vss. 19-20). Third person accusations
isolate this account. Third, she details her discovery of this misdeed (vs.
21). First person speech narrates this disclosure.

וַתֹּאמֶר הָאִשָּׁה הָאַחַת

And the first woman said,

בִּי אֲדֹנִי

"Please, my Lord,

אֲנִי וְהָאִשָּׁה הַזֹּאת יֹשְׁבֹת בְּבַיִת אֶחָד

I and this woman were living in one house.

וָאֵלֵד עִמָּהּ בַּבָּיִת:

And I gave birth with her in the house. (vs. 17)

---

[41]Fontaine, "The Bearing of Wisdom on the Shape of 2 Samuel 11–12 and
1 Kings 3," 67; and A. Brenner, *The Israelite Woman—Social Role and Literary
Type in Biblical Narrative* (Sheffield: JSOT Press, 1985) 78-83.

[42]Trible, *God and the Rhetoric of Sexuality*, 31.

וַיְהִי בַּיּוֹם הַשְּׁלִישִׁי לְלִדְתִּי

And on the third day after I gave birth,

וַתֵּלֶד גַּם־הָאִשָּׁה הַזֹּאת

This woman also gave birth.

וַאֲנַחְנוּ יַחְדָּו

And we were together,

אֵין־זָר אִתָּנוּ בַּבַּיִת

there was no one else with us in the house,

זוּלָתִי שְׁתַּיִם־אֲנַחְנוּ בַּבָּיִת:

only the two of us were in the house. (vs. 18)

וַיָּמָת בֶּן־הָאִשָּׁה הַזֹּאת לָיְלָה אֲשֶׁר שָׁכְבָה עָלָיו:

And the son of this woman died at night
   when she lay on him. (vs. 19)

וַתָּקָם בְּתוֹךְ הַלַּיְלָה

And she arose in the middle of the night.

וַתִּקַּח אֶת־בְּנִי מֵאֶצְלִי וַאֲמָתְךָ יְשֵׁנָה

And she took my son from my side while your servant slept.

וַתַּשְׁכִּיבֵהוּ בְּחֵיקָהּ

And she laid him at her breast.

וְאֶת־בְּנָהּ הַמֵּת הִשְׁכִּיבָה בְחֵיקִי:

And her dead son, she laid at my breast. (vs. 20)

וָאָקֻם בַּבֹּקֶר לְהֵינִיק אֶת־בְּנִי

And when I arose in the morning to nurse my son,

וְהִנֵּה־מֵת

Behold! he was dead.

וָאֶתְבּוֹנֵן אֵלָיו בַּבֹּקֶר

And when I looked at him in the morning,

וְהִנֵּה לֹא־הָיָה בְנִי אֲשֶׁר יָלָדְתִּי:

Behold! he was not my son to whom I gave birth." (vs. 21)

By means of her opening salutation, בִּי אֲדֹנִי "Please, my Lord,"[43]
the first woman (הָאִשָּׁה הָאַחַת) suggests her subservient status. At
the same time, her courtly courtesy acknowledges the sovereignty of the

---

[43] בִּי is probably the imperative of the verb אבה "to be willing." Only the
original final consonant survived. See Gray, *I & II Kings. A Commentary*, 129;
DeVries, *I Kings*, 59; and Montgomery and Gehman, *The Book of Kings*, 112.

king.[44] Her initial description (vss. 17-18) establishes a context for her story. The form and content of her account underscores the social kinship between the women.

וַתֹּאמֶר הָאִשָּׁה הָאַחַת

And the first woman said,

בִּי אֲדֹנִי

"Please, my Lord,

אֲנִי וְהָאִשָּׁה הַזֹּאת יֹשְׁבֹת בְּבַיִת אֶחָד

I and this woman were living in one house.

וָאֵלֵד עִמָּהּ בַּבָּיִת:

And I gave birth with her in the house. (vs. 17)

וַיְהִי בַּיּוֹם הַשְּׁלִישִׁי לְלִדְתִּי

And on the third day after I gave birth,

וַתֵּלֶד גַּם־הָאִשָּׁה הַזֹּאת

This woman also gave birth.

וַאֲנַחְנוּ יַחְדָּו

And we were together,

אֵין־זָר אִתָּנוּ בַּבַּיִת

there was no one else with us in the house,

זוּלָתִי שְׁתַּיִם־אֲנַחְנוּ בַּבָּיִת:

only the two of us were in the house. (vs. 18)

Her references to herself and the other woman ("I and this woman") render both women nameless. Her description of their activity, "I gave birth," "this woman also gave birth," underscores their sameness.[45] The fourfold repetition "in the house" locates the two women and contributes to their togetherness. Her three-stage elaboration of their mutual proximity reinforces their oneness.

וַאֲנַחְנוּ יַחְדָּו

And we were together,

---

[44]S. Bar-Efrat, *Narrative Art in the Bible* (Sheffield: The Almond Press, 1989) 66, notes that "the speaker's social standing is often reflected in speech."

[45]Some variants of this story further the sameness between the women by suggesting that the births occurred at the same hour, and in the same room. See Gressman, "Das Salomonische Urteil," 219; and Josephus, *Jewish Antiquities V–VIII*, trans. H. St. J. Thackeray and R. Marcus, LCL (Cambridge MA: Harvard University Press, 1934) 585-87.

אֵין־זָר [46]אִתָּנוּ בַּבַּיִת

there was no one else with us in the house,

זוּלָתִי שְׁתַּיִם־אֲנַחְנוּ בַּבָּיִת׃

only the two of us were in the house. (vs.18)

At the same time, this literary redundancy highlights their social isolation. The significance of this isolation becomes apparent as the woman
continues her story.

וַיָּמָת בֶּן־הָאִשָּׁה הַזֹּאת לָיְלָה אֲשֶׁר שָׁכְבָה עָלָיו׃

And the son of this woman died at night
        when she lay on him. (vs. 19)

וַתָּקָם בְּתוֹךְ הַלַּיְלָה

And she arose in the middle of the night.

וַתִּקַּח אֶת־בְּנִי מֵאֶצְלִי וַאֲמָתְךָ יְשֵׁנָה

And she took my son from my side while your servant slept.

וַתַּשְׁכִּיבֵהוּ בְּחֵיקָהּ

And she laid him at her breast.

וְאֶת־בְּנָהּ הַמֵּת הִשְׁכִּיבָה בְחֵיקִי׃

And her dead son, she laid at my breast. (vs. 20)

Tragedy "at night" (vs. 19), leads to a thievery "of the night" (vs.
20). Repetition of the temporal phrase "at/of the night" demarcates these
two phases.[47] A death separates a woman and her son. This separation
between a mother and her child dissociates the women. The iteration of
the verb שכב traces the course of this social rupture. Initially, שכב narrates
the act that killed.

And the son of this woman died . . . when she lay (שכב) on him.

In the subsequent repetitions, the verb שכב discloses the act that deceived.

---

[46]The term זר may refer to "lodger" or "alien." Based upon his assessment
of Josh. 2, T. J. Walsh, "I and II Kings," *The New Jerome Biblical Commentary*,
ed. R. Brown et al. (Englewood Cliffs NJ: Prentice Hall, 1990) 165, suggests that
prostitution and hostelry may have been frequent companions in ancient times.
More comparative evidence is needed to confirm this observation.

[47]Bar-Efrat, *Narrative Art in the Bible*, 142, notes that such references to time
serve as structuring devices in the story.

and my son . . . she laid (שכב) at her breast.
and her dead son she laid (שכב) at my breast.

A litany of third-person accusations dramatizes the new antagonisms between the women, as well as details the crime.

she lay on him.
she arose in the middle of the night.
she took my son from my side. . . .
she laid him at her breast.
she laid him at my breast.

Charge by charge, the woman erects a case against her adversary. Their togetherness "in the house" has become the occasion for their estrangement. Amidst this incriminating hostility, the woman maintains courtly courtesy with a third person reference to herself.[48] Her testimony "while your servant slept" emphasizes her role as innocent prey. Moreover, this description of her restive state contrasts with the active machinations of her opponent. But the difficulty of her testimony merits the king's cross-examination. She reports events which occurred while she slept.[49] Moreover, as she herself testifies, only in the morning light was the deed discovered.

וָאָקֻם בַּבֹּקֶר לְהֵינִיק אֶת־בְּנִי

And when I arose in the morning to nurse my son,

וְהִנֵּה־מֵת

Behold! he was dead.

וָאֶתְבּוֹנֵן אֵלָיו בַּבֹּקֶר

And when I looked at him in the morning,

וְהִנֵּה לֹא־הָיָה בְנִי אֲשֶׁר יָלָדְתִּי:

Behold! he was not my son to whom I gave birth." (vs. 21)

---

[48]Bar-Efrat, ibid., 66, identifies this as the polite form of speech in biblical narrative which characterizes the encounters with the king.

[49]H. Rand, "Justice in Solomon's Court—Anonymous vs. Anonymous," *Dor le Dor* 10 (1982): 172, who offers a legal analysis of the proceedings, makes this observation. See also E. and G. Leibowitz, "Solomon's Judgment," *Beth Mikra* 35 (1989–1990): 242-44.

The woman arose (אקם) in the morning and discovered the crimes of the woman who arose (אקם) in the night. The two phases of night time activity are countered by two phases of morning disclosure. The repetition of the temporal phrase "in the morning" introduces the discoveries. The repetition of "behold" (הנה) signals two climaxes. The tragedy and thievery in the darkness give way to the detection of death and deception in the light of day. The discovery of death and deception annul this woman's effort to sustain life (להינק).

The repetition of "I gave birth" (ילד) yokes the conclusion of the woman's tale with its opening.

> I and this woman were living in the same house
>> when I gave birth (אלד) . . . (vs. 17)
> And behold, it was not the son whom I bore (ילדתי). (vs. 21).

She begins and ends her speech with her first-person statement about birth. This inclusio illustrates and circumscribes the woman's social crisis.[50] Encircled in the events of childbirth (ילד), the woman is trapped in a demeaning nightmare. This sociorhetorical interplay narrates her discomfiture. Having told her story, the plaintiff now falls silent.

Speech Two, vs. 22a

For the first time in the narrative, the other woman (הָאַחֶרֶת הָאִשָּׁה) speaks. She speaks as defendant and denies the charges. Though she defends herself before the king, she directs her response to her accuser.

וַתֹּאמֶר הָאִשָּׁה הָאַחֶרֶת

But the other woman said,

לֹא כִּי בְּנִי הַחַי

"Not so, my son is the living one,

וּבְנֵךְ הַמֵּת

and your son is the dead one."

---

[50]Here the inclusio functions to delimit the woman's testimony. See R. G. Moulton, *The Literary Study of the Bible* (Boston: D. C. Heath, 1899) 53-54, 150-51, on inclusios. See also W. Watson, *Classical Hebrew Poetry—A Guide to Its Techniques* (Sheffield UK: JSOT Press, 1986) 286-87, on the function of this literary device.

Despite the commonness of their social circumstances and careers, the sameness between the women has eroded. The form and content of the "other woman's" (הָאִשָּׁה הָאַחֶרֶת) address corroborate this social alienation. In contrast to the courtly style of the first woman's presentation, this speaker does not even acknowledge the king. Instead, she argues with the other woman. Unlike the first woman's wordy account, this speaker's remarks are brief and confrontational.[51] She has no opposing account of the events. Though she speaks as the defendant, she does not defend herself. Instead, she only reverses the charges. Her cold-clipped accusation incites the first woman's repetitive retort.

Speech Three, vs. 22b

In the third and final speech in this episode, the first woman levels a countercharge. Her initial presentation before the king now yields a forensic stalemate.

וְזֹאת אֹמֶרֶת

But this one said,

לֹא כִי בְּנֵךְ הַמֵּת

"Not so, your son is the dead one,

וּבְנִי הֶחָי

and my son is the living one."

The woman's repetition of the key words "living," "dead," captures the heart of the dispute. Issues of life and death define the woman's struggle. Her response to the other woman's words reverberates to and fro to create a chiastic deadlock.[52]

וַתֹּאמֶר הָאִשָּׁה הָאַחֶרֶת

But the other woman said,

לֹא כִי בְּנִי הַחַי

A   "Not so, my son is the living one,

---

[51]Long, *I Kings with an Introduction to Historical Literature*, 68.

[52]The chiastic structure of this verse has also been observed by Trible, *God and the Rhetoric of Sexuality*, 31, and Long, *I Kings with an Introduction to Historical Literature*, 69. On chiasms, see A. R. Ceresko, "The A:B:B:A Word Pattern in Hebrew and Northwest Semitic, with Special Reference to the Book of Job," *UF* 7 (1975): 73-88, and "The Chiastic Word Pattern in Hebrew," *CBQ* 38 (1976): 303-11.

וּבְנֵךְ הַמֵּת

B   and your son is the dead one."

וְזֹאת אֹמֶרֶת

But this one said,

לֹא כִי בְּנֵךְ הַמֵּת

B[1] "Not so, your son is the dead one,

וּבְנִי הֶחָי

A[1] and my son is the living one."

Rhetoric reveals the social dynamic between the two women. The chiastic structure of their argumentation illustrates the cross-purposes of their feud. The content of this chiastic formation narrates the dualism of their dispute.[53] The women are locked in a formidable impasse. The narrator summarizes their forensic stalemate.

Conclusion, vs. 22c

Narrated discourse offers a reprieve from the tension of the preceding first person speeches. This conclusion to these events provides a transition to the next episode.

וַתְּדַבֵּרְנָה לִפְנֵי הַמֶּלֶךְ:

And so they argued before the king. (vs. 22)

This episode, which began "before the king" (vs. 16), now concludes "before the king" (vs. 22). Focus on the king anticipates the next episode. The unit opens with the monarch's response.

Episode II, vss. 23-28

Direct discourse introduces the second episode and determines its course. First, a speech by the king (vss. 23-25) addresses the dispute between the women. The narrated discourse which follows describes a mother's sentiments for her threatened child (vs. 26a). This narrative disclosure anticipates a new direction for the story. Speeches by the plaintiff, defendant, and king immediately follow (vss. 26b-27). Their exchanges achieve a judgment. The story concludes with the narrator's report of Israel's response to the outcome (vs. 28).

---

[53]Trible, *God and the Rhetoric of Sexuality*, 31-32.

The King's Speech, vss. 23-25

Three recitations by the king introduce this episode and address the women's presentation. First, the king repeats the women's testimony. Next, he issues an order for a sword. Finally, he levels a further mandate in order to resolve the dispute.

וַיֹּאמֶר הַמֶּלֶךְ

And the king said,

זֹאת אֹמֶרֶת

"This one says,

זֶה־בְּנִי הַחַי

'My son is the living one,

וּבְנֵךְ הַמֵּת

and your son is the dead one.'

וְזֹאת אֹמֶרֶת

But the other one says,

לֹא כִי בְּנֵךְ הַמֵּת

'Not so, your son is the dead one,

וּבְנִי הֶחָי:

and my son is the living one.'" (vs. 23)

וַיֹּאמֶר הַמֶּלֶךְ

And the king said,

קְחוּ לִי־חָרֶב

"Bring me a sword."

וַיָּבִאוּ הַחֶרֶב לִפְנֵי הַמֶּלֶךְ:

And they brought a sword before the king. (vs. 24)

וַיֹּאמֶר הַמֶּלֶךְ

And the king said,

גִּזְרוּ אֶת־הַיֶּלֶד הַחַי לִשְׁנָיִם

"Divide the living child in two.

וּתְנוּ אֶת־הַחֲצִי לְאַחַת

Give half to one,

וְאֶת־הַחֲצִי לְאֶחָת:

half to the other." (vs. 25)

As the episode opens, the king proceeds to act as a supreme court and address the unresolvable problem.[54] The protection and adjudication on behalf of the widow and the poor were the hallmarks of a virtuous king.[55] Moreover, such protection was not only the work of monarchs, it was the activity and concern of the gods.[56] Mesopotamian texts credit the sun god Shamash with the protection of the weak.[57] In Egypt, the sun god Re or his supplanter Amon was regarded as the protector of the poor.[58] In a late Egyptian text, Amon-Re is called the vizier of the poor.[59] In Israel, the activity was also linked to the Supreme Judge, Yahweh.[60] In Deuteronomy 10:18, the protection of the poor was the prerogative of Israel's God. Psalm 82 extols Yahweh as the only true judge and protector of the weak.

As mediator of God's judgment, the king in Israel attended to the needs of the poor. Despite his hesitation, David legislated on behalf of the Tekoite widow (2 Sam. 14:1-22). Similarly, he also judged in favor of a fictitious poor man who had been cheated (2 Sam. 12:5-6). David's provisions for Mephibosheth guaranteed sustenance for the life time of this crippled man (2 Sam. 9:1-13). Accordingly, the picture of these poor women before Solomon anticipates his judicial action on behalf of at least one of them.

Solomon commences his involvement by repeating the women's testimony.

---

[54] R. de Vaux, *Ancient Israel* (New York/Toronto/London: McGraw-Hill, 1961) 152, characterizes the king in such instances as a final court of appeal even though "recourse could also be made to him in the first instance."

[55] F. C. Fensham, "Widow, Orphan, and the Poor in Ancient Near Eastern Legal and Wisdom Literature," *JNES* 21 (1962): 129.

[56] Ibid., 130.

[57] F. M. Theo de Liagre Bohl, "De zonnegod als Bsechermer der Nood druftigen," *Opera Minora* (1953): 188-206.

[58] J. A. Wilson, trans., "Egyptian Texts," *Ancient Near Eastern Texts*, ed. J. Pritchard (Princeton: Princeton University Press, 1955) 408.

[59] Fensham, "Widow, Orphan, and the Poor in Ancient Near Eastern Legal and Wisdom Literature," 133.

[60] M. Brettler, *God Is King: Understanding an Israelite Metaphor* (Sheffield: JSOT Press, 1989) 44-45.

And the king said,
        וַיֹּאמֶר הַמֶּלֶךְ

   "This one says,
        זֹאת אֹמֶרֶת

      'My son is the living one,
        זֶה־בְּנִי הַחַי

      and your son is the dead one.'
        וּבְנֵךְ הַמֵּת

   But the other one says,
        וְזֹאת אֹמֶרֶת

      'Not so, your son is the dead one,
        לֹא כִי בְּנֵךְ הַמֵּת

      and my son is the living one.'" (vs. 23)
        וּבְנִי הֶחָי:

The king's monotonous repetition of the women's words and sounds captures the wearisome dynamic of the dispute. Further, his recitation of their impasse hints at the king's own perplexity. "In this context, the king's restating of the dispute (vs. 23) amounts to a verbalized scratching of the head at the impossible conundrum."[61] Subsequently, the king issues an order.

And the king said,
        וַיֹּאמֶר הַמֶּלֶךְ

   "Bring me a sword."
        קְחוּ לִי־חָרֶב

Though the command moves beyond the chiastic confines of the opposing claims, it engenders further confusion. No explanation accompanies the startling injunction. Instead, it generates an unsettling ambiguity.

    The sword (חרב) was an instrument of violence and punishment in Israel.[62] Ehud slew Eglon, the king of Moab with a sword (Judg. 3:12ff.).

---

[61]Long, *I Kings with an Introduction to Historical Literature*, 69.

[62]Other instances where (חרב) "sword" occurs as an instrument of punishment and violence include Lev. 26:6, 25; 2 Sam. 3:27; 11:25; 12:10; 20:8; Isa. 34:5f; 66:16; Ps. 7:12.

Nathan prophesied that the sword would never depart from David's house because of his sin against Uriah (2 Sam. 12:10). At the same time, the sword often symbolized authority to execute justice. In the Song of Moses, Yahweh, the Divine Judge, is portrayed with a sword in hand (Deut. 32:41-42). Similarly, the sword is associated with authority in judgment throughout the prophetic texts.[63] Hence, Solomon's summons for a sword courts an ambiguous meaning. The image connotes his authority to judge, as well as his potential to do violence.

A precise description of the order's implementation directly follows.

וַיָּבִאוּ הַחֶרֶב לִפְנֵי הַמֶּלֶךְ:

And they brought a sword before the king. (vs. 24)

This immediate literary progression suggests obedience to the king's injunctions. Further, the narrative description matches the abbreviated sharpness of the king's command.[64]

Rhetoric yokes these vulnerable supplicants with the grave order and its fulfillment. The impasse caused by the women who "came before the king" (באו, vs. 16) is about to be resolved by the "sword brought before the king" (בא, vs. 24). The king's judicial directive builds narrative tension and begs a rapid resolution. A second command by the king anticipates the settlement.

וַיֹּאמֶר הַמֶּלֶךְ

And the king said,

גִּזְרוּ אֶת־הַיֶּלֶד הַחַי לִשְׁנָיִם

"Divide the living child in two.

וּתְנוּ אֶת־הַחֲצִי לְאַחַת

Give half to one,

וְאֶת־הַחֲצִי לְאֶחָת:

half to the other." (vs. 25)

---

[63]See Isa. 14:19; 22:2; 27:1; 34:5; 46:16; Jer. 12:12; 47:6f.; Ezek. 21:1-5; 31:17-18; 32:29-30; 35:8; Amos 9:1; Zeph. 2:12; Zech. 13:7-8.

[64]The repetition in language between Solomon's command and the narration of fulfillment adds emphasis to these terms or events. See R. Alter, *The Art of Biblical Narrative* (New York: Basic Books, 1981) 77.

The king issues an order for death to remedy a dispute over life.[65] The sociorhetorical interplay dramatizes the dynamics of this judicial scene.[66] The form and content of the king's order convey the disinterested character of these official proceedings. Repetition in language, "half to one," "half to the other," represents an equal allocation for each party. The king's references to the women underscore the impartiality of his decision. Neither the defendant nor the plaintiff are afforded identity as "women" (נשים) or even as "prostitutes" (זנות). Instead, he designates them as "the one . . . the other." This impersonal speech intensifies the chilling aloofness which surrounds his dire decision. Such rigorous judicial practice does not guarantee a just judgment.

The king's order contradicts Israel's regard for and legislation on human life. Not only does the decalogue in Exodus prohibit murder (Exod. 20:13), the law in Leviticus specifically forbids child sacrifice (Lev. 18:21; 20:2-5). In Israel's traditions, stories reinforce this reverence for human life. An angel of the Lord prevented Abraham's sacifice of his son Isaac (Gen. 22:12).[67] Shiphrah and Puah, who feared God, defied Pharaoh in order to save the life of Hebrew children (Exod. 1:15-17).[68] Further, the king's order runs contrary to the life-giving role of the monarch. Protection of the most vulnerable in society was not only a

---

[65]R. Juddah remarked "If I had been there, I would have wound a rope of wool around Solomon's neck when . . . he said fetch me a sword." See *Middrash Rabbah VIII/2 Ecclesiastes*, trans. A. Cohen (New York/London: Soncino Press, 1983) 277.

[66]The story has been described by Rand, "Justice in Solomon's Court—Anonymous vs. Anonymous," 170, as "a concise record of a courtroom scene." H. J. Broecker, *Redeformen des Rechtsleben im Alten Testament* (Neukirchen Verlag: Neukirchen-Vluyn, 1964) 73, 85, and 98, suggests that the terminology in 1 Kings 3:15-28 may represent forensic terminology. However, he does not offer a systematic investigation of the language.

[67]See C. Westermann, *Genesis 12–36: A Commentary*, trans. J. Scullion (Minneapolis: Augsburg, 1985) 353-58, for an elaboration of these events in the story.

[68]For a further exposition of these midwives as divine agents, see J. C. Exum, "'You shall let every daughter live': A Study of Exodus 1:8–2:10," *Semeia* 28 (1983): 63-82.

characteristic of a virtuous king; it was the duty of the Israelite king. In his judicial role, the king was God's vicegerent.[69]

Prior to and during the transition to monarchy, a leader secured divine will with the aid of sacral devices. In the book of Exodus, Moses instituted oaths of purgation (Exod. 22:9-10). These declarations before God determined guilt in disputes between two parties. On another occasion, Joshua cast lots in order to identify an evildoer in the Israelite community. Later, Saul in his role as king, consulted the Urim and Thummim in the indictment of his own son Jonathan (1 Sam. 14:36-46).

The disappearance of these sacral devices in Israel coincided with the story of Solomon's kingship. The legal decision of the king appears to have replaced these sacral maneuvers. God's gift of wisdom now guided the king's decisions.[70] The story of the Tekoite woman before David foreshadowed the bestowal of this charism.[71] Solomon's dream at Gibeon confirmed the infusion of God's gift.

Yet, how God's wisdom informed Solomon's judgment in this story remains a question. Though Solomon assumes the appearance of a judge,[72] he seeks no recourse to investigative procedures. He does not cross-examine either woman. He does not seek evidence or even a witness. He ignores the difficulties of the woman's story who spoke as an eyewitness in the night. He disregards the other woman's lack of an alternate account.[73] Instead, Solomon, who acts on behalf of a life-sustaining God, utters a daring death-engendering order. Further, the order yields only an apparent justice. This ruling, which assigns an equal share to both women, generates further inequity. The life of a child will be sacrificed.[74]

---

[69]T. N. D. Mettinger, *King and Messiah*, 244; Whitelam, *The Just King—Monarchical Judicial Authority in Ancient Israel*, 164.

[70]M. Noth, "Die Bewahrung von Salomos 'gottliche Weisheit,'" *VTSup* 3 (Leiden: Brill, 1955) 230-37; N. W. Porteous, "Royal Wisdom," *VTSup* 3 (Leiden: Brill, 1955) 164ff.; and Mettinger, *King and Messiah*, 243.

[71]See discussion in chap. 5, pp. 77-121.

[72]See preceding analysis, 145-46.

[73]Contra W. McKane, *Prophets and Wise Men* (Naperville IL: Allenson, 1965) 59, who applauds Solomon's "skill in sifting the evidence."

[74]Despite the usual benefit of the doubt afforded Solomon, the text gives no indication that the king was only proposing this as a test. Moreover, in one

Narrative Discourse, vs. 26a

Direct discourse has governed the course of the story until this point. A narrative moment interrupts the flood of direct speech and navigates a new direction for the plot.[75]

וַתֹּאמֶר הָאִשָּׁה אֲשֶׁר־בְּנָהּ הַחַי אֶל־הַמֶּלֶךְ

And the woman whose son was the living one spoke to the king,

כִּי־נִכְמְרוּ רַחֲמֶיהָ עַל־בְּנָהּ

because her compassion burned for her son.

A relative clause (הָאִשָּׁה אֲשֶׁר־בְּנָהּ) specifies the woman's identity. She is the mother of the living child. A further description verifies her motherhood.

כִּי־נִכְמְרוּ רַחֲמֶיהָ עַל־בְּנָהּ

because her compassion burned for her son.

In the book of Genesis, the verb כמר captures Joseph's burning sentiments for his estranged brother, Benjamin (Gen. 43:30). "Joseph hurried out for his heart was moved (כמר) at the sight of his brother and he was near to weeping." In another text, כמר describes God's delirium at the thought of giving up parentage of Israel (Hos. 11:8). In the present story, the woman's maternal sentiments burn within her. In keeping with the maternal motif of the tale, the Hebrew noun רחם traces the woman's sentiments to her "womb." The plural form of "compassion" (רחמים) which occurs here,[76] broadens the meaning of the image. The fullness of a metaphor embodies the locus and character of these stirrings.[77] Compassion wells up from the depths of this woman's womb. The rousing of these sentiments overrides her self-righteous claims on a life. This selfless love replaces all previous possessive inclinations. The particle "because" (כִּי) introduces and designates these maternal stirrings

---

Indian parallel cited at length by Gressmann, "Das Salomonische Urteil," 214, it is the mother's demands that reverse the deity's intent to slay her baby.

[75]See also Trible, *God and the Rhetoric of Sexuality*, 32, who notes the significance of this narrative intrusion.

[76]G. Schmuttermayr, "RHM—Eine lexikalische Studie," *Bib* 51 (1970): 499-532; and I. Eitan, "An Unknown Meaning of Rahamim," *JBL* 53 (1934): 269-71.

[77]Trible, *God and the Rhetoric of Sexuality*, 33.

as incentive.[78] "The woman spoke . . . to the king *because* (כִּי) her compassion burned for her son."

Three Speeches, vss. 26-27

The three speeches that follow achieve a reversal of the king's initial decision (vs. 25). First, one woman offers to relinquish the living child. Second, the other woman argues in favor of the king's plan to divide the child. Finally, the king issues a new order which assigns the child to the real mother.

Speech One

Moved by maternal stirrings, one woman pleads with the king and offers to give up the child.

וַתֹּאמֶר

And she said,

בִּי אֲדֹנִי

"Please, my Lord,

תְּנוּ־לָהּ אֶת־הַיָּלוּד הַחַי

Give her the living child,

וְהָמֵת אַל־תְּמִיתֻהוּ

Indeed, do not kill him." (vs. 26b)

The woman proposes a different sacrifice in lieu of Solomon's proposed sacrifice of her child. She offers to relinquish the child in order to save him. Her reference to the infant as "the living child" (הַחַי הַיָּלוּד) replaces her previous designation of him as "my son" (בְּנִי, vs. 22). The shift in language verifies the social distance necessary to make such an offer. The compassionate self-sacrifice of this mother incites a vindictive retort from the other woman.

Speech Two, vs. 26

In the second speech, the other woman opposes the first woman's proposal.

---

[78]On the rhetorical uses of the particle כִּי, see J. Muilenburg, "The Linguistic and Rhetorical Uses of כִּי in the Old Testament," *HUCA* 32 (1961): 135-60.

וְזֹאת אֹמֶרֶת

But the other one said,

גַּם־לִי

"Neither mine,

גַּם־לָךְ לֹא יִהְיֶה

nor yours will he be.

גְּזֹרוּ:

Divide him!" (vs. 26)

Rhetoric crafts a social kinship between this "other one" and the king. The form and content of her speech collaborates with the king's mandate.

(king)	Give half to one
	half to the other (vs. 25)
(woman)	He shall be neither mine
	nor yours (vs. 26)

The two-part format of her retort parallels the two-part format of the monarch's mandate. Further, she details a two-stage outcome of the king's two-stage order. Moreover, the content of this woman's curt response replicates the king's dire order.

| (king) | Divide him (vs. 25) |
| (woman) | Divide him (vs. 26) |

Like the king, she favors the clear-cut justice of equal distribution. Like the king, she remains dispassionate. Like the king, she appears immune to the consequences for the child.

The contrasting responses of the women reveal their true social identities. One is fit for motherhood. One is not. Despite the king's judicial office, the women judge themselves. This disclosure nullifies the king's initial judgment, as well as threatens his credibility. The king seizes upon the evidence and hurries to amend his decision.

Speech Three, vs. 27

In this final speech, the king reverses his previous command (vs.25). He rules on behalf of one of the women and on behalf of the child.

וַיַּעַן הַמֶּלֶךְ וַיֹּאמֶר

Then the king spoke and he said,

תְּנוּ־לָהּ אֶת־הַיָּלוּד הַחַי

"Give her the living child.

וְהָמֵת לֹא תְמִיתֻהוּ

Indeed, do not kill him.

הִיא אִמּוֹ:

She is his mother." (vs. 27)

The king rules in favor of the true mother. For the first time in the narrative, the woman is afforded a social identity by the king. Her willingness to relinquish her child renders her "mother."[79]

Rhetoric illustrates a shift in the social dynamics of the tale. The monarch depends upon the decision of a woman. The king's revised ruling occurs after the innocent woman's plea. Further, the king's new decision is an exact reproduction of the innocent woman's words.

(woman)   Give her the child, do not slay him. (vs. 26b)
(king)   Give her the child, do not slay him. (vs. 27)

Only at this juncture of the story is Solomon's decision recognized as "wise."

Conclusion, vs. 28

A report of Israel's response signals the conclusion of this trial. The narrator's summary draws closure to these events.

וַיִּשְׁמְעוּ כָל־יִשְׂרָאֵל אֶת־הַמִּשְׁפָּט אֲשֶׁר שָׁפַט הַמֶּלֶךְ

And when all Israel heard the judgment which the king judged,

וַיִּרְאוּ מִפְּנֵי הַמֶּלֶךְ

they marveled before the king,

כִּי רָאוּ כִּי־חָכְמַת אֱלֹהִים בְּקִרְבּוֹ לַעֲשׂוֹת מִשְׁפָּט:

because they saw that the wisdom of God was within him
     to do justice. (vs. 28)

The epilogue establishes the king's reputation. Solomon is a wise judge! The threefold repetition of the root שפט celebrates this judicial prowess. The witness by "all Israel" (כָל־יִשְׂרָאֵל) affords him unani-

---

[79]Trible, *God and the Rhetoric of Sexuality*, 33.

mous endorsement. The "wisdom of God" (חָכְמַת אֱלֹהִים) characterizes his judicial capacity, as well as credits Solomon with the highest praise.

The sociorhetorical dynamics across these exchanges disclose a different evaluation. "The judgment which the king judged" is skillfully juxtaposed between two purpose clauses.

כִּי־נִכְמְרוּ רַחֲמֶיהָ עַל־בְּנָהּ

because her compassion burned for her son.

וַיַּעַן הַמֶּלֶךְ וַיֹּאמֶר

Then the king spoke and he said,

תְּנוּ־לָהּ אֶת־הַיָּלוּד הַחַי

"Give her the living child.

וְהָמֵת לֹא תְמִיתֻהוּ

Indeed, do not kill him.

הִיא אִמּוֹ:

She is his mother." (vs. 27)

כִּי רָאוּ כִּי־חָכְמַת אֱלֹהִים בְּקִרְבּוֹ לַעֲשׂוֹת מִשְׁפָּט:
because they saw that the wisdom of God was within him
to do justice. (vs. 28)

Narrated discourse houses both clauses. The particle "because" (כִּי) introduces both phrases. Parallels in rhetoric between these two phrases invite recognition of correspondences in the social realm. Israel recognized the wisdom of God in Solomon in line with what had taken place in the woman. This rhetorical artistry defines the mechanics of the social interactions of this tale. The woman's compassion and action make possible the recognition of God's wisdom in the king.

Sociorhetorical features in this tale challenge the unequivocal prominence of Solomon and his wisdom in the surrounding Solomonic Narrative. The progression of speech in this story makes Israel's perception of God's wisdom in Solomon contingent upon the compassion and action of one of his subjects. Patterns of speech disclose that the true mother's words ("Give her the child . . . " vs. 26b) form a climax which supersedes the king's pronouncement ("Give her the child. . . . " vs. 27). This repetition in speech makes the king's wise decision subordinate to the woman's bold decision.

The sociorhetorical interplay of this story offers a qualified portrait of kingship, as well as exposes the underside of royal ideology.[80] Solomon's rule manifests the "wisdom of God" only when it is informed by the compassion and self-sacrifice of a woman. Left to his own devices, the king acts foolishly. When Solomon speaks on his own, he summons a sword and orders a slaying. At best, such judicial strategy constitutes a dangerous move for justice. At worst, it manifests itself as a cruel trick. It blackmails motherhood. It puts God's gift of wisdom on trial. It gambles human life. When a king threatens the fate of an innocent baby in the name of justice, the whole nation is at risk. Literary images embody the potential social consequences. The judicial policies of a king who would propose to divide an innocent child in two could eventually sever a whole nation.

---

[80]Ideological literature is designed to promote a certain interest, idea, or value system. At the same time, it may expose the limitations and failings of the very ideology it is designed to promote. See P. Macherey, *A Theory of Literary Production* (London/Boston: Routledge and Kegan Paul, 1978) 155; C. Belsey, *Critical Practice* (London/ New York: Methuen, 1980) 116-17; and F. Jamison, "Reification and Utopia in Mass Culture," *Social Text* 1 (1979): 141, 144.

Conclusion

The interpretation of biblical texts qualifies as a central concern in biblical studies. The ongoing development of new methods reflects the seriousness and centrality of this concern.[1] Approaches adapted from other disciplines open up new possibilities.[2] Each new criticism proposes a well defined avenue for interpretation of biblical writings.[3] As the shortcomings of a method become apparent, other methods develop and offer alternate routes.[4] The gains of specialization in the methods of biblical

---

[1]See L. Alonso Schokel's review of recent developments in Old Testament studies: "Trends: Plurality of Methods, Priority of Issues," *VTSup* (Leiden: E. J. Brill, 1988) 285-92. See also his presidental address at the Pontifical Institute in Rome on the questions raised by the new literary methods in biblical studies: "Of Methods and Models," *VTSup* (Leiden: E. J. Brill, 1983) 3-13.

[2]E.g., a recent work which draws upon the nomenclature and philosophy of deconstruction is Peter Miscall, *The Workings of Old Testament Narrative* (Philadelphia: Fortress Press, 1983).

[3]For an overview of these various methods, see R. Davidson and A. R. C. Leaney, *Biblical Criticism* (London: Pelican Press, 1970); and J. H. Hayes and C. R. Holladay, *Biblical Exegesis* (Atlanta: John Knox Press, 1987). The series *Guides to Biblical Scholarship*, published by Fortress Press, Philadelphia, offers individual studies on the development and appropriation of many of these methods as well as valuable bibliographies. John Barton has prepared an introduction to methods for O.T. study which surveys the older traditional (source, form, redaction) criticisms and the newer "text-immanent" (canonical, structuralist) approaches. See John Barton, *Reading the Old Testament—Method in Biblical Study* (Philadelphia: Westminster Press, 1984). For a review of reader-oriented literary approaches, see Edgar McKnight, *The Bible and the Reader: An Introduction to Literary Criticism* (Philadelphia: Fortress Press, 1985).

[4]For a history of the development of methods of O.T. interpretation, see R. E. Clements, *One Hundred Years of Old Testament Interpretation* (Philadelphia: Westminster Press, 1976); and H. Hahn, *The Old Testament in Modern Research* (London: S.C.M. Press, 1966). The impact of synchronic methods upon the long-standing diachronic approaches is discussed in R. Polzin, "Literary and

interpretation have been noted.[5] Each new critical method endeavors to interpret the text by the study of *one or more of its parts.* Yet, the narrow spectrum of these individual criticisms can compromise one's vision of the text as a *whole.*

Sociorhetorical criticism seeks to elucidate the whole text by a study of *the social and rhetorical elements in relation to one another.* The social and rhetorical features in a story are investigated for potential points of collaboration and interplay. How rhetoric shapes the social elements, how the social features anchor the rhetoric, and how the evaluation of the interplay of the social and rhetorical findings inform the interpretation, guide the approach to exegesis.

In the past, historical criticism studied biblical texts in order to trace the compositional history of these writings. Further, historical and social science investigations viewed the biblical texts as data with which to reconstruct a portrait of ancient Israel. In recent years, the paradigm of interpretation has shifted away from historical studies toward literary studies. Concern for the extrinsic world of the Bible has been supplanted by studies of the intrinsic world of the text. As a result, an impasse exists between methods that focus on texts and those that focus on context. Sociorhetorical exegesis wrestles with this predicament. It draws upon data from outside the text, from studies on the social and historical context of Israel to clarify the social realm of the story. It interprets rhetoric in light of the social data and considers how the social world is shaped and animated by the rhetoric.

Three texts served as illustrations of this sociorhetorical approach to exegesis. Upon analysis, each of these stories produced a vast array of social and rhetorical findings. When these two sets of findings were viewed concurrently, each text also manifested a network of interconnec-

---

Historical Criticism of the Bible: Crisis in Scholarship," *Orientation by Disorientation: Studies in Literary Criticism and Biblical Literary Criticism,* ed. Richard Spencer (Pittsburg: Pickwick Press, 1980) 99-114; R. B. Crotty, "Changing Fashions in Biblical Interpretation," *Australian Bible Review* 33 (1985): 15-30; R. Rendtorff, "Between Historical Criticism and Holistic Interpretation: New Trends in Old Testament Exegesis," *VTSup* (Leiden: E. J. Brill, 1988) 298-305; and E. Greenstein, *Essays on Biblical Method and Translation* (Atlanta: Scholars Press, 1989) 3-84.

[5]See the introduction, pp. 1-2.

tions between the social and rhetorical features. While the sociorhetorical interplay varied in each story, some general observations can be made. The results can be catalogued according to the following three principles.

1. Rhetoric shapes and animates the social world in a story.

The social medium of characters' identities, interactions, customs, behaviors, and institutions makes up the content of a tale. Like a potter's clay, the social data serve as subject matter out of which a story can be formed. The particular formulation of this content (i.e., structure, scope, design, stylistics) shapes and animates these social elements. The identity of characters comes to life. Patterns of interactions reinforce or undercut their identity. Form and content govern the dynamics of their exchanges. Further, rhetoric determines the character of the social conditions prevailing in a story. As a result of the artistic formulation of content, familiar behaviors and actions, assume a particularity; conventional institutions, customs, and values take on a specificity. Rhetoric crafts the social data to create a unique story world. This principle can be seen at work in each of the three texts studied.

The content of an interaction in 1 Samuel 14.36 tells of the relationship between the king and a people.[6] The particular formulation of that exchange, namely the grammatical patterns, qualifies the terms of the relationship. Saul's cohortative language to the people reveals his tentative status as king. In turn, the people's imperative to Saul confirms their residual collective power.

In 1 Kings 3.22, two women argue over custody of a child.[7] The content of their interaction reveals their status as opponents. The particular formulation of that exchange, namely, a chiastic structure, illustrates the dynamic of their interaction. The women are trapped in a forensic deadlock.

In 2 Samuel 14.5, the content of a woman's speech conveys her crisis as a widow.[8] The particular formulation of her story dramatizes her plight. "A mourning woman am I, for my husband is dead." Assonance (אבל, אשה, אלמנה אני, אשי) amplifies the anguish which she reports. Thus

---

[6]See chap. 4, pp. 49.
[7]See chap. 6, pp. 140-41.
[8]See chap. 5, pp. 92-93.

do form and content cohere in rhetoric that gives a particular shape to each story's social world.

2. *The exposition of the social realm of the story anchors and informs the interpretation of rhetoric.*

The integrity of form and content conveys meaning in a story. Knowledge of the social elements embedded in this rhetorical artistry influences an understanding of the tale. An exposition of these social elements corroborates the rhetoric and furthers an appreciation of the rhetorical achievement.

Over the past thirty years, New Criticism's emphasis on the self-sufficiency of the text has been far-reaching. In the case of rhetorical studies, the coherence of form and content are often evaluated without reference to any extrinsic factors. This exclusive attention to text in rhetorical studies has had an abundant yield. At the same time, it has disclosed some shortcomings. Whether the interpretation of a text on its own terms is even possible is questionable. Moreover, critics object that the interpretation of rhetorical artistry has been grounded solely in the biases and beliefs of the critic. A sociorhetorical approach to exegesis heeds these objections. The interpretation of rhetorical features is no longer the prerogative and product of the critic's subjectivity alone. Exposition of the social elements of the story world anchor and inform the interpretation of the rhetoric. That is not to disclaim the part that every reader/interpreter plays in the outcome of sociorhetorical exegesis. It is impossible to leave behind one's own situation when reading and interpreting texts. Moreover, one who conducts sociorhetorical *exegesis* of biblical texts probably does so from a confessional stance. The clarification of the social elements of a story, as well as the interpretation of the rhetoric, is necessarily governed by the questions one asks. However, the elaboration of the social elements of the narrative establishes parameters within which the rhetorical artistry can be appraised. The spectrum of the critic's influence in the interpretative process narrows. This social data rather than solely the critic's evaluation anchors and informs the rhetorical interpretation.

The social exposition may elaborate the roles of characters, designate the parameters of a king's military authority, or enumerate the features of a cultic ritual. The results of this exposition serve as a the point of reference for the rhetorical assessment. The social roles of characters coincide with patterns of discourse. The description of the limits of a king's military authority concurs with the literary boundaries of the story. The features of a ritual constitute the structural elements of the tale. How this principle operates varies with each text.

The social features in 1 Samuel 14:36-46 invite an investigation of Saul's judicial authority.[9] The integrity of his military authority is found to be integrally tied to his skill in judicial matters. Hence, Saul's failure in the judgment of Jonathan anticipates a curtailment of his military escapades. In the opening of the story (1 Sam. 14.36), Saul plans to battle the Philistines. In the account which follows, Saul fails in his judicial responsibility. The story's conclusion (1 Sam. 14.46) reports that Saul abandoned his battle plan. Hence, the connection between the two realms of his authority is borne out in the rhetorical boundaries of the tale.

The social referents in 1 Kings 3:16-28 warrant an investigation of the character of kingship in the Solomonic era.[10] The exposition of these social clues discloses as unconventional the behavior of Solomon in this story given the otherwise aloof and remote nature of the kingship. The atypical picture of kingship corroborates the rhetoric. A profusion of direct speech governs the form of the story, while content shows the king interacting directly with his subjects.

The social clues in 1 Samuel 14:1-21 summon an exposition of David's social standing.[11] This investigation exposes the dual nature of his social role. He is both father and judge of Absalom. The complexity of this twofold status concurs with the form and content of the disclosure. Content discloses the complexity of this role. The formulation of this content conveys the inherent ambiguity of this position. David's heart is both "on" and "against" Absalom. Hence, the elaboration of the social relations in this story collaborates with the rhetoric. Moreover, the exposition of the social realm confines and anchors the rhetorical achievement.

---

[9]See chap. 4, pp. 75-76.
[10]See chap. 6, pp. 126-29.
[11]See chap. 5, p. 85.

3. The evaluation of the sociorhetorical interplay in texts yields meaning

The interplay between the social and rhetorical features of the story world discloses congruences, oppositions, parallels, and confluences. Rhetoric shapes, illustrates, reinforces, undercuts, and dramatizes the social dimensions of the story world. Concurrently, the exposition of the social data corroborates the rhetoric and highlights the compositional artistry.

anchors and informs

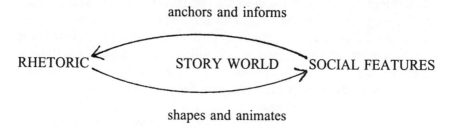

RHETORIC   STORY WORLD   SOCIAL FEATURES

shapes and animates

A story unfolds as a result of this interaction. The interplay of the social and rhetorical elements influences the coherence of characters, the tenor of their conversations, the course of events, and the resolution of the plot.

In 2 Samuel 14:1-21, the exposition of the social cues of the story established the social distance between David as king and the woman as widow.[12] The form and content of the woman's speech oppose these social categories. Though she is powerless, the form of their conversation discloses her initiative and her control over the course of their exchange. Further, the content of her speech instructed the king in the nature of his authority. Hence, the exposition of social elements of the story is undercut by the rhetoric. The interpretation of this sociorhetorical interplay informs meaning. Though a powerful king mediates God's judgment to Israel, a powerless woman first mediated God's wisdom to the king.

In 1 Samuel 14:36-46, the exposition of the social referents qualified the tentative nature of Saul's kingly authority before the people.[13] The course and content of the story set the king and people at cross-purposes. The particular formulation of the vow of the people which opposes the vow of Saul narrates this hostility. The people profess that God is responsible for Jonathan's success. By contrast, the vows and lot casting

---

[12]See chap. 5, pp. 77-121.
[13]See chap. 4, pp. 39-76.

of Saul compelled God's judgment of Jonathan. Monarchical improvidence on the part of Saul fostered this theological dilemma. He manipulated rather than mediated divine ways.

In 1 Kings 3:16-28, the social exposition revealed the unequivocal power of Solomon's kingship.[14] Rhetoric undercuts this social portrait and exposes a monarch's facade. Patterns and repetition of speech make the judicial decision and pronouncement of the all powerful king subordinate to the woman's declaration. Moreover, the words of the king's judgment replicate the words of the woman's proposal. Interpretation of the sociorhetorical interchange contributes to meaning in the story. The recognition of divine wisdom in the king was contingent upon the compassion and self-sacrifice of a woman.

Sociorhetorical interplay is not limited to select biblical texts. All literature is stamped with social features.[15] Because social data inscribe the rhetorical elements of form and content, sociorhetorical interplay takes place in all the biblical texts. However, several factors determine and limit the sociorhetorical analysis.

First, some texts are more artistically fashioned and rhetorically rich. These writings are more receptive to rhetorical analysis. Undoubtedly, the yield in a rhetorical study of Second Isaiah 40–55 would easily surpass the rhetorical analysis of 1 Kings 6–7, the description of the Solomonic temple construction. Texts which are noted for their rhetorical achievement would necessarily accommodate a sociorhetorical analysis more readily.

Second, while all texts embody social data, some texts do not afford a warehouse of explicit social indicators. The lack of specific referents in a text will limit the sociological investigation which can be made. For example, the exposition of the social referents surrounding the generic wife in Proverbs 31:10-31 would produce diminished returns as compared to an exposition of Sarah and her role in the Genesis stories. Hence, the specificity and quantity of a text's social data will affect its receptivity to sociorhetorical analysis.

---

[14]See chap, 6, pp. 123-53.

[15]Kenneth Burke, *On Symbols and Society* (Chicago/London: University of Chicago Press, 1989) 44.

Third, sociorhetorical analysis is limited by a factor extraneous to biblical texts. Relevant social science investigations and/or comparative studies are needed to clarify the social referents. All texts contain social cues. These elements govern the exposition of the implicit social realm of the tale. The studies necessary for the exposition of this social data may not exist, however. For example, extensive social science studies have been conducted on prophets, monarchy, and cult. By contrast, few studies exist which detail child-rearing practices or the status of slaves during monarchy. The lack of relevant investigations or comparative studies could seriously hamper the description of the social world implicit in a story. In turn, this gap in information limits the prospects for a sociorhetorical analysis.

Finally, the reader/interpreter will influence the outcome of the socio-rhetorical method. One's attention to and subsequent exposition of the social referents in texts will limit or enhance the analysis, as will one's sensitivity to and facility with rhetoric. At the same time, the social and rhetorical elements in the text urge the reader to listen and respond to the interplay as one seeks to understand the story.[16] A dialogue serves as analogue for this exchange between text and reader. As in real conversation, the purpose is not simply to agree with or to impose one's own position on the other. A dialogue aims at an understanding of the matter at hand.[17] Hence, both the text and reader maintain some autonomy in the interpretive process. Not only may the reader have his or her way with the text, but "the text must be allowed to have its way with the reader."[18] Hence, the interpretation of the interplay between the social and rhetorical features necessarily involves an interplay between the reader and the text.

Such an understanding invites a brief reflection on sociorhetorical analysis as "method." In biblical studies, the notion of "method" has

---

[16]See P. Ricoeur, *Interpretation Theory: Discourse and the Surplus of Meaning* (Fort Worth TX: Texas Christian University Press, 1976) 25-44, for a discussion of the priority of the text in interpretation.

[17]H. G. Gadamer, *Truth and Method* (New York: Seabury, 1975) 325-41. Gadamer focuses on the nature of dialogue as a genuine engagement between parties who are mutually interested in the subject matter at hand.

[18]J. Muilenburg, "A Study in Hebrew Rhetoric: Repetition and Style," *VTSup* 1 (Leiden: Brill, 1953) 109.

become synonymous with "criticism." Each method prescribes a set of procedures aimed at ascertaining *the meaning* of texts.[19]

Sociorhetorical analysis as method resists this connotation. While it does aim at the interpretation of meaning in texts, it does not claim to uncover *the meaning* of texts. As method, sociorhetorical analysis proposes one avenue for interpreting texts. The sociorhetorical features of the texts themselves instigated this proposal. The development of a sociorhetorical approach "codified" these observations. John Barton describes the matter aptly.

> Texts are perceived as having certain sorts of meaning - or, just as interestingly, as failing to convey meaning—by reading them with certain vague expectations about genre, coherence and consistency, which are either confirmed and clarified, or disappointed and frustrated. Then reading begins again, this time with a sharper focus; and at the end of the process there emerges a distinct impression of what the text means, together with an explanatory theory as to how it comes to mean it. But the theory—which when codified, will become source analysis or redaction criticism or whatever—is logically subsequent to the intuition about meaning.[20]

Sociorhetorical exegesis, like other methods "codifies" "how texts mean." It begins with the recognition of the hypothetical nature of methods, as well as the legitimacy of different approaches. Hence, sociorhetorical analysis is not proposed over and against other methods. Moreover, sociorhetorical criticism is not set forth as an alternative to other approaches. Rather, it engages the procedures and outcomes of several methods. Form and text criticisms contribute to the sociorhetorical analysis.

---

[19]E. D. Hirsch offers the classical statement of this position. Throughout his works, he defines the two tasks of interpretation as determining "the meaning" and "the significance" of a work. See E. D. Hirsch Jr., *Validity in Interpretation* (New Haven CT: Yale University Press, 1967) and *The Aims of Interpretation* (Chicago: University of Chicago Press, 1976). J. Derrida, by contrast argues for the radical indeterminancy of the meaning of texts. On J. Derrida, see Jonathan Culler, *On Deconstruction: Theory and Criticism after Structuralism* (Ithaca NY: Cornell University Press, 1982) 131-34.

[20]Barton, *Reading the Old Testament—Method in Biblical Study*, 205.

This receptivity to other methods of interpretation does not undermine one's own approach or invite anarchy in interpretation. Rather, it
cultivates a mode of interpretation which recognizes the legitimacy and
contributions of other frameworks. Such a context opens opportunities for
collaboration between previously unreconcilable methods. This study
results from such collaborations. The outcome has been twofold. First,
sociorhetorical criticism and the accompanying analysis of texts sow
seeds for further study. What other avenues exist for traversing the intrinsic and extrinsic world of texts. Already, a new current in literary studies
is mapping the ways literary productions reap the consequences of the
historical, social, and political conditions. "New Historicism" or "Cultural
Poetics" as it is called, is soon to attract the interest of and beckon implementation by biblical critics.[21] Finally, the exploration of sociorhetorical
criticism accomplishes something more. It occasions a collaborative
forum for the examination of seemingly disparate matters . . . in this
study, the matters of methods, monarchs, and meanings.

---

[21]For an introduction to the New Historicism, see the collection of essays
edited by A. Veeser, *The New Historicism* (London: Routledge and Kegan Paul,
1989).

Bibliography

Abrams, M. H. *The Mirror and the Lamp*. New York: W. W. Norton & Company, 1958.

Achtemeier, P., and G. Tucker, "Biblical Studies: The State of the Discipline." *Bulletin of the Council of Societies for the Study of Religion* 3 (June 1980): 72-76.

Ackroyd, P. "The Succession Narrative (so-called)." *Int* 35 (1981): 383-96.

Adam, A. K. M. "The Future of Our Allusions." In *SBLSP 1992*, ed. E. Lovering. Atlanta: Scholars Press, 1992.

Ahlstrom, G. W. *Royal Administration and National Religion in Ancient Palestine*. Leiden: E. J. Brill, 1982.

Alt, A. "The Formation of the Israelite State in Palestine." In *Essays on the Old Testament History and Religion*, 171-238. Garden City NY: Doubleday, 1968.

Alter, R. *The Art of Biblical Narrative*. New York: Basic Books, 1981.

Andersen, Francis I. *The Sentence in Biblical Hebrew*. The Hague: Mouton, 1974.

Andersen, Kirsten M., ed. "Reading Scripture: Literary Criticism and Biblical Hermeneutics." *Literature and Theology* 6 (1992): 217-79.

Anderson, A. A. *2 Samuel*. WBC 11. Waco TX: Word Books, 1989.

Anderson, B. "The New Frontier of Rhetorical Criticism. A Tribute to James Muilenburg." In *Rhetorical Criticism: Essays in Honor of James Muilenburg*, ed. J. J. Jackson and M. Kessler, ix-xvii. Pittsburgh: Pickwick Press, 1974.

Aristotle. *The Art of Rhetoric*. Translated by J. H. Freese. LCL. Cambridge MA: Harvard University Press, 1926.

Arthurs, Jeffrey Dean. "Biblical Interpretation through Rhetorical Criticism: Augmenting the Grammatical/Historical Approach." Ph.D. diss., Purdue University, 1992.

Bal, M. *Lethal Love: Feminist Literary Readings of Biblical Love Stories*. Bloomington: Indiana University Press, 1987.

Baldwin, J. *1 & 2 Samuel*. Leicester UK: InterVarsity Press, 1988.

Ball, I. J., Jr. "Additions to a Bibliography of James Muilenburg's Writings." In *Rhetorical Criticism: Essays in Honor of James Muilenburg*, ed. J. J. Jackson and M. Kessler, 285-87. Pittsburgh: Pickwick Press, 1974.

Baltzer, K. *The Covenant Formulary in Old Testament, Jewish, and Early Christian Writings*. Philadelphia: Fortress Press, 1971.

Bar-Efrat, S. *Narrative Art in the Bible*. Sheffield UK: Almond Press, 1984.

Barkun, M. *Law without Sanctions: Order in Primitive Societies and the World Community*. New Haven and London: Yale University Press, 1968.

Barr, J. *Holy Scripture*. Philadelphia: Westminster, 1983.

Barrett, C. "The Language of Ecstasy and the Ecstasy of Language." In *The Bible as Rhetoric: Studies in Biblical Persuasion and Credibility*, ed. M. Warner, 205-31. Warwick Studies in Philosophy and Literature. London: Routledge, 1990.

Barton, J. *Reading the Old Testament: Method in Biblical Study*. Philadelphia: Westminster Press, 1984.

Bellefontaine, E. "Customary Law and Chieftainship: Judicial Aspects of 2 Samuel 14.4-21." *JSOT* 38 (1987): 47-72.

Belsey, C. *Critical Practice*. London and New York: Methuen, 1980.

Berhardt, C. L. *The New Century Handbook of English Literature*. New York: Appleton/Century/Crofts, 1967.

Berger, P. "Charisma and Religious Innovation: The Social Location of Israelite Prophecy." *American Sociological Review* 28 (1963): 940-50.

Best, T., ed. *Hearing and Speaking the Word*. Chico CA: Scholars Press, 1984.

Betz, H. D. *2 Corinthians 8 and 9: A Commentary on Two Administrative Letters of the Apostle Paul*. Hermeneia. Philadelphia: Fortress Press, 1985.

Beuken, W. A. M. "No Wise King without a Wise Woman (I Kings iii 16-28)." In *New Avenues in the Study of the Old Testament*, ed. A. S. Van der Woude, 1-10. Leiden: E. J. Brill, 1989.

Birch, B. C. *The Rise of the Israelite Monarchy: The Growth and Development of I Samuel 7-15*. Missoula MT: Scholars Press, 1976.

Bird, P. "Male and Female He Created Them: Gen. 1.27b in the Context of the Priestly Account of Creation." *HTR* 77 (1981): 129-59.

_____. "The Harlot as Heroine: Narrative Art and Social Presupposition in Three Old Testament Texts." *Semeia* 46 (1989): 119-39.

Black, C. "Rhetorical Criticism and Biblical Interpretation." *ExpTim* 100 (1989): 252-58.

Blenkinsopp, J. "Jonathan's Sacrilege." *CBQ* 26 (1964): 423-49.

_____. "Theme and Motif in the Succession History (2 Sam. XI 2ff) and the Yahwist Corpus." *VTSup* 15 (1966): 44-57.

Boecker, H. J. *Law and the Administration of Justice in the Old Testament and Ancient East*. Minneapolis: Augsburg Publishing House, 1980.

Bossman, David M., ed. "Rhetoric of Hate, Instruments of War." *BTB* 21 (1991): 13-39.

Brenner, A. *The Israelite Woman: Social Role and Literary Type in Biblical Narrative*. Sheffield UK: JSOT Press, 1985.

Brettler, M. *God Is King. Understanding an Israelite Metaphor*. Sheffield UK: JSOT Press, 1989.

Brichto, Herbert Chanan. *Toward a Grammar of Biblical Poetics: Tales of the Prophets*. New York: Oxford University Press, 1992.

Brock, B., R. Scott, and J. Chesebro, eds. *Methods of Rhetorical Criticism: A Twentieth-Century Perspective*. Detroit: Wayne State University Press, 1989.

Broecker, H. J. *Redeformen des Rechtsleben im Alten Testament*. Neukirchen-Vluyn: Neukirchen Verlag, 1964.

Brosend, William F., II. "The Limits of Metaphor." *Perspectives in Religious Studies* 21 (1994): 23-41.

Brueggemann, W. "At the Mercy of Babylon: A Subversive Rereading of the Empire." *JBL* 110 (1991): 3-22.

_____. "Crisis-Evoked, Crisis-Resolving Speech." *BTB* 24 (1994): 95-105.

_____. *First and Second Samuel.* Interpretation. Louisville: John Knox Press, 1990.

_____. "The Social Significance of Solomon as a Patron of Wisdom." In *The Sage in Israel and the Ancient Near East*, ed. J. Gammie and L. Perdue, 117-32. Winona Lake IN: Eisenbrauns, 1990.

Budd, P. J. *Numbers.* WBC 5. Waco TX: Word Books, 1984.

Budde, K. D. *Die Bücher Samuel.* KHC 8. Tübingen: J. C. B. Mohr, 1902.

Burke, K. *On Symbols and Society.* Edited by J. R. Gusfield. Chicago and London: University of Chicago Press, 1989.

Camp, C. "The Wise Women of 2 Samuel: A Role Model for Women in Early Israel." *CBQ* 43 (1981): 14-29.

_____. "The Female Sage in Biblical Wisdom Literature." In *The Sage in Israel and the Ancient Near East*, ed. J. G. Gammie and L. Perdue, 185-204. Winona Lake IN: Eisenbrauns, 1990.

Carlson, R. A. *David the Chosen King.* Uppsala: Almquist and Wiksells, 1964.

Carroll, R. *When Prophecy Failed: Cognitive Dissonance in the Prophetic Traditions of the Old Testament.* New York: Seabury, 1979.

Ceresko, Anthony R. "The Rhetorical Strategy of the Fourth Servant Song." *CBQ* 56 (1994): 42-55.

_____. "The A:B:B:A Word Pattern in Hebrew and Northwest Semitic, with Special Reference to the Book of Job." *UF* 7 (1975): 73-88.

_____. "The Chiastic Word Pattern in Hebrew." *CBQ* 38 (1976): 303-11.

_____. "The Function of Chiasmus in Hebrew Poetry." *CBQ* 40 (1978): 1-10.

Childs, B. *Introduction to the Old Testament as Scripture.* Philadelphia: Fortress Press, 1979.

Cicero. *Rhetorica and Herennium.* LCL. Cambridge MA: Harvard University Press, 1931.

Claessen, H., and P. Skalnik, eds. *The Early State.* The Hague: Mouton, 1978.

Clark, W. M. "A Legal Background of the Yahwist's Use of 'Good and Evil' in Genesis 2-3." *JBL* 88 (1969): 266-78.

Clements, R. E. *One Hundred Years of Old Testament Interpretation.* Philadelphia: Westminster Press, 1976.

Clines, D. "The Arguments of Job's Three Friends." In *Art and Meaning: Rhetoric in Biblical Literature*, ed. D. Clines, D. Gunn, and A. Hauser, 199-214. Sheffield UK: JSOT Press, 1982.

_____. *What Does Eve Do to Help? And Other Readerly Questions to the Text.* Sheffield UK: Sheffield Academic Press, 1990.

_____, S. E. Fowl, and S. E. Porter, eds. *The Bible in Three Dimensions: Essays in Celebration of Forty Years of Biblical Studies in the University of Sheffield*. Sheffield UK: Sheffield Academic Press, 1990.

Coats, G. W. "Parable, Fable, and Anecdote. Storytelling in the Succession Narrative." *Interpretation* 35 (1981): 368-82.

Coggins, Richard J. *Introducing the Old Testament*. Oxford: Oxford University Press, 1990.

Cohen, M. A. "The Role of the Shilonite Priesthood in the United Monarchy of Ancient Israel." *HUCA* 36 (1964): 59-98.

_____. "The Rebellions during the Reign of David: An Inquiry into the Social Dynamics in Ancient Israel." In *Studies in Jewish Bibliography, History, and Literature in Honor of I. E. Kiev*, ed. C. Berlin, 91-112. New York: Ktav Publishers, 1971.

Cohen, R., and R. Elman, eds. *Origins of the State. The Anthropology of Political Evolution*. Philadelphia: ISHI Publications, 1978.

Conley, T. M. *Philo's Rhetoric: Studies in Style, Composition and Exegesis*. Berkeley CA: Center for Hermeneutical Studies, 1987.

Conroy, C. *Absalom! Absalom!* Rome: Biblical Institute Press, 1978.

Cook, S. A. "Notes on the Composition of 2 Samuel." *AJSL* 16 (1899/1900): 158-59.

Corbett, E. J. *Classical Rhetoric for the Modern Student*. Third ed. New York: Oxford University Press, 1990.

Crafton, Jeffrey A. "The Dancing of an Attitude: Burkean Rhetorical Criticism and the Biblical Interpreter." In *Rhetoric and the New Testament*, ed. S. Porter. Minneapolis: Fortress Press, 1990.

Craig, Kenneth M., Jr. "Rhetorical Aspects of Questions Answered with Silence in Samuel 14:37 and 28:6." *CBQ* 56 (1994): 221-39.

Craven, T. *Artistry and Faith in the Book of Judith*. SBLDS 70. Chico CA: Scholars Press, 1983.

Crenshaw, J. L. *Old Testament Wisdom*. Atlanta: John Knox, 1981.

Cross, F. M. *Canaanite Myth and Hebrew Epic*. Cambridge MA: Harvard University Press, 1973.

Crossan, J. D. "Ruth Amid the Corn: Perspectives and Methods in Contemporary Biblical Criticism." In *The Biblical Mosaic: Changing Perspectives*, ed. R. Polzin and E. Rothman, 199-210. Philadelphia: Fortress Press, 1982.

Crow, Loren D. "The Rhetoric of Psalm 44." *Zeitschrift für die Alttestamentliche Wissenschaft* 104 (1992): 394-401.

Culler, J. *The Pursuit of Signs: Semiotics, Literature, Deconstruction*. Ithaca NY: Cornell University Press, 1981.

Culley, R. "An Approach to the Problem of Oral Tradition." *VT* 13 (1963): 113-25.

_____. *Oral Formulaic Language in the Biblical Psalms*. Toronto: University of Toronto Press, 1967.

_____. "Oral Tradition and Historicity." In *Studies on the Ancient Palestinian World*, ed. J. W. Weavers and D. B. Redford, 106-216. Toronto: University of Toronto Press, 1972.

_____. "Oral Tradition and the Old Testament: Some Recent Discussion." *Semeia* 5 (1976): 1-33.

_____. "Action Sequences in Genesis 2–3." *SBLSP* 1, ed. P. Achtemeier, 51-59. Missoula MT: Scholars Press, 1978.

_____. "Exploring New Directions." In *The Hebrew Bible and Its Modern Interpreters*, ed. D. Knight and G. Tucker, 167-200. Philadelphia: Fortress Press, 1985.

Davidson, R., and A. R. C. Leany. *Biblical Criticism*. London: Pelican Press, 1970.

Davies, E. W. "Inheritance Rights and the Hebrew Levirate Marriage." *VT* 31 (1981): 138-44.

de Boer, P. A. H. "Vive de roi." *VT* 5 (1955): 225-31.

DeGeus, C. H. J. *The Tribes of Israel*. Assen: Van Gorcum, 1976.

de Liagre Bohl, F. M. T. "De zonnegod als Bsechermer der Nood druftigen." *Opera Minora* (1953): 188-206.

Deurloo, K. A. "The King's Wisdom in Judgment-Narration as Example (I Kings iii)." In *New Avenues in the Study of the Old Testament*, ed. A. S. Van der Woude, 11-21. Leiden: E. J. Brill, 1989.

de Vaux, R. *Ancient Israel: Its Life and Institutions*. London: Dartman, Longman & Todd, 1961; 2-vol. pbk. repr.: New York: McGraw-Hill, 1965.

DeVries, S. *1 Kings*. WBC 12. Waco TX: Word Books, 1985.

Dhorme, P. *Les Livres de Samuel*. Ebib. Paris: J. Gabalda, 1910.

Di Marco, Angelico. "Rhetoric and Hermeneutic—on a Rhetorical Pattern: Chiasmus and Circularity." In *Rhetoric and the New Testament*, ed. S. Porter. Minneapolis: Fortress Press, 1990.

Dionysius. *On Literary Composition*. Translated by R. Roberts. Cambridge: Cambridge University Press, 1910.

Dorsey, David A. "Can These Bones Live? Investigating Literary Structure in the Bible." *Evangelical Journal*. 9 (1991): 11-25.

Driver, S. R. *Notes on the Hebrew Text of the Books of Samuel*. Oxford: Clarendon Press, 1913.

Duke, P. *Irony in the Fourth Gospel*. Atlanta: John Knox Press, 1985.

Duke, R. *The Persuasive Appeal of the Chronicler: A Rhetorical Analysis*. Bible and Literature Series 25. Sheffield UK: Almond Press, 1990.

Earle, T. K. *Economic and Social Organization of a Complex Chiefdom: The Halelea District, Kahua'i, Hawaii*. Ann Arbor: Museum of Anthropology, University of Michigan, 1978.

Eco, A. *The Role of the Reader: Explorations of the Semiotics of Texts*. Bloomington: Indiana University Press, 1979.

Edgerton, W. F. "The Government and the Governed in the Egyptian Empire." *JNES* 6 (1947): 152-60.

Elliott, John Hall. *What Is Social-Scientific Criticism?* Guides to Biblical Scholarship, New Testament Series. Minneapolis: Fortress Press, 1993.

Eitan, I. "An Unknown Meaning of Rahamim." *JBL* 53 (1934): 269-71.

Enos, R. L. "The Epistemology of Gorgias's Rhetoric: A Reexamination." *Southern Speech Communication Journal* 42 (1979): 35-51.

Erickson, K., ed. *Aristotle: The Classical Heritage of Rhetoric.* Metuchen NJ: Scarecrow Publishers, 1974.

_____. *Aristotle's Rhetoric: Five Centuries of Philological Research.* Metuchen NJ: Scarecrow Publishers, 1975.

Eslinger, L. "Inner-Biblical Exegesis and Inner-Biblical Allusion: The Question of Category." *VT* 42 (1992): 47-58.

Evans, W. "An Historical Reconstruction of the Emergence of Israelite Kingship and the Reign of Saul." In *Scripture in Context: Essays on the Comparative Method*, ed. W. Hallo, J. Moyer, and L. Perdue, 61-77. Winona Lake IN: Eisenbrauns, 1983.

Evans-Pritchard, E. E., and M. Fortes, *African Political Systems.* London: Oxford University Press, 1940.

Exum, J. Cheryl, and David J. A. Clines, eds. *The New Literary Criticism and the Hebrew Bible.* JSOTSup 143. Sheffield UK: JSOT Press, 1993.

Exum, J. Cheryl. *Tragedy and Biblical Narrative: Arrows of the Almighty.* New York: Cambridge University Press, 1992.

_____. "'You shall let every daughter live': A Study of Exodus 1.8–2.10." *Semeia* 28 (1983): 63-82.

Farenga, V. "Periphrasis on the Origin of Rhetoric." *Modern Language Notes* 94 (1979): 1033-55.

Fensham, F. C. "A Few Aspects of the Legal Practices in Samuel in Comparison with the Legal Material from the Ancient Near East." *Studies on the Books of Samuel*, 18-27. Pretoria: University of South Africa Press, 1960.

_____. "Widow, Orphan, and the Poor in Ancient Near Eastern Legal and Wisdom Literature." *JNES* 21 (1962): 129-39.

Fewell, D. N., ed. *Reading between Texts: Intertextuality and the Hebrew Bible.* Literary Currents in Biblical Interpretation. Louisville: Westminster/John Knox Press, 1992.

_____, and D. M. Gunn. *Gender, Power, and Promise: Stories of Desire and Division in the Hebrew Bible.* Nashville: Abingdon Press, 1993.

Flanagan, J. "Chiefs in Israel." *JSOT* 20 (1981): 47-73.

_____. "Models for the Origin of Iron Age Monarchy: A Modern Case Study." In *SBLSP 1982*, 135-56. Chico CA: Scholars Press, 1982.

_____. *David's Social Drama: A Hologram of Israel's Early Iron Age.* Sheffield UK: The Almond Press, 1988.

Fohrer, G. *Introduction to the Old Testament.* Translated by D. Green. London: S.P.C.K., 1970.

Fokkelman, J. P. *Narrative Art and Poetry in the Books of Samuel.* Vol. 1. *King David (II Samuel 9–20 and I Kings 1–2).* Assen: Van Gorcum, 1981.

_____. *Narrative Art and Poetry in the Books of Samuel*. Vol. 2. *The Crossing Fates*. Assen: Van Gorcum, 1986.

Fontaine, C. "The Bearing of Wisdom on the Shape of 2 Samuel 11–12 and 1 Kings 3." *JSOT* 34 (1986): 61-77.

Fowler, R. *Linguistic Criticism*. Oxford and New York: Oxford University Press, 1986.

Frankfort, H. *Kingship and the Gods*. Chicago: University of Chicago Press, 1948.

Frazer, J. *Folklore in the Old Testament*. London: Macmillan, 1918.

Frei, H. *The Eclipse of Biblical Narrative*. New Haven: Yale University Press, 1974.

Frick, F. *The City in Ancient Israel*. Missoula MT: Scholars Press, 1977.

_____. "Religion and Sociopolitical Structure in Early Israel: An Ethno-archaeological Approach." In *SBLSP 1979*, ed. P. J. Achtemeier, 233-53. Missoula MT: Scholars Press, 1979.

_____. *The Formation of the State in Ancient Israel. A Survey of Models and Theories*. Social World of Biblical Antiquity series 4. Sheffield UK: Almond Press, 1985.

Fried, M. *The Evolution of a Political Society. An Essay in Political Anthropology*. New York: Random House, 1967.

Frisch, A. "Structure and Its Significance: The Narrative of Solomon's Reign (1 Kgs. 1-12.24)." *JSOT* 51 (1991): 3-14.

Fry, P. *Spirits of Protests*. Cambridge and New York: Cambridge University Press, 1976.

Fuchs, Esther. "Contemporary Biblical Literary Criticism: The Objective Phallacy." In *Mappings of the Biblical Terrain. The Bible as Text*, ed. Vincent L. Tollers and John Maier. Bucknell Review 33. Lewisburg PA: Bucknell University Press, 1990.

Gabel, J. B., and C. B. Wheeler. *The Bible as Literature. An Introduction*. Second ed. New York: Oxford University Press, 1990.

Gadamer, H. G. *Truth and Method*. New York: Seabury, 1975.

_____. *Kleine Schriften I. Philosophie. Hermeneutik*. Tübingen: Mohr, 1976.

Gagon, J. "Prostitution." In *International Encyclopedia of the Social Sciences*, ed. D. Silk, 592-98. New York: Macmillan and the Free Press, 1968.

Garsiel, Moshe. "The Story of David and Bathsheba: A Different Approach." *CBQ* 55 (1993): 244-62.

Gealy, F. D. "Lots." *IDB*, K–Q: 163-64. New York and Nashville: Abingdon Press, 1962.

Geertz, C. *Islam Observed: Religious Development in Morocco and Indonesia*. Chicago/London: University of Chicago Press, 1968.

_____. "Deep Play: Notes on the Balinese Cockfight." *The Interpretation of Cultures*, 412-54. New York: Basic Books, 1973.

_____. "Thick Description: Toward an Interpretive Theory of Culture." *The Interpretation of Cultures*, 3-30. New York: Basic Books, 1973.

_____. "On the Nature of Anthropological Understanding." *American Scientist* 28 (1975): 1-26.

_____. "Blurred Genres." *The American Scholar* 49 (1980): 165-79.

Geller, S. *Parallelism in Early Biblical Poetry*. Ann Arbor MI: Scholars Press, 1979.

Gitay, Y. *Prophecy and Persuasion: A Study of Isaiah 40–48*. Forum Theologiae Linguistics 14. Rome: Linguistica Biblica, 1981.

_____. "Rhetorical Criticism." In *To Each Its Own Meaning: An Introduction to Biblical Criticisms and Their Application*, ed. Stephen R. Haynes and Steven L. McKenzie. Louisville: Westminster/John Knox Press, 1993.

_____. "Rhetorical Criticism and the Prophetic Discourse." In *Persuasive Artistry: Studies in New Testament Rhetoric in Honor of George A. Kennedy*, ed. Duane F. Watson. JSOTSup 50. Sheffield UK: JSOT Press, 1991.

Gluckman, M. *The Judicial Process Among the Barotse of Northern Rhodesia*. New Haven: Yale University Press, 1965.

_____. *Politics, Law, and Ritual in Tribal Society*. Oxford: Blackwell, 1965.

Goldman, S. *Samuel: Hebrew Text and English Translation*. London amd Bournemouth: Soncino Press, 1951.

Goodwin, David. "Rhetorical Criticism." In *Encyclopedia of Contemporary Literary Theory*, ed. Irena R. Makaryk, 174-78. Toronto: University of Toronto Press, 1993.

Gordis, R. "A Rhetorical Use of Interrogative Questions in Biblical Hebrew." *AJSL* 49 (1932/1933): 212-17.

Gordon, R. P. *1 and 2 Samuel*. Exeter: The Pater Noster Press, 1986.

Gottwald, N. "Literary Criticism of the Hebrew Bible: Retrospect and Prospect." In *Mappings of the Biblical Terrain: The Bible as Text*, ed. Vincent L. Tollers and John Maier. Bucknell Review 33. Lewisburg PA: Bucknell University Press, 1990.

_____. "Sociological Method in the Study of Ancient Israel." In *Encounter with the Text: Form and History in the Hebrew Bible*, ed. M. J. Buss, 69-81. Philadelphia: Fortress Press, 1979.

_____. *The Tribes of Yahweh: A Sociology of the Religion of Liberated Israel 1250–1050 B.C.E.* Maryknoll NY: Orbis; London: SCM, 1979.

_____. *The Hebrew Bible: A Socioliterary Introduction*. Philadelphia: Fortress Press, 1985.

Gray, J. "Hebrew Conception of the Kingship of God: Its Origin and Development." *VT* 6 (1956): 268-85.

_____. *I & II Kings. A Commentary*. Second edition. Old Testament Library. London: SCM Press; Philadelphia: Westminster Press, ²1970; ¹1964.

Graham, M. Patrick. "Aspects of the Structure and Rhetoric of 2 Chronicles 25." In *History and Interpretation: Essays in Honor of John H. Hayes*, ed. Graham M. Patrick, William P. Brown, and Jeffrey K. Kuan. JSOTSup 173. Sheffield UK: JSOT Press, 1993.

Gressmann, H. "Das Salomonische Urteil." *Deutsche Rundschau* 130 (1907): 212-28.

Gulliver, P. H. *Social Control in an African Society.* London: Routledge and Kegan Paul, 1963.

Gunkel, H. "Fundamental Problems of Hebrew Literary History." In *What Remains of the Old Testament.* Translated by A. K. Dallas. New York: Macmillan, 1928.

_____. *The Legends of Genesis.* Repr.: New York: Schocken, 1964; [1]1901. Originally the introduction to Gunkel's *Die Genesis*, HKAT 1/1 (1901;[4]1917).

Gunn, D. "Narrative Patterns and Oral Tradition in Judges and Samuel." *VT* 24 (1974): 286-317.

_____. *The Story of King David: Genre and Interpretation.* JSOTSup 6. Sheffield UK: JSOT Press, 1978.

_____. *The Fate of King Saul.* Sheffield UK: JSOT Press, 1980.

Gunn, G. "The Semiotics of Culture and the Interpretation of Literature: Clifford Geertz and the Moral Imagination." *Studies in the Literary Imagination* 12 (1977): 109-28.

Gusfield, J., ed. *Kenneth Burke: On Symbols and Society.* Chicago and London: University of Chicago Press, 1989.

Hagan, H. "Deception as Motif and Theme in 2 Sam. 9–20; 1 Kgs. 1–2." *Bib* 60 (1979): 301-26.

Hahlen, Mark Allen. "The Literary Design of Habakkuk." Ph.D. diss., Southern Baptist Theological Seminary, 1992.

Hahn, H. F. *The Old Testament in Modern Research.* Third revised and expanded edition. Philadelphia: Fortress Press; London: SCM Press, [3]1970; [2]1966.

Halpern, B. *The Constitution of the Monarchy in Israel.* Chico CA: Scholars Press, 1981.

Halpern, B., and J. D. Levenson, eds. *Traditions in Transformation: Turning Points in Biblical Faith.* Winona Lake IN: Eisenbrauns, 1981.

Hamnett, I. *Chieftainship and Legitimacy. An Anthropological Study of Executive Law in Lesotho.* London and Boston: Routledge and Kegan Paul, 1975.

Harris, M. *Cultural Materialism: The Struggle for a Science of Culture.* New York: Random House, 1979.

Hayes, J. H., and C. R. Holladay. *Biblical Exegesis.* Atlanta: John Knox Press, 1987.

Hayes, J. H., and J. M. Miller, eds. *Israelite and Judaean History.* Philadelphia: Trinity Press International, 1977.

Haynes, Stephen R., and Steven L. McKenzie, eds. *To Each Its Own Meaning: An Introduction to Biblical Criticisms and Their Application.* Louisville: Westminster/John Knox Press, 1993.

Heaton, E. W. *Solomon's New Men: The Emergence of Ancient Israel as a National State.* New York: Pica Press, 1974.

Held, M. "Rhetorical Questions in Ugaritic and Biblical Hebrew." *ErIs* 9 (1969): 71-79.

Hermission, H. J. "Weisheit und Geschichte." In *Probleme biblische Theologie*, ed. H. W. Wolff, 136-54. München: Kaiser, 1971.

Hermogenes. "On Ideas of Style." In *Ancient Literary Criticism: The Principle Texts in New Translations*, ed. D. A. Russell and M. Winterbottom, 561-79. Oxford: Clarendon Press, 1972.

Hertzberg, H. W. *I and II Samuel. A Commentary.* Old Testament Library. Philadelphia: Westminster Press, 1964.

Hicks, R. L. "A Bibliography of James Muilenburg's Writings." In *Israel's Prophetic Heritage*, ed. B. Anderson and W. Harrelson, 233-42. New York: Harper & Row, 1962.

Hillers, D. *Covenant: The History of a Biblical Idea.* Baltimore: Johns Hopkins University Press, 1969.

Hoftijzer, J. "David and the Tekoite Woman." *VT* 20 (1970): 419-44.

Holmberg, B. *Sociology and the New Testament: An Appraisal.* Philadelphia: Fortress Press, 1990.

Honeyman, A. M. "Merismus in Biblical Hebrew." *JBL* 71 (1952): 11-18.

House, Paul R., ed. *Beyond Form Criticism: Essays in Old Testament Literary Criticism.* Sources for Biblical and Theological Study, Old Testament 2. Winona Lake IN: Eisenbrauns, 1992.

_____. "The Rise and Current Status of Literary Criticism of the Old Testament." In *Beyond Form Criticism: Essays in Old Testament Literary Criticism.* Sources for Biblical and Theological Study, Old Testament 2. Winona Lake IN: Eisenbrauns, 1992.

_____Hutton, Rodney R. *Charisma and Authority in Israelite Society.* Minneapolis: Fortress Press, 1994.

Hyde, M. J., and C. R. Smith. "Hermeneutics and Rhetoric: A Seen but Unobserved Relationship." *Quarterly Journal of Speech* 65 (1979): 347-63.

Hyman, Ronald T. "God, Abraham, and Moses, A Comparison of Key Questions." *Jewish Bible Quarterly* 19 (1990–1991): 250-59.

Ishida, T. *The Royal Dynasties in Ancient Israel.* Berlin and New York: Walter de Gruyter, 1977.

Jacobsen, T. *The Sumerian King List.* Assyrian Studies 11. Chicago: University of Chicago Press, 1940.

Jamison, F. "Reification and Utopia in Mass Culture." *Social Text* 1 (1979): 141-44.

Jeffrey, David L. "How to Read the Hebrew Prophets." In *Mappings of the Biblical Terrain: The Bible as Text*, ed. Vincent L. Tollers and John Maier. Bucknell Review 33. Lewisburg PA: Bucknell University Press, 1990.

Jewett, R. "Romans as an Ambassadorial Letter." *Int* 36 (1982): 5-20.

Jobling, D. "Saul's Fall and Jonathan's Rise: Tradition and Redaction in 1 Samuel 14:1-46." *JBL* 95 (1970): 367-76.

_____. *The Sense of Biblical Narrative.* Sheffield UK: JSOT Press, 1978.

_____. "A Structural Analysis of Genesis 2:4b–3:24." *SBLSP* 1, ed. P. Achtemeier, 61-69. Missoula MT: Scholars Press, 1978.

_____. *The Sense of the Biblical Narrative: Structural Analyses in the Hebrew Bible II*. Sheffield UK: JSOT Press, 1986.

_____. "Sociological Literary Approaches to the Bible: How Shall the Twain Meet?" *JSOT* 38 (1987): 85-93.

_____, Peggy L. Day, and Gerald T. Sheppard, eds. *The Bible and the Politics of Exegesis: Essays in Honor of Norman K. Gottwald on His Sixty-Fifth Birthday*. Cleveland: Pilgrim Press, 1991.

Johnson, A. R. *Sacral Kingship in Ancient Israel*. Cardiff: University of Wales, 1967.

_____. *The Cultic Prophet and Israel's Psalmody*. Cardiff: University of Wales, 1979.

Johnson, B. "Urim and Thummim as Alphabet." *ASTI* 9 (1973): 23-29.

Jolles, A. *Einfache Formen*. Tübingen: Max Niemeyer, 1958.

Josephus. *Jewish Antiquities V–VIII*. LCL. Translated by H. St. J. Thackeray and R. Marcus. Cambridge MA: Harvard University Press, 1934.

Jung, K. N. "Court Etiquette in the Old Testament." Ph.D. diss., Drew University, 1979.

Kautzsch, E., and A. E. Cowley, E., eds. *Gesenius' Hebrew Grammar*. Second edition. Repr.: Oxford: Clarendon Press, 1988; [2]1910; [1]1898.

Keil, C. F., and F. Delitzsch. *Biblical Commentary on the Old Testament*. Repr.: Grand Rapids: Eerdmans, 1962.

Kenik, H. A. *Design for Kingship*. Chico CA: Scholars Press, 1983.

Kennedy, G. *The Art of Persuasion in Greece*. Princeton: Princeton University Press, 1963.

_____. *Quintilian*. Twayne World Author Series. New York: Twayne Publishers, 1969.

_____. *Classical Rhetoric and Its Christian and Secular Tradition from Ancient to Modern Times*. Chapel Hill: University of North Carolina Press, 1980.

_____. *New Testament Interpretation through Rhetorical Criticism*. Chapel Hill and London: University of North Carolina Press, 1984.

Kessler, M. "Rhetorical Criticism of Genesis 7." In *Rhetorical Criticism: Essays in Honor of James Muilenburg*, ed. J. Jackson and M. Kessler, 1-17. Pittsburgh: Pickwick Press, 1974.

_____. "Inclusion in the Hebrew Bible." *Semiotics* 6 (1978): 44-49.

Kimelman, Reuven. "Theme, Structure, and Impact." *JBL* 113 (1994): 37-58.

Kirkpatrick, A. F. *The First and Second Books of Samuel*. Cambridge: Cambridge University Press, 1930.

Klein, R. *1 Samuel*. WBC 10. Waco TX: Word Books, 1983.

Knierim, R. "Criticism of Literary Features, Form, Tradition, and Redaction." In *The Hebrew Bible and Its Modern Interpreters*, ed. D. Knight and G. Tucker, 123-66. Philadelphia: Fortress Press, 1985.

Krentz, Edgar. "Biblical Interpretation for a New Millenium." *Currents in Theology and Mission* 20 (1993): 345-59.

Kurz, W. "Hellenistic Rhetoric in the Christological Proof of Luke-Acts." *CBQ* 42 (1980): 171-95.

Langlamet, F. "Pour ou contre Salomon? La redaction prosalomonienne de I Rois I-II." *RB* 83 (1976): 321-79.

Lanham, Richard A. *A Handlist of Rhetorical Terms*. Second edition. Berkeley: University of California Press, 1991.

Lasine, Stuart. "Reading Jeroboam's Intentions: Intertextuality, Rhetoric, and History in 1 Kings 12." In *Reading between Texts*, ed. D. Fewell. Literary Currents in Biblical Interpretation. Louisville: Westminster/John Knox Press, 1992.

_____. "The Riddle of Solomon's Judgment." *JSOT* 45 (1989): 61-86.

Lategan, Bernard C. "Textual Space as Rhetorical Device." In *Rhetoric and the New Testament*, ed. S. Porter. Minneapolis: Fortress Press, 1990.

Lausberg, H. *Handbuch der literarischen Rhetorik*. Two volumes. Third edition. Stuttgart: Franz Steiner, 1990.

Leemans, W. F. "King Hammurabi as Judge." In *Symbolae Ivridicae et Historicae Martino David Dedicatae*, 107-29. Leiden: E. J. Brill, 1968.

Leggett, D. A. *The Levirate and Goel Institutions in the Old Testament with Special Attention to the Book of Ruth*. Cherry Hill NJ: Mack Publishing Company, 1974.

Lehmann, M. R. "Biblical Oaths." *ZAW* 81 (1969): 74-92.

Leibowitz, E. and G. "Solomon's Judgment." *Beth Mikra* 35 (1989–1990): 240-46.

Lemche, N. P. *Early Israel: Anthropological and Historical Studies on the Israelite Society Before the Monarchy*. Leiden: E. J. Brill, 1985.

Lenchak, Timothy A. *Choose Life: A Rhetorical-Critical Investigation of Deuteronomy 28, 69-30, 20*. Rome: Editrice Pontificio Instituto Biblico, 1993.

Lerner, G. "The Origin of Prostitution in Ancient Mesopotamia." *Signs: Journal of Women in Culture and Society* 11 (1986): 236-54.

Lindblom, J. "Lot-Casting in the Old Testament." *VT* 12 (1962): 164-78.

Liver, J. "The Book of the Acts of Solomon." *Bib* 48 (1967): 75-101.

Loades, Ann, and Michael McLain. *Hermeneutics, the Bible, and Literary Criticism*. New York: St. Martin's Press, 1992.

Long, B. O. "Social Dimensions of Prophetic Conflict." In *Anthropological Perspectives on Old Testament Prophecy*, ed. R. Culley. *Semeia* 21 (1982): 29-53.

Long, B. O. *1 Kings*. Forms of the Old Testament Literature. Grand Rapids: Eerdmans, 1984.

_____. "The 'New' Biblical Poetics of Alter and Sternberg." *JSOT* 51 (1991): 71-84.

Long, V. P. *The Reign and Rejection of King Saul: A Case for Literary and Theological Coherence*. Atlanta GA: Scholars Press, 1989.

Longinus on the Sublime. Translated by W. R. Roberts. Cambridge: Cambridge University Press, 1899.

Lundbom, J. *Jeremiah: A Study in Ancient Hebrew Rhetoric*. Atlanta GA: Scholars Press, 1975.

_____. "Rhetorical Structures in Jeremiah 1." *Zeitschrift für die Alttesta-mentliche Wissenschaft* 103 (1991): 193-210.

McCarter, P. K., Jr. *I Samuel.* AB 8. Garden City NY: Doubleday, 1980.

_____. "Plots, True and False: The Succession Narrative as Court Apologetic." *Int* 35 (1981): 355-67.

McCarthy, D. *Treaty and Covenant: A Study in Form in the Ancient Oriental Documents and in the Old Testament.* AnBib 21. Rome: Pontifical Biblical Institute, 1963.

Macherey, P. *A Theory of Literary Production.* London and Boston: Routledge and Kegan Paul, 1978.

Macholz, G. C. "Zur Geschichte der Justizorganisation in Juda." *ZAW* 84 (1972): 314-40.

Mack, B. *A Myth of Innocence: Mark and Christian Origins.* Philadelphia: Fortress Press, 1988.

_____. *Rhetoric and the New Testament.* Minneapolis: Fortress Press, 1990.

McKane, W. *Prophets and Wise Men.* Studies in Biblical Theology 44. Naperville IL: Alec R. Allenson; London: SCM Press, 1965.

McKeating, H. "Vengeance Is Mine." *ExpTim* 74 (1963): 239-45.

_____. "The Development of the Law on Homicide in Ancient Israel." *VT* 25 (1975): 46-68.

McKenzie, J. L. "Elders in the Old Testament." *Studia Biblica et Orientalia* 10 (1959): 388-406.

Mair, L. P. *An Introduction to Social Anthropology.* Oxford: Clarendon Press, 1972.

Malamat, A. "Organs of Statecraft in the Israelite Monarchy." *BAR* 3 (1970): 163-98.

Marcus, D. *Jephthah and His Vow.* Lubbock TX: Texas Tech Press, 1986.

Martin, Dale B. "Social-Scientific Criticism." In *To Each Its Own Meaning: An Introduction to Biblical Criticisms and Their Application,* ed. Stephen R. Haynes and Steven L. McKenzie. Louisville: Westminster/John Knox Press, 1993.

Mattu, H. "Jeremiah vs. Hananiah: Ideology and Truth in Old Testament Prophecy." In *The Bible and Liberation,* ed. N. Gottwald, 235-51. Maryknoll, New York: Orbis Press, 1983.

Mauchline, J. *1 and 2 Samuel.* London: Oliphants, 1971.

May, David M. *Social Scientific Criticism of the New Testament: A Bibliography.* National Association of Baptist Professors of Religion Bibliographic Series 4, ed. David M. Scholer. Macon GA: Mercer University Press, 1991.

Mayes, A. D. H. *The Story of Israel between Settlement and Exile.* London: SCM Press, 1983.

Mazar, B. "The Military Elite of David." *VT* 13 (1963): 310-20.

_____. *II Samuel.* AB 9. Garden City NY: Doubleday, 1984.

Mendelsohn, I. "Urim and Thummim." *IDB* R-Z:739-40. New York and Nashville: Abingdon Press, 1962.

Mendenhall, G. E. *Law and Covenant and the Ancient Near East*. Pittsburgh: Presbyterian Board of Colportage of Western Pennsylvania, 1955.

_____. "The Hebrew Conquest of Palestine." *Biblical Archaeologist* 25 (1962): 66-87.

_____. *The Tenth Generation: The Origins of the Biblical Tradition*. Baltimore and London: Johns Hopkins University Press, 1973.

_____. "The Shady Side of Wisdom: The Date and Purpose of Genesis 3." In *A Light unto My Path: Old Testament Studies in Honor of Jacob M. Myers*, ed. H. N. Bream, R. D. Heim, and C. A. Moore, 319-34. Philadelphia: Temple University Press, 1974.

_____. "Monarchy." *Int* 29 (1975): 155-70.

_____. "Social Organization in Early Israel." In *Magnalia Dei: The Mighty Acts of God*, ed. F. M. Cross et al., 132-51. Garden City NY: Doubleday, 1976.

Mettinger, T. N. D. *Solomonic State Officials: A Study of the Civil Government Officials of the Israelite Monarchy*. Lund: C. W. K. Gleerup, 1971.

_____. *King and Messiah: The Civil and Sacral Legitimation of Israelite Kings*. Lund: C. W. K. Gleerup, 1976.

Meyers, C. *Discovering Eve: Ancient Israelite Women in Context*. New York and Oxford: Oxford University Press, 1988.

_____. "Gender Roles and Genesis 3.16 Revisited." In *The Word of the Lord Shall Go Forth*, ed. C. Meyers and M. O'Connor, 337-54. Philadelphia: Americal Schools of Oriental Research, 1983.

Middrash Rabbah VIII/2 Ecclesiastes. Translated by A. Cohen. New York and London: Soncino Press, 1983.

Miller, Dane Eric. "Micah and Its Literary Environment: Rhetorical Critical Case Studies." Ph.D. diss., University of Arizona, 1991.

Miller, J. M. "Saul's Rise to Power: Some Observations Concerning 1 Sam. 9:1–10:16; 10:26–11:15; and 13:2–14:46." *CBQ* 36 (1974): 157-74.

Miller, P., and J. M. Roberts. *The Hand of the Lord*. Baltimore and London: Johns Hopkins University Press, 1977.

Minor, Mark. *Literary-Critical Approaches to the Bible: An Annotated Bibliography*. West Cornwall CT: Locust Hill Press, 1992.

Miscall, P. *1 Samuel, a Literary Reading*. Bloomington: Indiana University Press, 1986.

Montgomery, J. A., and H. S. Gehman. *A Critical and Exegetical Commentary on the Books of Kings*. ICC. Edinburgh: T. & T. Clark, 1951.

Moor, S. F. *Law as Process: An Anthropological Approach*. London and Boston: Routledge and Kegan Paul, 1978.

Moulton, R. G. *The Literary Study of the Bible*. Boston: D. C. Heath and Co., 1899.

Mowinckel, S. *The Psalms in Israel's Worship*. Translated by D. R. Ap-Thomas. New York: Abingdon Press, 1962.

Muecke, D. C. *Irony*. London: Methuen, 1970.

Muilenburg, J. "The Book of Isaiah. Chapters 40–66." *IB* 5, ed. G. A. Buttrick et al., 381-419. Nashville: Abingdon Press, 1956; repr. 1978.

_____. "Form Criticism and Beyond." *JBL* 88 (1969): 1-18.

_____. "The Linguistic and Rhetorical Usages of the Particle *KY* in the Old Testament." *HUCA* 32 (1961): 135-60.

_____. "A Liturgy on the Triumphs of Yahweh." In *Studia Biblica et Semitica*, ed. W. C. van Unnik and A. S. van der Woude, 233-57. Wageningen, Netherlands: H. Veenman en Zonen, 1966.

_____. "A Study in Hebrew Rhetoric." VTSup 1, 97-111. Leiden: E. J. Brill, 1953.

_____. "The Terminology of Adversity in Jeremiah." In *Translating and Understanding the Old Testament*, ed. H. T. Frank and W. L. Reed, 42-63. Nashville: Abingdon Press, 1970.

Muraoka, T. *Emphatic Words and Structures in Biblical Hebrew*. Leiden: E. J. Brill, 1985.

Nichol, G. G. "The Wisdom of Joab and the Wise Woman of Tekoa." *ST* 36 (1982): 97-104.

Nicholson, E. W. *God and His People: Covenant and Theology in the Old Testament*. Oxford: Clarendon Press, 1986.

Niditch, Susan, ed. *Text and Tradition: The Hebrew Bible and Folklore*. Atlanta: Scholars Press, 1990.

Niehoff, M. "Do Biblical Characters Talk to Themselves? Narrative Modes of Representing Inner Speech in Early Biblical Fiction." *JBL* 111 (1992): 577-95.

Niehr, H. "Zur Gattung von Jes. 5.1-7." *BZ* 30 (1986): 99-104.

Noort, E. "Eine weitere Kurzbemerkung zu I Samuel xiv.41." *VT* 21 (1971): 112-16.

Noth, M. "Die Bewahrung von Solomos 'gottlicher Weisheit'." VTSup 3:225-37. Leiden: Brill, 1955.

_____. *The History of Israel*. New York: Harper, 1958.

_____. *Könige*. 1 Teilband. Neukirchen-Vluyn: Neukirchen Verlag, 1968.

Ochs, Peter. *The Return to Scripture in Judaism and Christianity: Essays in Postcritical Scriptural Interpretation*. Mahwah NJ: Paulist Press, 1993.

O'Connell, Robert H. "Deuteronomy vii.1-26: Asymmetrical Concentricity and the Rhetoric of Conquest." *VT* 42 (1992): 248-65.

_____. "Deuteronomy ix.7–x.7, 10-11: Panelled Structure, Double Rehearsal and the Rhetoric of Covenant Rebuke." *VT* 42 (1992): 492-509.

O'Grady, John F. "Biblical Methodologies." *Chicago Studies* 29 (1990): 87-100.

Osiek, C. "The New Handmaid: The Bible and the Social Sciences." *Theological Studies* 50 (1989): 260-78.

Overholt, T. "The Ghost Dance of 1890 and the Nature of the Prophetic Process." *Ethnohistory* 21 (1974): 37-63.

Parker, K. I. "Repetition as a Structuring Device in I Kings 1–11." *JSOT* 42 (1988): 19-27.

Patrick, D., and A. Scult. *Rhetoric and Biblical Interpretation*. Sheffield UK: Almond Press, 1990.

Patrick, Dale. "The Rhetoric of Revelation." *HBT* 16 (1994): 20-40.

Pedersen J. *Israel, Its Life and Culture*. Four volumes in two. Translated by Mrs. Aslaug Møller. London: Oxford University Press, [2]1963–1964; [1]1926–1940; orig. Danish, 1920–1934.

Perdue, L. "'Is There Anyone Left of the House of Saul . . . ?' Ambiguity and the Characterization of David in the Succession Narrative." *JSOT* 30 (1984): 67-84.

Perry, T. Anthony. "A Poetics of Absence: The Structure and Meaning of Genesis 1:2." *JSOT* 58 (1993): 3-11.

Petersen, N. *Rediscovering Paul: Philemon and the Sociology of Paul's Narrative World*. Philadelphia: Fortress Press, 1984.

Pfeiffer, R. H. *Introduction to the Old Testament*. New York: Harper Brothers, 1941.

Phillips, A. "Some Aspects of Family Law in Preexilic Israel." *VT* 23 (1973): 349-61.

Phillips, A. "Another Look at Murder." *JJS* 28 (1977): 105-26.

Pisano, S. *Additions or Omissions in the Books of Samuel*. Göttingen: Vanderhoeck und Ruprecht, 1984.

Plato. *Gorgias*. Translated by W. R. M. Lamb. LCL. Cambridge MA: Harvard University Press, 1925.

_____. *Phraedrus*. Translated by H. N. Fowler. LCL. Cambridge MA: Harvard University Press, 1932.

Poland, L. "The Bible and the Rhetorical Sublime." In *The Bible as Rhetoric: Studies in Biblical Persuasion and Credibility*, ed. Margin Warner. Warwick Studies in Philosophy and Literature. London: Routledge, 1990.

Polzin, R. *Moses and the Deuteronomist: A Literary Study of the Deuteronomic History*. New York: Seabury Press, 1980.

_____. *Samuel and the Deuteronomist: A Literary Study of the Deuteronomic History*. San Francisco: Harper & Row, 1989.

Pope, M. "Oaths." *IDB* K-Q:575-77. New York and Nashville: Abingdon Press, 1962.

Porten, B. "Structure and Theme of the Solomonic Narrative (1 Kings 3–11)." *HUCA* 38 (1967): 93-128.

Porteous, N. W. "Royal Wisdom." VTSup 3. Leiden: E. J. Brill, 1955.

Porter, J. R. *The Extended Family in the Old Testament*. Occasional Papers in Social and Economic Administration 6. London: Edutext, 1967.

Pospisil, L. "Legal Levels and Multiplicity of Legal Systems in Human Society." *The Journal of Conflict Resolution* 11 (1967): 2-26.

Powell, Mark Allan, compiler, with Cecile G. Gray and Melissa C. Curtis. *The Bible and Modern Literary Criticism: A Critical Assessment and Annotated Bibliography*. New York: Greenwood Press, 1992.

Preminger, A., and E. Greenstein, eds. *The Hebrew Bible in Literary Criticism*. New York: Ungar, 1986.

Prickett, Stephen, ed. *Reading the Text: Biblical Criticism and Literary Theory*. Cambridge: Blackwell, 1991.

Pritchard, J., ed. *Ancient Near Eastern Texts Relating to the Old Testament.* Princeton: Princeton University Press, 1955.

_____. *The Ancient Near East: Supplementary Texts and Pictures Relating to the Old Testament.* Princeton: Princeton University Press, 1969.

Quintilian. *Institutio Oratoria.* LCL. Cambridge MA: Harvard University Press, 1930.

Rabinowitz, I. " *'AZ* Followed by the Imperfect Verb Form in Preterite Contexts: A Redactional Device in Biblical Hebrew." *VT* 34 (1984): 53-62.

Radday, Y. T., and A. Brenner, eds. *On Humor and the Comic in the Hebrew Bible.* Sheffield UK: Sheffield Academic Press, 1990.

Rand, H. "Justice in Solomon's Court: Anonymous vs. Anonymous." *Dor le Dor* 10 (1982): 170-76.

Ratner, Robert J., Lewis M. Barth, Marianne Luijken Gevirtz, and Bruce Zuckerman. "Let Your Colleagues Praise You: Studies in Memory of Stanley Gevirtz." *Maarav* 8 (1992).

Redford, D. B. "Studies in the Relations between Palestine and Egypt during the First Millenium B.C." In *Studies in the Ancient Palestinian World,* ed. J. W. Weavers and D. B. Redford. Toronto: University of Toronto Press, 1972.

Rendtorff, R. "The Paradigm Is Changing: Hopes and Fears." *Biblical Interpretation* 1 (1993): 34-53.

Renfrew, C. "Beyond a Subsistence Economy: The Evolution of Social Organization in Prehistoric Europe." In *Reconstructing Complex Societies,* ed. C. B. Moore, 65-88. Cambridge MA: American Schools of Oriental Research, 1974.

Reumann, John. "After Historical Criticism, What? Trends in Biblical Interpretation and Ecumenical, Interfaith Dialogues." *JES* 29 (1992): 55-86.

Reviv, H. "Structure of Society." In *The Age of the Monarchies: Culture and Society. The World History of the Jewish People,* ed. A. Malamat. Jerusalem: Masada Press, 1979.

_____. *The Elders in Ancient Israel: A Study of a Biblical Institution.* Jerusalem: Magnes Press, 1989.

Richter, W. *Traditionsgeschichtliche Untersuchungen zum Richterbuch.* Bonn: Peter Hanstein, 1963.

Ridout, George P. "Prose Compositional Techniques in the Succession Narrative (2 Sam. 7, 9–20; 1 Kings 1–2)." Thesis, Graduate Theological Union, Berkeley CA, 1971.

Rhoads, David. "Social Criticism: Crossing Boundaries." In *Mark and Method: New Approaches in Biblical Studies,* ed. Janice Capel Anderson and Stephen D. Moore. Minneapolis: Fortress Press, 1992.

_____. "Die *nagid* Formel: Ein Beitrag zur Erhellung des *nagid* Problems." *BZ* 9 (1965): 71-84.

Ricoeur, P. *Interpretation Theory: Discourse and the Surplus of Meaning.* Fort Worth TX: Texas Christian University Press, 1976.

Ridderbos, N. "Psalmen und Kult." In *Zur neuren Psalmenforschung,* ed. P. Neumann, 234-79. Darmstadt: Wissenschaftliche Buchgesellschaft, 1976.

Robbins, V. *Jesus the Teacher: Sociorhetorical Interpretation of Mark.* Philadelphia: Fortress Press, 1984.

_____, "Rhetoric and Culture: Exploring Types of Cultural Rhetoric in a Text." In *Rhetoric and the New Testament,* ed. S. Porter. Minneapolis: Fortress Press, 1990.

_____, ed. "The Rhetoric of Pronouncement." *Semeia* 64 (1994).

Robertson, E. "The Urim and Thummim: What Were They?" *VT* 14 (1964): 66-74.

Robinson, J. *The First Book of Kings.* Cambridge MA: Harvard University Press, 1972.

Rogerson, J. W. *Anthropology and the Old Testament.* Atlanta: John Knox Press, 1978.

Rohrbaugh, Richard L. "Social Science and Literary Criticism: What Is at Stake?" *Hervormde Teologiese Studies* 49 (1993): 221-33.

Rosenblatt, J. P., and J. C. Sitterson, Jr. *"Not in Heaven": Coherence and Complexity in Biblical Narrative.* Bloomington: Indiana University Press, 1991.

Rosenthal, E. I. J. "Some Aspects of the Hebrew Monarchy." *JJS* 9 (1958): 1-18.

Rost, L. *Die Uberlieferung von der Thronnachfolge Davids.* Stuttgart: Kohlhammer, 1926. ET: *The Succession Throne of David.* Sheffield UK: Almond Press, 1982.

_____. "Konigsherrschaft Jahwes in Vorkoniglicher Zeit?" *TLZ* 85 (1960): 721-24.

Sacon, K. "A Study of the Literary Structure of the Succession Narrative." *Studies in the Period of David and Solomon and Other Essays,* ed. T. Ishida, 27-54. Tokyo: Yamakawa Shuppansha, 1982.

Said, E. "Opponents, Audiences, Constituencies and Community." In *Politics of Interpretation,* ed. W. J. Mitchell, Chicago and London: University of Chicago Press, 1983.

Salmon, J. M. "Judicial Authority in Early Israel: A Historical Investigation of Old Testament Institutions." Th.D. diss., Princeton Theological Seminary, 1968.

Savran, G. "1 and 2 Kings." In *The Literary Guide to the Bible,* ed. R. Alter and K. Kermode, 146-64. Cambridge MA: Harvard University Press, 1987.

Schlossberg, Eliezer. "Ten Observations on Rhetoric and Expression by Saadia Gaon." *Journal of Semitic Studies* 38 (1993): 269-77.

Schmidt, T. "Sociology and New Testament Exegesis." In *Introducing New Testament Interpretation.* Guides to New Testament Exegesis, ed. S. McKnight, 115-32. Grand Rapids: Baker Book House, 1990.

Schmuttermayr, G. "RHM. Eine lexikalische Studie." *Bib* 51 (1970): 499-532.

Schwartz, Regina M., ed. *The Book and the Text: The Bible and Literary Theory.* Cambridge: Basil Blackwell, 1990.

Scott, R. B. Y. "Solomon and the Beginnings of Wisdom in Israel." In *Wisdom in Israel and in the Ancient Near East.* VTSup 3:262-79. Leiden: E. J. Brill, 1955.

_____. "Folk Proverbs of the Ancient Near East." In *Studies in Ancient Israelite Wisdom*, ed. J. Crenshaw, 417-28. New York: KTAV, 1976.
Service, E. *Origins of the State and Civilization*. New York: W. W. Norton, 1975.
Shaw, Charles S. *The Speeches of Micah: A Rhetorical-Historical Analysis*. JSOTSup 145. Sheffield UK: Sheffield Academic Press, 1993.
Shelly, Patricia Joyce. "Amos and Irony: The Use of Irony in Amos's Prophetic Discourse." Ph.D. diss., Iliff School of Theology and University of Denver, 1992.
Simon, U. "Minor Characters in Biblical Narrative." *JSOT* 46 (1990): 11-19.
_____. "The Poor Man's Ewe-Lamb. An Example of a Juridical Parable." *Bib* 48 (1967): 207-42.
Smith, H. P. *A Critical and Exegetical Commentary on the Books of Samuel* ICC. New York: Charles Scribner's Sons; Edinburgh: T. & T. Clark, 1899.
Smith, W. R. *The Religion of the Semites: The Fundamental Institutions*. Repr.: New York: Schocken, 1972; orig. pub. 1927.
Speiser, E. A. "'People' and 'Nation' in Israel." *JBL* 79 (1960): 157-63.
Stager, L. "The Archaeology of the Family in Ancient Israel." *BASOR* 260 (1985): 1-35.
Staley. J. *The Print's First Kiss: A Rhetorical Investigation of the Implied Reader in the Fourth Gospel*. SBLDS 82. Atlanta: Scholars Press, 1988.
Stamps, Dennis L. "Rhetorical Criticism and the Rhetoric of New Testament Criticism." *Literature and Theology* 6 (1992), 268-79.
Sternberg, M. "Biblical Poetics and Sexual Politics: From Reading to Counter-Reading." *JBL* 111 (1992): 463-88.
_____. "The Bible's Art of Persuasion: Ideology, Rhetoric, and Poetics in Saul's Fall." *HUCA* 54 (1983): 45-82.
_____. *The Poetics of Biblical Narrative*. Bloomington: Indiana University Press, 1987.
Stipp, Hermann-Josef. "Das Verhältnis von Textkritik und Literarkritik in neuren alttestamentlichen Veröffentlichungen." *BZ* 34 (1990): 16-37.
Stoebe, H. J. *Das Erste Buch Samuelis*. KAT 8. Gütersloh: Gerd Mohr, 1973.
Stowers, S. "Social Status, Public Speaking and Private Teaching: The Circumstances of Paul's Preaching Activity." *NovT* 26 (1984): 59-82.
Sulzberger, M. *The Ancient Hebrew Law*. London: Julius H. Greenstone, 1915.
Tadmor, H. "The People and the Kingship in Ancient Israel: The Role of the Political Institutions in the Biblical Period." *Journal of World History* 11 (1968): 46-68.
_____. "Traditional Institutions and the Monarchy: Social and Political Tensions in the Time of David and Solomon." In *Studies in the Period of David and Solomon*, ed. T. Ishida, 239-58. Tokyo: Yamakawa-Shuppansha, 1982.
Talmon, S. *Literary Studies in the Hebrew Bible: Form and Content: Collected Studies*. Jerusalem: Magnes Press, 1993.

_____. *King, Cult and Calendar in Ancient Israel*. Jerusalem: Magnes Press, 1986.

Tanner, James Paul. "Textual Patterning in Biblical Hebrew Narrative: A Case Study in Judges 6-8." Ph.D. diss., University of Texas at Austin, 1990.

Tate, W. R. *Biblical Interpretation: An Integrated Approach*. Peabody MA: Hendrickson Publishers, 1991.

Theissen, G. "Sociological Interpretation of Religious Traditions: Its Methodological Problems as Exemplified in Early Christianity." In *The Social Setting of Pauline Christianity: Essays on Corinth*, ed. J. H. Schutz, 175-200. Philadelphia: Fortress Press, 1982.

Tigay, J. *You Shall Have No Other Gods: Israelite Religion in Light of Hebrew Inscriptions*. Atlanta: Scholars Press, 1986.

Toeg, A. "A Textual Note on I Samuel xiv.41." *VT* 19 (1960): 493-98.

Tollers, Vincent L., and John Maier, eds. *Mappings of the Biblical Terrain: The Bible as Text*. Bucknell Review 33. Lewisburg PA: Bucknell University Press, 1990.

Trible, P. *God and the Rhetoric of Sexuality*. Philadelphia: Fortress Press, 1978.

_____, *Rhetorical Criticism: Context, Method, and the Book of Jonah*. Minneapolis: Fortress Press, 1994.

_____, *Texts of Terror*. Philadelphia: Fortress Press, 1984.

Tsevat, M. "Assyriological Notes on the First Book of Samuel." In *Studies in the Bible*, ed. J. M. Grintz and J. Liver. Jerusalem: Kiryat Sepher L. T. D., 1964.

Tubbs, Fred Charles. "The Nature and Function of Humor and Wit in the Old Testament Literary Prophets." Ph.D. diss., Southwestern Baptist Theological Seminary, 1990.

Tucker, G. *Form Criticism of the Old Testament*. Philadelphia: Fortress Press, 1971.

Ulrich, E. C. "4QSamc: A Fragmentary Manuscript of Samuel 14-15 from the Scribe of the *Serek Hay-yahad* (1QS)." *BASOR* 235 (1979): 1-25.

Untersteiner, M. *The Sophists*. Oxford: Basil Blackwell, 1953.

van Dijk, P. J. "The Function of So-Called Etiological Elements in Narratives." *ZAW* 102 (1990): 19-33.

Veeser, A. ed., *The New Historicism*. London: Routledge and Kegan Paul, 1989.

Vickers, B. *Rhetoric Revalued*. Binghamton NY: Center for Medieval and Renaissance Studies, 1982.

von Rad, G. *The Problem of the Hexateuch and Other Essays*. Translated by E. W. T. Dicken. New York: McGraw-Hill; Edinburgh: Oliver and Boyd, 1966; orig. German, 1938.

_____. *Holy War in Ancient Israel*. Translated by M. Dawn. Repr.: Grand Rapids: Eerdmans, 1991; orig. German, 1958.

von Waldow, H. E. "Social Responsibility and Social Structure in Early Israel." *CBQ* 32 (1970): 182-203.

Walsh, T. J., and Christopher T. Begg. "1–2 Kings." In *NJBC*, ed. R. Brown et al., 160-85. Englewood Cliffs NJ: Prentice Hall, 1990.

Walters, R. "Signs of the Times: Clifford Geertz and the Historians." *Social Research* 47 (1980): 537-56.

Waltke, B. K., and O'Connor, M. *An Introduction to Biblical Hebrew Syntax.* Winona Lake IN: Eisenbrauns, 1990.

Warner, Martin, ed. *The Bible as Rhetoric: Studies in Biblical Persuasion and Credibility.* Warwick Studies in Philosophy and Literature. London: Routledge, 1990.

Watson, D. F., and A. J. Hauser. *Rhetorical Criticism of the Bible: A Comprehensive Bibliography with Notes on History and Method.* Leiden: E. J. Brill, 1994.

Watson, W. *Classical Hebrew Poetry: A Guide to its Techniques.* Sheffield: JSOT Press, 1984.

Weber, M. *Ancient Judaism.* New York: Free Press, 1952. Originally published posthumously as vol. 3 of *Gesammelte Aufsatze zur Religion-Soziologie.* Tübingen: J. C. B. Mohr, 1921.

Webster, Edwin C. "The Rhetoric of Isaiah 63-65." *JSOT* 47 (1990): 89-102.

Welch, K. E. *The Contemporary Reception of Classical Rhetoric: Appropriations of Ancient Discourse.* Hillsdale NJ: Lawrence Erlbaum, 1990.

Wellek. R., and A. Warren. *Theory of Literature.* New York: Harcourt, Brace, and World, 1956.

Wellhausen, J. *Der Text der Bucher Samuelis.* Göttingen: Vanderhoeck und Ruprecht, 1871.

_____. *Einleitung in das Alte Testament.* Berlin: F. Bleek, 1878.

_____. *Prolegomena to the History of Israel.* Edinburgh: A. and C. Black, 1885.

Westermann, C. "Die Begriffe fur Fragen und Suchen in Alten Testament." *KD* 6 (1960): 2-20.

_____. *Genesis 12–36. A Commentary.* Translated by J. Scullion. Minneapolis: Augsburg Publishing House, 1985.

Wharton, J. A. "A Plausible Tale: Story and Theology in II Samuel 9–20, I Kings 1–2." *Int* 35 (1981): 341-54.

Wheelwright, P. *Metaphor and Reality.* Bloomington: Indiana University Press, 1962.

Whitelam, K. *The Just King: Monarchical Judicial Authority in Ancient Israel.* Sheffield: JSOT Press, 1979.

Whybray, R. N. *The Succession Narrative.* Studies in Biblical Theology second series 9:56-95. London: SCM, 1968.

Wilder, Amos N. "Holy Writ and Lit Crit." *Christian Century* 107 (1990): 790-91.

Willis, Timothy M. "So Great Is His Steadfast Love: A Rhetorical Analysis of Psalm 103." *Biblica* 72 (1991): 525-37.

Wilson, R. *Genealogy and History in the Biblical World.* New Haven: Yale University Press, 1979.

_____. *Prophecy and Society in Ancient Israel.* Philadelphia: Fortress, 1980.

_____. "Enforcing the Covenant: The Mechanisms of Judicial Authority in Early Israel." In *The Quest for the Kingdom of God: Studies in Honor of G. E. Mendenhall*, ed. H. B. Huffmon, F. A. Spina, and A. R. W. Green, 59-76. Winona Lake IN: Eisenbrauns, 1983.

_____. "Israel's Judicial System in the Preexilic Period." *JQR* 74 (1983): 229-48.

_____. *Social Science Approaches to the Old Testament.* Philadelphia: Fortress Press, 1984.

Wink, W. *The Bible in Human Transformation.* Philadelphia: Fortress Press, 1973.

Wolff, H. W. *Obadiah and Jonah. A Commentary.* Minneapolis: Augsburg Publishing House, 1977.

Wright, G. E. "The Provinces of Solomon (I Kings 4.7-19)." *ErIs* 8 (1967): 58-68.

Wuellner, W. "Biblical Exegesis in the Light of the History and Historicity of Rhetoric and the Nature of the Rhetoric of Religion." In *Rhetoric and the New Testament*, ed. S. Porter. Minneapolis: Fortress Press, 1990.

_____. "Paul as Pastor: The Function of Rhetorical Questions in First Corinthians." In *L'Apotre Paul: personalite, style et conception du ministere*, ed. A. Vanhoye, 49-77. Leuven: Leuven University Press, 1986.

Würthwein, E. *Die Bucher der Konige. 1 Konige 1–16.* Göttingen: Vanderhoeck und Ruprecht, 1977.

Zannoni, Arthur E. *The Old Testament: A Bibliography.* Collegeville MN: Liturgical Press, 1992.

Zulick, Margaret Diefenderfer. "Rhetorical Polyphony in the Book of the Prophet Hosea." Ph.D. diss., Northwestern University, 1994.

Indexes

Author Index

Subject index

Of Methods, Monarchs, and Meanings.
A Sociorhetorical Approach to Exegesis.
by Gina Henz-Piazza. Studies in Old Testament Interpretation (SOTI) 3.

Mercer University Press, Macon, Georgia 31210-3960.
Isbn 0-86554-503-0. MUP/H394.
Text, titles, and cover design, composition, and layout by Edd Rowell.
Camera-ready pages composed on a Gateway 2000
 (via WordPerfect 5.1/5.2) and printed on a LaserMaster 1000.
Text font: TimesNewRomanPS 11/13 and 10/12.
 Titles: Helvetica. Hebrew: ATECH. Greek: ATECH.
Printed and bound by Braun-Brumfield Inc., Ann Arbor, Michigan 48106
 Via offset lithography on 50# Natural Hi-Bulk paper.
 Smyth sewn and cased in .088 binder boards,
  rounded and backed, and with matching headbands.
 Cloth: Roxite C 56548 (blue) vellum finish,
  one hit on spine and c. 4 with gold foil S19.
 Dust jacket: 80# Rainbow Antique (blue-gray)
  printed PMS 539 (dark blue) (endleaves match dust jacket).
                    [November 1996]

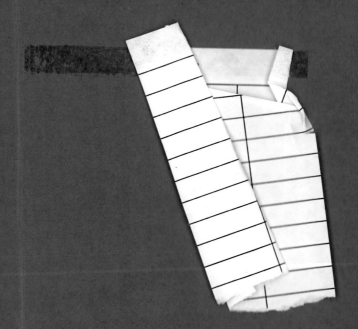